Leading the Project Revolut

CW01483759

People play a vital part in the success of projects, initiatives and organisations, yet traditional project management sources offer limited guidance and insights that extend beyond technical roles and prescriptions. *Leading the Project Revolution* delves into the dynamics of people, teams and organisations, exploring their impact on leadership, strategy, success and achievement.

The book offers a progressive agenda for improving project practice, enabling the dialogue to advance from the typical coverage of static toolsets towards an understanding of flexible mindsets. Flexibility, agility and resilience are addressed as the social, cultural and complexity dimensions of leadership, strategy, organisations and project execution are examined and practical insights are synthesised into pragmatic models and frameworks.

The volume brings together some of the best writing by leading authorities on teams, leadership, corporate culture, human behaviour, organisational dynamics, psychology, complexity, strategy, execution, innovation, social media and decision sourcing.

Darren Dalcher is Professor in Strategic Project Management at Lancaster University Management School. He has written over 200 papers and book chapters and published over 30 books. He is Editor-in-Chief of the *Journal of Software: Evolution and Process* and of two established book series published by Routledge.

Advances in Project Management Series
Edited by Darren Dalcher

Project management has become a key competence for most organisations in the public and private sectors. Driven by recent business trends such as fewer management layers, greater flexibility, increasing geographical distribution and more project-based work, project management has grown beyond its roots in the construction, engineering and aerospace industries to transform the service, financial, computer, and general management sectors. In fact, a Fortune article rated project management as the number one career choice at the beginning of the 21st century. Yet many organizations have struggled in applying the traditional models of project management to their new projects in the global environment.

Project management offers a framework to help organisations to transform their mainstream operations and service performance. It is viewed as a way of organising for the future. Moreover, in an increasingly busy, stressful, and uncertain world it has become necessary to manage several projects successfully at the same time. According to some estimates the world annually spends well over $10 trillion (US) on projects. In the UK alone, more than £250 billion is spent on projects every year. Up to half of these projects fail! A major ingredient in the build-up leading to failure is often cited as the lack of adequate project management knowledge and experience. Some organizations have responded to this situation by trying to improve the understanding and capability of their managers and employees who are introduced to projects, as well as their experienced project managers in an attempt to enhance their competence and capability in this area.

Advances in Project Management provides short, state of play, guides to the main aspects of the new emerging applications including: maturity models, agile projects, extreme projects, six sigma and projects, human factors and leadership in projects, project governance, value management, virtual teams, project benefits.

For a complete list of titles in this series, please visit https://www.routledge.com/business/series/APM

Managing Projects in a World of People, Strategy and Change
Edited by Darren Dalcher

The Evolution of Project Management Practice
From Programmes and Contracts to Benefits and Change
Edited by Darren Dalcher

Net Present Value and Risk Modelling for Projects
By Martin Hopkinson

Performance Coaching for Complex Projects
Influencing Behaviour and Enabling Change
By Tony Llewellyn

Leading the Project Revolution

Reframing the Human Dynamics of Successful Projects

Edited by
Darren Dalcher

Routledge
Taylor & Francis Group

LONDON AND NEW YORK

First published 2019
by Routledge
2 Park Square, Milton Park, Abingdon, Oxon OX14 4RN

and by Routledge
605 Third Avenue, New York, NY 10017

First issued in paperback 2020

Routledge is an imprint of the Taylor & Francis Group, an informa business

British Library Cataloguing-in-Publication Data
A catalogue record for this book is available from the British Library

Library of Congress Cataloging-in-Publication Data
A catalog record has been requested for this book

ISBN 13: 978-0-367-73172-4 (pbk)
ISBN 13: 978-0-367-02873-2 (hbk)

Typeset in Bembo
by Deanta Global Publishing Services, Chennai, India

MIX
Paper from
responsible sources
FSC
www.fsc.org
FSC™ C013985

Printed in the United Kingdom
by Henry Ling Limited

Contents

Figures

Tables

About the Editor

Darren Dalcher Ph.D. (Lond), HonFAPM, FRSA, FCMI, FBCS, CITP, SMIEEE, SFHEA is Professor in Strategic Project Management at Lancaster University Management School and holds visiting appointments at Warwick Manufacturing Group, Drexel University, SKEMA Business School, Vienna University of Economics and Business, and the University of Iceland. He is the founder and Director of the National Centre for Project Management (NCPM), an interdisciplinary centre of excellence operating in collaboration with industry, government, academia, third sector organisations and the learned societies.

Following industrial and consultancy experience in managing technology projects, Professor Dalcher gained his PhD from King's College London for his work on continuous delivery, dynamic feedback and extended software project cycles. In 1992, he founded an IEEE taskforce focused on learning from project failures. He is active in numerous international committees, standards bodies, steering groups and editorial boards. He is heavily involved in organising international conferences, and has delivered many international keynote addresses and tutorials. He has written over 200 refereed papers and book chapters and published over 30 books. His work has been translated into French, German, Spanish, Italian, Russian, Chinese and Portuguese. He is Editor-in-Chief of Wiley's *Journal of Software: Evolution and Process* and of two established book series focused on managing projects and change initiatives published by Routledge.

He has built a reputation as leader and innovator in the area of practice-based education and reflection in project management and has designed, developed and launched the UK's first professional doctorate in project management, alongside an extensive suite of executive and professional masters programmes and diplomas. In 2008 he was named by the Association for Project Management as one of the top 10 influential experts in project management and has also been voted Project Magazine's Academic of the Year for his contribution in 'integrating and weaving academic work with practice'. He has been chairman of the influential APM Project Management Conference for an unprecedented five years, expanding the scope and content of the event, setting consecutive attendance records and bringing together the most influential speakers.

He received international recognition in 2010 with his appointment as a member of the PMForum International Academic Advisory Council. In October 2011 he was awarded a prestigious lifetime Honorary Fellowship from the Association for Project Management for outstanding contribution to the discipline of project management.

He has delivered lectures and courses in many institutions across Europe and North America and has won multiple awards and prizes, including most recently, the 2015 Best Paper Award from the British Academy of Management, the 2016 CMI's Management Articles of the Year competition, a 2017 Outstanding Paper Award in the Emerald Literati Network Awards for Excellence, the 2017 and 2018 PM World Journal Editor's Choice Awards, and the 2018 Project Management Review Outstanding Contributor Award. His research interests focus on rethinking project success and project agility, as well as maturity and capability; process improvement; systems engineering; decision making; change management; ethics, complexity; project leadership; knowledge management and reflective practice.

Professor Dalcher is an Honorary Fellow of the Association for Project Management, a Chartered Fellow of the British Computer Society, a Senior Fellow of the Higher Education Academy, a Fellow of the Chartered Management Institute and the Royal Society of Arts, a Senior Member of the IEEE and a Member of the Project Management Institute and the British Academy of Management. He has also been invited into the 'Ordre des Arts et Des Technologie' as a Chevalier (Knight), at Crypto Chain University, the leading non-profit research-only institute, focused on the public policy issues facing blockchain, cryptocurrency and decentralised computing technologies, in recognition of 'significant contributions to the technological arts, or the propagation of these fields'. He sits on numerous senior research and professional boards, including the PMI Academic Member Advisory Group, the APM Research Advisory Group, the International Advisory Council of PM World Today, the CMI Academic Council and the APM Group Ethics and Standards Governance Board.

Contributors

David Bentley has many years of experience working in business planning and improvement through change management at the corporate level, both in the private sector and embedded with public sector organisations, with a multi-national engineering consulting company and more recently in delivering organisational and cultural change programmes as an independent consultant. As a Chartered Civil Engineer, his background is in construction planning and managing projects in the highways, water and power sectors. Working on the introduction of IT systems and quality management led to a career in business and change management and a Director level position with a major international engineering consultant, working on highway network management in the UK and Australia. Supported by an MBA and a PhD in Business, David has strong leadership experience with teams of change agents and works to deliver significant benefits in business development and cultural improvement. David's particular skills in training and coaching in management, systems development, process mapping and improvement, procedure development, audit and systems accreditation inform David's approach to successful change delivery.

Joana Bértholo is a researcher, novelist and playwright. She first attended the Fine-Arts in Portugal, with a focus on Communication Design, and later obtained a PhD in Cultural Studies in Germany. Art processes are her preferred mode of research, using writing as a platform to investigate on a wide scope of interests, such as technology, ecology, sustainability and the darker aspects of groups and communities.

Richard Bolden is Professor of Leadership and Management and Director of Bristol Leadership and Change Centre at Bristol Business School, University of the West of England. He has over 20 years' experience in applied leadership, management and organisational research and education, including previous roles at the Universities of Exeter and Sheffield. His teaching and research explores the interface between individual and collective approaches to leadership and leadership development, with a particular focus on issues of identity, culture and collaboration. He has published widely on topics including distributed leadership, leadership in higher education, African leadership and leadership development evaluation. His books include *Exploring Leadership: Individual, Organizational and Societal Perspectives* (Oxford University Press, 2011) and *Leadership Paradoxes: Rethinking Leadership for an Uncertain World* (Routledge, 2016), the latter of which was shortlisted for the 2017 CMI Management Book of the Year Award. He is Associate Editor for the journal *Leadership* and engages extensively with external organisations and partnerships, including the NHS Leadership Academy and Bristol Golden Key.

David Booth has over 20 years of business management experience working for companies such as United Biscuits, Grand Metropolitan and Smith & Nephew, in marketing and then HR and strategic development at the senior management level, followed by working for the past 16 years as an independent management consultant helping organisations with their 'strategy journeys': clients include a range of large and medium-sized organisations from international financial services companies to specialist NHS Foundation Trusts. These projects have involved working intensively with client organisations, guiding and complementing their internal knowledge and resources to help steer their strategic planning processes and develop effective strategic plans: there has been a strong emphasis on organisational learning, and clients have remarked on the continuing value and relevance of the work.

Constance Dierickx is a sought-after advisor to boards and senior executives in high-stakes situations such as rapid growth, mergers and acquisitions, CEO succession and crisis. Her merger and acquisition clients succeed 400% more often than the average. Constance has been quoted in and asked to write for publications such as *The Wall Street Journal, Chief Executive, Chief Financial Officer, Directorship, Boards and Directors* and *Corporate Board Member*. Constance has consulted with dozens of boards and over 500 executives on five continents. She has worked with companies from the Fortune 50 to high-tech start-ups. Some of her clients include EWI Risk, Johnson Controls, Joy Global, Milliken Research, Porsche, Schnabel Engineering, Tennessee Valley Authority and Vulcan Materials. She is Vice-Chair of the board of The Partnership Against Domestic Violence and a member of the Advisory Board of Executive Women of Goizueta (Emory University). She is a member of the National Association of Corporate Directors and the Association for Psychological Science. Constance received her undergraduate degree from the University of North Carolina-Asheville, with faculty bestowed '*high honors*'. Her M.A. and Ph.D. are from Georgia State University where she studied psychology and decision science.

Ronald Meijers is senior partner Leadership, Transformation and Governance at Deloitte. For years, Ronald has been engaged in boardroom coaching and consulting, while fulfilling various management roles in professional services firms, such as co-chairman of the executive board of Krauthammer. He sits on various supervisory and advisory boards, e.g. at Dunamare, an education group. He gives keynotes on topics such as corporate culture, organizational collaboration, change management, creative thinking, leadership and governance. He has (co-)authored numerous articles, books and columns, among others in *Management Team* and *Management Scope*.

Ron Meyer is Professor of Strategic Leadership at Tias School for Business and Society, Tilburg University in the Netherlands, and Managing Director of the Center for Strategy & Leadership. For years, Ron has been combining boardroom consulting with in-house management training and applied management research. Besides that, Ron gives speeches and presentations on topics such as corporate strategy, business innovation, change management, strategic thinking, leadership and organizational development. He has (co-)authored numerous articles and books, among which the internationally leading textbook *Strategy – Process, Content, Context: An International Perspective*.

Gabrielle O'Donovan has clocked up more than 30,000 hours over 20+ years working on change programmes that have covered the full spectrum. Clients have included Bank of America Merrill Lynch, Unilever, the London Metropolitan Police, Lloyds Banking Group, Friends Life Insurance, the Ministry of Justice UK, Invensys Plc, Dublin Airport Authority, Cathay Pacific Airways and HSBC Hong Kong. Projects have been global, regional and country-specific in scale. Gabrielle O'Donovan has some significant achievements under her belt: her culture transformation programme for HSBC Hong Kong plus five subsidiary companies embedded a customer-centric culture and won an ASTD Excellence in Practice Award (USA, 2005); at Dublin Airport Authority, Ireland, her work as Stakeholder Management Lead for the building of Terminal 2 was instrumental in securing capital expenditure; Gabrielle's first book *The Corporate Culture Handbook* was rated 'In the top 1% of best business books for 2005' by USA reviewer Business Book Review; in 2010, Edgar Schein, Professor Emeritus of Sloan School of Management, MIT and founding father of organisational culture, referenced Gabrielle and her HSBC culture change programme in his 4th Edition of *Organisational Culture and Leadership* (Jossey-Bass, 2010). Schein also shared Gabrielle's 'Characteristics of a Healthy Culture' typology in his book, referring to her 23 new culture dimensions as 'notable'.

Dale Roberts is VP of Professional Services for Clarabridge, author, commentator, columnist and speaker. As a professional services leader for Clarabridge in Europe, Roberts is advising some of the world's largest companies on optimising the customer experience using social and digital insights. Prior to this he was part of the founding circle of Artesian Solutions, an innovator in social CRM and a Director of Services for business intelligence giant Cognos. Dale was identified as a thought leader in big data and analytics by Analytics Week, is a contributor to business and technology publications including Wired and ClickZ and a Fellow of the Royal Society of Arts. His first book, *Decision Sourcing*, is an inspiring commentary on the impact of social on corporate decision making. His latest, *World of Workcraft*, is a timely piece on engagement, motivation and digital humanism in the workplace.

Kurt Verweire obtained his PhD at Erasmus University Rotterdam in 1999. He is Associate Professor in Strategic Management and Partner at Vlerick Business School. He is also Programme Director of the MBA-FSI programme, a general management programme that is entirely focused on the financial services industry. His research interests include formulating and implementing winning business strategies, performance management and change management and corporate strategy. Current research projects address how firms have to position themselves in the market, and how to create alignment and commitment within the organisation. Many of his research projects deal with financial services organisations.

PM World Journal

The *PM World Journal* (PMWJ) is an online publication produced by PM World Inc. in the United States, but is created by a virtual team of advisors, correspondents and contributing editors located worldwide. Each month, the PMWJ features dozens of new articles, papers and stories about programmes, projects and project management (P/PM) around the world. Objectives for the journal are to (1) support the creation of new P/PM knowledge; (2) support the transfer of that knowledge to individuals, organisations and locations where professional P/PM may be weak, less available or sorely needed; (3) provide recognition and visibility for authors, the creators of new P/PM knowledge; (4) provide an easily accessible and useful online repository of P/PM knowledge and information as a global resource for knowledge sharing and continuous learning; and (5) promote the application of modern, professional P/PM for solving more of the world's problems – to make this world a better place.

Introduction

In search of a revolution
From toolsets to mindsets

Darren Dalcher

Welcome to another title in the *Advances in Project Management* series. The series continues to provide new ideas and fresh perspectives related to project thinking and practice. In keeping with our overarching rationale, many of the authors endeavour to refine and define the knowledge and capabilities related to the management of projects, often by looking at other disciplines and importing ideas and concepts that work from other domains and contexts. While some of the topics covered in this collection are mentioned in the various guides and bodies of knowledge, albeit in name only, the majority are yet to feature within the more conventional project management literature. The common thread linking the different areas and interests is around capabilities, skills, attitudes, values and perspectives that are needed to sustain and improve project performance in contemporary project settings.

Conventional project management has traditionally been oriented around the delivery of a comprehensive toolset that continues to grow and expand. Indeed, tools and procedures are easy to enumerate and offer an attractive basis for training courses and accreditation programmes. As a result they become a focus of technical discussion and practitioner accreditation within the profession. However, mastery of a toolset does not make experts; more crucially, it does not provide a guarantee of success in project delivery, acceptance and the realisation of value from the project outcomes. Focusing on the means often results in ignoring the ends: For some organisations failure to deliver results in even greater scrutiny and increased diligence in utilising the tools and following the process, which may in turn lead to an ever widening mismatch with the expected results.

The growing fascination and obsession with agile methods indicate a certain degree of dissatisfaction with the traditional approaches and the resulting outcomes, suggesting a yearning for alternatives that place people and their needs and expectations at the core of development. Certainly, it is worth noting that the first value statement expressed in the *Manifesto for Agile Software Development* (2001), the basis for agile thinking and methods, places 'individuals and interactions over processes and tools'. Relationships and collaboration are clearly crucial for developing relevant software, as well as for the management and delivery of meaningful projects that address organisational concerns and encourage people to alter behavioural patterns, and engage with new systems and structures in order to bring about beneficial change and realise intended benefits.

The shift in emphasis reflects a growing interest in the role of people in projects, be it as users, participants, stakeholders, sponsors or project managers and leaders. People play a vital part in the success of projects, initiatives and organisations, yet traditional project management sources offer limited guidance and insights that extend beyond technical roles and prescriptions. *Leading the Project Revolution* delves into the dynamics of people, teams and organisations exploring their impact on leadership, strategy, success and achievement. The book offers a progressive agenda for improving project practice, enabling the dialogue to progress from the typical coverage of static toolsets towards an understanding of flexible and adaptable mindsets. Flexibility, agility and resilience are addressed as the social, cultural and complex dimensions of leadership, strategy, organisations and project teamwork are examined and practical insights are synthesised into practical models and frameworks.

Our own manifesto may suggest that we pursue a progressive agenda that encourages new ways of thinking and a broader consideration of issues related to people and their ability to operate and excel at project work within organisations in change-ridden, turbulent and dynamic environments. The corresponding shift in values advocated through the writing could be summarised as a series of moves:

- From a static toolset, towards flexible skillsets and pragmatic mindsets;
- From the pursuit of process, towards an appreciation of people;
- From technical and instrumental rationality, towards a wider social, cultural, political and institutional awareness; and
- From passive conformance, towards professional reflection, agility, flexibility and adaptability.

It is becoming increasingly clear that as professionals we need to pursue a better informed agenda and that some of the learning and insights will need to be sourced from other domains. Identifying specific sources to sustain this growing awareness could be challenging, and perusing other domains and disciplines may be both time-consuming and problematic without an initial roadmap and knowledge of the vocabulary and local terrain. This volume therefore offers a starting point and sample of some of the best writing centred on leadership, people, strategy, execution and complexity.

The content is divided into nine main areas. Each area is explored from two distinct perspectives. First, an introductory narrative sets the scene and explains the context, typically focusing on the key ideas and main thinkers or re-visiting seminal writing or sharing a significant narrative. The areas explored often borrow from other disciplines or perspectives, and the writing tries to address an important question, explore paradoxes or review progress to date. Second, the main guest-authored chapter features new ideas, ways of thinking or perspective. Readers are strongly encouraged to pursue the additional sources listed in the chapters, which can offer further insight and detail. The seminal works indicated in the introductory narrative are also worth pursuing.

The chapters in this collection bring together leading authorities on topics that are relevant to managing, leading and directing projects. Topics include leadership, followership, agility, team dynamics, crises, organisational culture, change management, planning, strategy, mapping, complexity, shadow working, alignment, strategy execution and innovation.

The volume offers an introduction to a range of brand new and established ideas. It also introduces different perspectives and ways of thinking, as well as a host of new writers, thinkers and scholars from other domains and areas. The main aims of the collection are to reflect on and summarise the state of practice, to propose new extensions and additions to existing practice, to distil new insights and to provide a way of sampling a range of the most promising ideas, perspectives, approaches, perspectives and styles of writing from leading thinkers and practitioners.

Leading the revolution

'A revolution is an idea which has found its bayonets'.

– Napoleon Bonaparte

The title of this book is inspired by Professor Gary Hamel's relentless effort to rejuvenate management thinking and encourage innovation in the prevailing mindset and approach of mainstream management:

> Something **has** changed. Something is different. The signs are all around you. CEOs have been losing their jobs at a record pace. Newcomers have been capturing a growing share of the market value in a host of industries. Customers have been growing more restless, demanding and fickle. Web-enabled connectivity has been reshaping value chains. New technologies have been undermining old business models – from publishing to radio to pharmaceuticals. Traditional strategies for pumping up profits and the share price – incremental cost cutting, mega-mergers, share buybacks, outsourcing and financial engineering – have been losing their punch. Something **is** going on here.
>
> (Hamel, 2002: p. ix)

Hamel's contention is that the age of progress is over, requiring a new way of engaging with increasingly turbulent times.

> We are now standing on the threshold of a new age—an age of revolution. Change has changed. No longer is it additive. No longer does it move in a straight line. In the twenty-first century, change is discontinuous, abrupt, seditious.
>
> (ibid.: p. 5)

The key move that can be discerned is from a world of punctuated equilibrium, typified by episodic change, towards today's modern pace that is all punctuation and no equilibrium. A key implication is an inevitable move from harnessing, what Hamel terms 'the disciplines of progress', expressed through well-established ideas such as rigorous planning, continuous improvement, statistical control, six sigma and enterprise resource planning, towards a more innovative and responsive form of leadership. Hamel is therefore agitating for a more radical form of innovation that extends beyond mere refinement as befitting the age of revolution.

Hamel's radical view of innovation calls for (ibid.: p. 64):

- Reconfiguring products and processes;
- Creating entirely new business concepts; and
- Inventing new industry structures.

Pausing to reflect on achievement against the three bullet points would indicate that some progress has already been made. Radical product-centred innovation can boast transformative successes in terms of new online platforms and the introduction of disruptive technologies, including well-recognised names such as Facebook, PayPal, Alibaba and Uber. At the other end of the scale, new industry developments such as Industry 4.0 (Brettel et al., 2014; Lee, Bagheri & Kao, 2015; Lasi et al., 2014) indicate a new manufacturing and industrialisation landscape from a global industry-wide perspective. The middle ground, focused on the creation of radically innovative new models at the business level, seems to boast less, if any, progress.

> New business models are more than disruptive technologies, they are completely novel business concepts. They are more than replacements for what already is, instead they open up entirely new opportunities.
>
> (Hamel, 2002: p. 69)

Business concept innovation introduces greater strategic variety into a domain or industry. Project management has proved largely immune to such incursions. Hamel suggests that business concept innovation is a meta-innovation as it takes the entire business concept as a starting point (ibid.: p. 70).

The quote heading this section positions a revolution as an idea that has found its bayonets. However, a revolution requires its revolutionaries, active agents who believe and are willing to spread the word and promote the idea more widely, whatever the consequences.

What does it take to become a revolutionary? Hamel develops a list of essential qualities, which is expanded below with additional commentary. Revolutionaries have the abilities to (ibid.: pp. 122–148):

- Forget the future – invent it instead;
- See different, be different – develop an alternative point of view;

- Be a novelty addict – find discontinuities; buck the trend; agitate for new experiences; and
- Be a heretic – eschew orthodoxy and dogma; keep asking why.

In Hamel's view, the new revolutionaries are simply activists with a live and passionate interest:

> Activists are not anarchists. They are instead the 'loyal opposition'. Their loyalty is not to any particular person or office, but to the continued success of their organization and to all those who labor on its behalf. They are patriots intent on protecting the enterprise from mediocrity narrow and self-interest and veneration of the past. They seek to reform rather than to destroy. Their goal is to create a movement within their company and a revolution outside it.
>
> (ibid.: pp. 156–7)

A good example of such intense and passionate activism is provided by John Patrick and David Grossman of IBM who ultimately developed their own manifesto for creating web-enabled software as a complete antithesis to and in direct contravention of IBM's traditional way of doing things. The manifesto identified a set of essential principles required to compete in a web-enabled environment by focusing on rapid action to get the stuff out there, quick learning and continuous improvement.

The specific steps offer a steeped approach to managing in rapid environments (ibid.: p. 167):

1   Start simple; grow fast;
2   Trial by fire;
3   Just don't inhale (the stale air of orthodoxy);
4   Just enough is good enough;
5   Skip the krill (go to the top of the food chain when you're trying to sell your idea);
6   Wherever you go, there you are (the Net has no bounds);
7   No blinders;
8   Take risks; make mistakes quickly; fix them fast; and
9   Don't get pinned down (to any one way of thinking).

Agile enthusiasts may identify with many of the principles, which will also resonate with innovation aficionados. Simple steps can thus add up to a radical agenda supporting a fundamental shift in developing new business concepts and fostering much-needed management innovation. While the effort to embed them may be challenging, they offer a significant transformation from traditional thinking and established, self-sustaining orthodoxy, thus enabling a more responsive, radical and adaptive mode of innovation and operation.

It is perhaps not the bayonets which are needed to promulgate a new revolution, but an army of activists ready and willing to identify core principles, share new concepts, experiment and build a new reality.

In engaging in a journey of continuous activism and discovery, it is often through the conversations and discussions with other radicals and enthusiasts that new perspectives are unearthed, and new ideas are shared. This book offers a glimpse into some of the more promising ideas, models, and new ways of thinking that have been successfully applied within the context of project practice. It thus enables a further dialogue about what is feasible and desirable in the world of projects and change.

Advances in project management

The majority of the individual chapters build on articles that have been selected to feature in the 'Advances in Project Management' series of articles published in the *PM World Journal*. The main purpose of the series is to make the ideas and principles of the knowledge and skills required to manage projects more accessible. *Advances in Project Management* was introduced in order to improve understanding and project capability further up the organisation; amongst strategy and senior decision makers and amongst professional project and programme managers. Our ambition has been to provide project sponsors, project management leaders, practitioners, scholars and researchers with thought-provoking, cutting-edge information that combines conceptual insights with interdisciplinary rigour and practical relevance, thus offering new insights and understanding of key areas and approaches.

In order to identify the potential authors, a wide range of books and resources have been consulted. Contributions were selected by the editor on the basis of their individual merit, usefulness and applicability. The chapters offered here will feature many leading practitioners, researchers and leaders and highlight concepts, ideas and tools that will be of benefit to practising project managers. Indeed, many of the individual authors in this volume may be the radicals and revolutionaries needed to deliver a new agenda and share new business concepts and ways of thinking and working.

To this end, the individual chapters aim to:

1 share and embrace new ways of thinking around the challenges faced by project and programme managers;
2 identify and focus on *key* aspects of project, programme and portfolio management;
3 offer practical case examples of how new applications have been tackled in a variety of industries;
4 provide access to appropriate new models in these areas, as they emerge from either academic research or practical application.

In other words, the book aims to provide those people and organisations who are involved with the development in project management with the kind of structured information that will inform their thinking, their practice and improve their decisions. In effect, it is new food for thought intended to invigorate and stimulate the journey of discovery.

Geography and scope

'The only way to support a revolution is to make your own'.

— Abbie Hoffman

Project management is practised in many different sectors and environments. Such different perspectives allow for a diversity of ideas and ways of thinking. Many of the new ideas develop in different sectors and it is important to find a shared platform to present and highlight the impacts of such innovations and their potential for invigorating current thinking and engendering new insights. This publication offers such a shared environment, which will be of use to practitioners regardless of where they are based and whatever the geography of the projects that they are running.

The book offers a rich variety of ideas, lessons and insights that are ready to be shared and adopted. The topics emphasise key areas required to improve the delivery of projects and programmes in a wide range of environments and contexts. The experts and authors come from a variety of backgrounds and bring organisational, psychological, sociological or other influences they can share. Others are experts in coaching, strategy, innovation, leadership, human behaviour, organisational dynamics, complexity and transformational change. The value of the publication is in integrating the multitude of insights and perspectives and offering the opportunity to discuss, engage and adapt the ideas.

The management of projects offers an exciting space for sharing, collaboration and exploration. The ambition, scale and scope of many of the new endeavours are breathtaking. But an injection of new insights and approaches, especially in regard to human participants, is desperately needed. Many of our authors will not regard themselves as radicals or revolutionaries, but they are happy to guide new conversations and offer some of the new perspectives and mindsets needed for starting new and meaningful conversations. Together we can continue to develop and grow by embracing new skills and perspectives and improving the state of practice. We encourage readers who would like to share their insights and ideas with the wider community to get in touch with the editor. We look forward to continuing the dialogue about enduring success in projects and programmes and encouraging impactful revolutions in project thinking and practice.

Darren Dalcher
Lancaster, UK

References

Brettel, M., Friederichsen, N., Keller, M., & Rosenberg, M. (2014). How virtualization, decentralization and network building change the manufacturing landscape: An industry 4.0 perspective. *International Journal of Mechanical, Industrial Science and Engineering, 8*(1), 37–44.

Hamel, G. (2002). *Leading the revolution: How to thrive in turbulent times by making innovation a way of life*, updated edition. Boston, MA: Harvard Business School Press.

Lee, J., Bagheri, B., & Kao, H. A. (2015). A cyber-physical systems architecture for industry 4.0-based manufacturing systems. *Manufacturing Letters, 3*, 18–23.

Lasi, H., Fettke, P., Kemper, H. G., Feld, T., & Hoffmann, M. (2014). Industry 4.0. *Business & Information Systems Engineering, 6*(4), 239–242.

The Agile Alliance (2001). *Manifesto for Agile Software Development*, http://agilemanifesto.org/, accessed 14 December 2018.

1
Leadership

The leaders we deserve?

Darren Dalcher

Over the years, many of us have must have looked at our own bosses and wondered how they ever became leaders. We all recognise the profile; bereft of strategic thinking, enmeshed in local and personal considerations, unable to see the horizon of opportunities, antagonistic, incapable of inspiring others, lacking a vision, unable to consider consequences and options, incapable of making informed decisions, uncaring and ignorant of how to engage with and motivate followers. Poor leaders deliver a toxic long-term legacy, which affects team members and followers, and ultimately, impacts the bottom line of the organisation, team or unit. The typical traits of poor leaders (Leviticus, 2017) include:

- Lack of communication;
- Tendency to micromanage;
- Unclear expectations;
- Intimidation and bullying; and
- Poor people skills.

Many of our appointed leaders would appear to exhibit such symptoms, causing untold damage to organisations. Management scholar Laurence J. Peter reasoned that people simply rise to their level of incompetence. Selection to higher office and new positions is often based on performance in previous assignments. The Peter Principle suggests that people rise, or get promoted, until they reach a job they cannot really manage, leaving many individuals to operate at their 'level of incompetence'.

'In time, every post tends to be occupied by an employee who is incompetent to carry out its duties' (Peter & Hull, 1969: p. 36).

Inevitably, therefore:

'Work is accomplished by those employees who have not yet reached their level of incompetence' (ibid.).

The *Peter Principle* became an international best seller, selling well over a million copies. The original manuscript had been rejected by 30 publishers, before William Morrow & Company accepted it and printed a small run of

10,000 copies. The book made it into the *New York Times* best-seller list, selling over 200,000 copies in the first year. It has since been translated into 38 languages.

A generalised form of the Peter Principle asserts that anything that works will continue to be utilised in the exact same format, in increasingly more demanding contexts and applications, until it ultimately fails. The temptation is to develop a habit that keeps replicating exactly what has worked previously and impose it on new situations as they are encountered.

Ironically, Peter and Hull also noted that highly competent individuals may struggle to progress through the system.

'In most hierarchies, super-competence is more objectionable than incompetence' (ibid.).

Peter and Hull duly warned that extremely skilled and productive employees often face criticism, and would be fired if they don't start performing worse as their presence 'disrupts and therefore violates the first commandment of hierarchical life: the hierarchy must be preserved'.

A crisis of leadership

In an increasingly uncertain world, leaders are called upon to deliver both hope and change. When there is a need for a clear direction, followers turn to their leaders for the courage to make the right decision and the inspiration and assurance that allow followers to believe.

Many of the leaders we encounter in all spheres of life place their desire to be right above the wish to achieve the right outcome. Ego boosts, quests for power and the thirst for greed are often confused with leadership.

As a result, many followers, citizens, and workers remain concerned by the apparent lack of leadership skills. The World Economic Forum identified lack of leadership as one of the major global challenges facing the world in 2015, and commissioned a survey to investigate further. A staggering 86 percent of respondents worldwide agreed that there is currently a global leadership crisis (World Economic Forum, 2015).

The figures divided by region support the global perception of the problem, with respondents acknowledging a leadership crisis divided by continent and region as shown in Table 1.1.

Table 1.1 The problem with leadership regional survey

Region	Recognising a global crisis
Asia	83%
Europe	85%
Latin America	84%
Middle East & North Africa	85%
North America	92%
Sub-Saharan Africa	92%

It appears that if there is one thing we all agree upon, regardless of location, is that leaders are unable to perform as needed.

When asked what skills would be needed to win back their confidence, respondents identified a set of virtues, including:

- A global interdisciplinary perspective;
- Long-term, empirical planning;
- Strong communication skills;
- A prioritisation of social justice and well-being over financial growth;
- Empathy;
- Courage;
- Morality; and
- A collaborative nature.

It is no longer enough to be inspirational. Leaders are expected to engage different stakeholder groups, listen, mediate and include the opinions of diverse constituencies before making their decisions.

Successful leaders of the future are expected to be good at execution, team building and delegation, combined with honing a positive and reassuring attitude in the face of growing uncertainty and adversity.

Leadership matters

US Professor Warren Bennis is widely recognised as a pioneer of the leadership movement. Indeed, the *Financial Times* referred to him in 2000 as 'the professor who established leadership as a respectable academic field'. In August 2007, *Business Week* ranked Bennis as one of the top ten thought leaders in business.

Professor Bennis and Professor Bert Nanus wrote the first book dedicated to leadership. *Leaders: The Strategies for Taking Charge* was released in 1985 providing an insightful and much-needed guide to the area of leadership. The book is based on a series of interviews with successful leaders. The original edition proved a success, and the book was translated into 21 languages.

The book has evolved over time. It might be instructive therefore to conduct a brief guided tour through the three different editions, paying particular attention to the changes in emphasis.

The first edition (1985) predates most other writing in the area of leadership. It identifies a tendency to replace management with leadership as people do not want to be managed, but would prefer to be led. Leaders were not 'incrementalists'; they were looking to create new ideas, new policies and new methodologies. The authors identified four major strategies that emerged from their research that all of their 90 subjects embodied:

- **Attention through vision** is the creation of focus which matches the leaders' agenda and grabs followers;

- **Meaning through communication** is used to capture imagination and create alignment;
- **Trust through positioning** is used to maintain organisational integrity; and
- **The deployment of self** is essential to ensuring that leaders manage themselves. Without it, leaders will do more harm than good as 'like incompetent physicians, incompetent managers can make people sicker and less vital'. (ibid.: p. 58)

The second edition (Bennis & Nanus, 1997) offers new emphases. In particular, upon reflection, the authors felt that the following points were important:

- Leadership is about character and character is a continuously evolving thing;
- To keep organisations competitive, leaders must be instrumental in creating a social architecture capable of generating intellectual capital;
- Strong determination to achieve a goal or realise a vision must be a conviction or even a passion;
- The capacity to generate and sustain trust is the central ingredient in leadership;
- True leaders have an uncanny way of enrolling people in their vision through their optimism; and
- Leaders have a bias towards action that results in success. It comes from their capacity to translate vision and purpose into reality.

More crucially, the book identifies a need to refresh and update leadership thinking as millions of new leaders will need to come on board and play a part in driving new achievements. Gazing into the future, the authors conclude that the leaders who succeed most will be those who are able to:

1 Set direction during turbulent times;
2 Manage change whilst still providing exceptional customer service and quality;
3 Attract resources and forge new alliances to accommodate new constituencies;
4 Harness diversity on a global scale;
5 Inspire a sense of optimism, enthusiasm, and commitment among their followers; and
6 Be a leader of leaders, especially regarding knowledge workers.

The final update of the book took place with the publication of the third edition in 2003, enabling the authors to reflect on 20 years of development in leadership. In summarising the achievements of the book over that period, the authors identified five key contributions to leadership:

1 **Distinguishing leadership from management**: Leaders serve a different organisational purpose from managers and have a unique perspective and responsibility. The distinction that 'managers do things right while leaders do the right thing' had been widely accepted and quoted.

2 **Empowerment**: Empowerment replaces power and control, enabling concepts such as collaborative leadership and servant leadership.

3 **Vision**: A clearly articulated vision, or a strong sense of direction, focuses the attention: Ultimately, a widely shared vision enables organisations to succeed.

4 **Trust**: Trustworthiness is a vital characteristic of successful leadership, whilst the lack thereof has proven to be a key ingredient in organisational failures, scandals and disasters.

5 **Management of meaning**: Leaders play a key part in shaping meaning and communicating the culture. Indeed, they have primary responsibility for articulating organisational values, interpreting reality, framing and mobilising meaning, and creating the necessary symbols and role models to communicate a coherent image of the principles that should guide organisational behaviour.

In a world that is becoming increasingly complex, interdependent, and vulnerable to disruption, few things may be more important than the quality and credibility of leaders who set worthwhile agendas, mobilize the necessary resources and empower others to act in the best interests of their organizations and the larger society.

(Bennis & Nanus, 2003: p. iii)

Seeking agility in leaders

Many of the challenges identified by Bennis and Nanus remain valid. Meanwhile, new ones continue to come to the fore. Turbulent times, new technologies and revolutionary platforms, speedier resolution, increased global connectedness, and wider dependence and impacts of supply and delivery chains require new leaders capable of adapting, changing, and making ever more critical and demanding decisions at an increasingly faster pace.

There is a clear need for fresh thinking around leadership to address such contemporary challenges. The chapter by Ron Meyer and Ronald Meijers offers just that. The contribution draws on their book *Leadership Agility: Developing Your Repertoire of Leadership Styles*, published by Routledge. Ron and Ronald's work stems from the recognition that leadership is about influencing others to move in a certain preferred direction and there are many ways of achieving such influence. Recognising that leaders require a more extensive playbook for tackling demanding new contexts, Ron and Ronald simply set about writing one that will offer the requisite variety and resilience for leaders in changing contexts.

John P. Kotter observed that 'because management deals mostly with the status quo and leadership deals mostly with change, in the next century we are going to have to try to become much more skilled at creating leaders'. Ron and Ronald acknowledge the need for creating agile leaders. Agile leaders are flexible, adaptable and responsive and are therefore adept at switching between behaviours and acquiring new behaviours and are acutely aware of the situation faced and therefore able to rapidly react and take appropriate action. Not following a recipe requires greater familiarity with the range of options and potential approaches to enacting leadership and the authors do a wonderful job of introducing an extensive variety of approaches and perspectives. Their vision of agility revolves around leaders who 'have the capacity to flexibly switch between leadership styles, and adaptively master new ones, in rapid response to the specific needs of the people and situation they want to influence' (Meyer & Meijers, 2017: pp. xvi–xvii).

Agility is permeating most aspects of organisations, forcing leaders to respond to changing situations and contexts. Situational leadership theories always emphasised the need for contextual recognition and alignment. Ron and Ronald recognise that the situational pressures on leaders have become more pressing and exponentially more complex. They acknowledge that leaders need to respond by making a step change in their capacity to become more agile and responsive.

Ron and Ronald identify new trends towards greater organisational agility; a need for greater organisational diversity; a requirement for increased employee empowerment; and greater career diversity. The new trends make it impossible for leaders to rigidly hold on to any particular leadership style and approach. Moreover, they make it unlikely that the same approach can be sustained indefinitely over the long-term horizon. The focus on agility in leadership makes it possible to develop a wider repertoire of styles and approaches that can be customised and contextualised to deliver a better targeted and more effective range of responses.

Ron and Ronald are thus able to make an important contribution to the ongoing development of leadership scholarship. Their focus on 20 leadership styles expressed in ten dimensions is organised through five clusters into their leadership rose. Utilising the rose, forces prospective and existing leaders to engage with the contradictions and opposite views, and make sense of the different dimensions and perspectives, thereby gaining a richer understanding of the range of potential approaches. It also chimes with the view of Warren Bennis that 'Leaders must encourage their organizations to dance to forms of music yet to be heard'.

The early identification of default styles of leadership as advocated in *Leadership Agility* can subsequently be contrasted with shifting priorities and needs, encouraging the recognition of the plurality and diversity of response styles. Rather than settling on providing recipes and guidelines, Ron and Ronald encourage the development of responsible, informed and competent leaders, ready to face the demanding challenges of modern environments and contexts. In doing so they continue the tradition of stretching leaders to be the best they can be and give followers a chance to be guided and supported by the leaders that they deserve.

References

Bennis, W., & Nanus, B. (1985/1997/2003). *Leaders: The strategies for taking charge*. New York: Harper & Row.

Leviticus, G. (2017). The top signs of poor leadership. *Chron*, http://smallbusiness.chron.com/top-signs-poor-leadership-31537.html, accessed 14 December 2018.

Meyer, R., & Meijers, R. (2017). *Leadership agility: Developing your repertoire of leadership styles*. New York: Routledge.

Peter, L. J., & Hull, R. (1969). *The Peter principle: Why things always go wrong*. London: Peter Morrow.

World Economic Forum (2015). *Outlook on the global agenda: Lack of leadership*. Cologny, Switzerland: World Economic Forum.

Developing leadership agility

Different projects, different approaches

Ron Meyer and Ronald Meijers

Every project manager knows that each project is essentially unique. The mix of different people, different objectives, different agendas, different circumstances, and different unfolding events leads to a different dynamic that project managers ignore at their peril. One-trick ponies never do well – only the agile flourish. To be successful, project managers need to be *flexible*, that is, they need to have a broad repertoire of potential behaviours and problem-solving approaches that they can tap into. But preferably they should also be *adaptive*, in other words, have the ability to learn new behaviours and problem-solving approaches if the current set is not sufficient. At the same time, this flexibility and adaptability should be coupled with *responsiveness* to the situational demands, meaning that they should quickly and accurately sense what the circumstances require and adjust their behaviour accordingly. Only when project managers master flexibility, adaptability and responsiveness will they be truly agile and ready to deal with the unpredictable nature of project work.

For leaders in a project setting, the need for agility is even higher. Not only is each project unique and shifting over time, but the people involved in projects have become increasingly more diverse. Not only does the workforce come from a wider variety of cultural backgrounds, but there is also a richer mix of genders, affiliations, lifestyles and career paths, each requiring leaders to adjust their behaviour to be able to strike the right chord and win hearts and minds in the most effective way. With so many different situations and different people, all demanding a different approach, to be successful leaders must exhibit leadership agility – *have the capacity to flexibly switch between leadership styles, and adaptively master new ones, in rapid response to the specific needs of the people and the situation they want to influence.*

Yet, the fundamental question is which leadership styles exist that leaders could potentially make use of, what the advantages and disadvantages are of each, and under which conditions one would be preferable over the others. As this is a huge question, this chapter will limit itself to mapping 20 important leadership styles, grouped into ten pairs of opposite styles (see Figure 1.1 for an overview). For the reader, the question is whether you master all 20 and can easily switch between them depending on the needs of the circumstances.

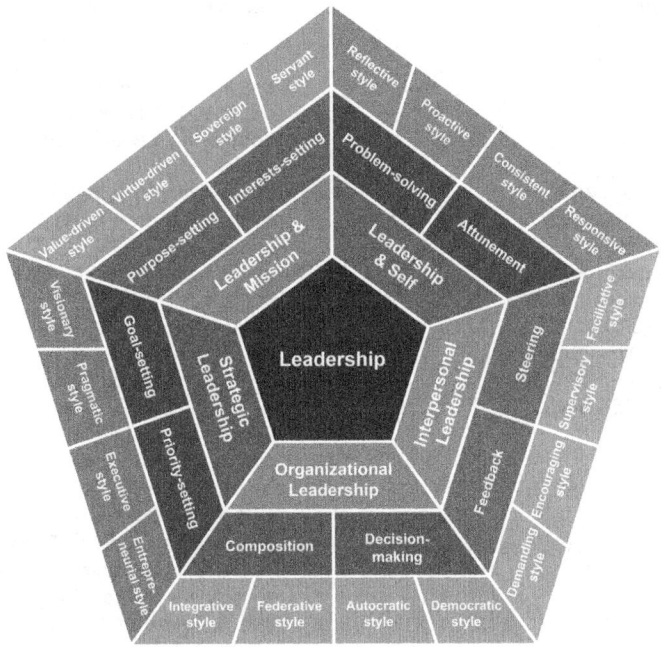

Figure 1.1 The leadership rose: leadership domains, tasks and styles.

That would make you highly agile. The more likely reality is that you will be better at some than at others, leading to the question of whether there are some leadership styles that you need to improve to become more agile. Generally, people tend to exhibit a preference for one side of a pair (we call this their 'default style'), making the other side of the pair the style requiring further development. If you would like to determine your own default styles, Table 1.2 provides a 'quick and dirty' assessment tool.

These ten dimensions are not the only ways in which leadership styles can differ, but they do represent the most important balancing acts faced by leaders in their drive to effectively influence people around them. The ten can be divided into five clusters, depending on the leadership domain involved. The first two dimensions fall into the domain of *interpersonal leadership*, which deals with how leaders interact with other individuals to achieve certain results. The second pair is concerned with *organisational leadership*, focusing on the ways in which leaders can get individuals to work together as a strong team. The third set of dimensions is concerned with *strategic leadership*, dealing with the question of which role a leader plays in the formulation and implementation of strategy. The fourth pair falls into the category of *leadership and mission*, which deals with the type of purpose that leaders emphasise to mobilise people to follow. And finally the fifth pair of dimensions revolves around the way in which

Table 1.2 The leadership style profiler

Left Style	Scale	Right Style
Supervisory Leadership Style I take hands on control of key tasks to ensure that people carry out the work correctly.	1.....2.....3.....4....5.....6	**Facilitative Leadership Style** I delegate key tasks to the right people and ensure that they are well-equipped to carry out the work independently.
Demanding Leadership Style I challenge people to do better, by emphasising the room for improvement.	1.....2.....3.....4....5.....6	**Encouraging Leadership Style** I show confidence in people, by emphasising their ability to do a good job.
Integrative Leadership Style I build teams of like-minded people, creating a shared sense of identity and uniform ways of working.	1.....2.....3.....4....5.....6	**Federative Leadership Style** I build teams of people with a diversity of attitudes and views, giving them room to think and act differently.
Autocratic Leadership Style I take the responsibility for making decisions and ensuring speed and clarity.	1.....2.....3.....4....5.....6	**Democratic Leadership Style** I take the responsibility for making sure decisions are taken jointly and ensuring quality and commitment.
Visionary Leadership Style I set strategic goals that are very ambitious and broad, challenging people to find ways of achieving them.	1.....2.....3.....4....5.....6	**Pragmatic Leadership Style** I set strategic goals that are realistic and specific, guiding people's progress in achieving them.
Executive Leadership Style I focus people on managing the current activities as efficiently and effectively as possible.	1.....2.....3.....4....5.....6	**Entrepreneurial Leadership Style** I focus people on renewing the organisation, taking the risk to seek out new opportunities.
Value-driven Leadership Style I explain to people that our mission is to do well by making money for our shareholders and ourselves.	1.....2.....3.....4....5.....6	**Virtue-driven Leadership Style** I explain to people that our mission is to do good by making a contribution to the well-being of our stakeholders.
Sovereign Leadership Style I strive to fulfil my own objectives, mobilising others to help me where possible.	1.....2.....3.....4....5.....6	**Servant Leadership Style** I strive to fulfil the group's objectives, offering others my help where possible.
Reflective Leadership Style I think before I act, reflecting on leadership issues and options before moving into action.	1.....2.....3.....4....5.....6	**Proactive Leadership Style** I think while I act, reflecting on leadership issues and managing responses along the way.
Consistent Leadership Style I approach each leadership situation in the same way, remaining predictable and authentic.	1.....2.....3.....4....5.....6	**Responsive Leadership Style** I flexibly adjust my approach to each leadership situation, depending on the specific circumstances.

a person deals with being a leader and behaves towards leadership challenges – *leadership and self.*

Interpersonal leadership

Two questions are key when it comes to steering the behaviour of individuals: *what* should leaders try to influence and *how* they should try to influence it. The issue of 'what to influence' is referred to as *interpersonal steering* and is concerned with determining the topics the leader wants to focus on to trigger the desired behaviour of the individual. The issue of 'how to influence' is referred to as *interpersonal feedback* and is concerned with the way the leader should stimulate the individual to actually move in the intended direction.

Interpersonal steering: The paradox of activities and conditions

To be successful, leaders need to get people to perform. They need to steer the behaviour of each individual, to enlarge the chance that the work actually gets done as intended. They need to have a lever of control – some way of ensuring that people carry out activities in an effective way (Blake & Mouton, 1964; Yukl & Fu, 1999). The most straightforward way of doing this is to tell each person which activities to complete and then to check whether these tasks are accomplished as instructed. This is direct control, whereby discussions between the leader and the follower generally have two agenda items: outlining the activities that will be delegated and evaluating the progress on each of the activities identified. The great advantage of this hands-on approach is that the leader knows exactly what is going on and can take corrective action quickly if necessary.

However, leaders can also trust that team members have the capacity to determine the necessary activities themselves. Leaders can delegate the activity definition, not only the activity execution. By giving individuals a clear mandate and the responsibility to reach the intended results in the way they believe works best, leaders can empower people to take initiative and ownership. This does not mean that the leader relinquishes control. The influence of the leader on the follower is not direct, by telling the individual what to do, but indirect, by shaping the conditions that enable followers to 'do it themselves'. The lever of control is not activity-oriented supervision, but condition-oriented facilitation, creating the optimal circumstances to trigger the intended behaviour. Typical enabling conditions include having the right training, information, resources, decision making authority and incentives.

In balancing between activities and conditions as the primary lever of control, leaders who prefer to influence on the basis of activities have a *supervisory leadership style*. These leaders tend to be personally involved in the nitty-gritty of day-to-day operations and very hands on, defining tasks and providing their team members with ideas, advice, and feedback. Leaders more inclined to indirect control by creating the optimal organisational conditions have a *facilitative leadership style*. These leaders focus on creating the right conditions, getting the right people, and then getting out of the way. They believe that the most effective way to bring out the best in people is to trust their competence and their willingness to perform.

Interpersonal feedback: The paradox of challenge and appreciation

Besides the issue of what to influence, leaders are faced with the question of how to influence. They must determine the tone of voice and posture they want to take to trigger people to move in the desired direction. Looking at the way that sports coaches give feedback to their athletes is very illustrative of how business leaders can approach this issue. Some coaches believe that the best way to spur an individual to an exceptional accomplishment is by continuously highlighting the upside potential and refusing to accept that the current performance is the best possible. These coaches challenge their charges to rise above themselves and to see that they are capable of operating at a higher level. Therefore, these coaches feel that their feedback needs to be critical, demanding, and sometimes even confrontational, constantly pushing their athletes to close the gap between their current and optimal performance.

Other coaches, however, do not emphasise the performance gap, as they find this stance too negative. Instead of instilling the urge to live up to their potential, they focus on instilling confidence in their athletes. They want their sportspeople to believe in themselves and to have the inner strength to go out and excel. Therefore, these coaches show appreciation for the talents and hard work that their athletes put in. They are understanding, encouraging and sometimes even overly complimentary, constantly expressing their belief in the ability of their athletes to give a top performance.

As business leaders try to find the best way to motivate their followers, they too must find the right stance, somewhere between being challenging and being appreciative. Where leaders lean over towards the side of challenge, they have a *demanding leadership style*. These leaders are constructively dissatisfied with the current level of performance and set higher standards to challenge followers to do better. Leaders more inclined towards the appreciation side of the balance have an *encouraging leadership style*. These leaders are positive towards their followers, expressing confidence in the capabilities and willingness of each individual to do a good job.

Organisational leadership

Organisational leadership is about the leader's role in building and maintaining an effective team of people. The organisational unit that the leader focuses on can be small (e.g. a department) or large (e.g. a corporation), formal (e.g. a unit) or informal (e.g. a community), and inside the company (e.g. a cross-functional team) or across the company's boundaries (e.g. an alliance).

Two issues are key when it comes to the leader's work of getting people organised: determining how to pull together the best possible team (*organisational composition*) and establishing how they should make choices (*organisational decision making*).

Organisational composition: The paradox of unity and diversity

Whether it is a taskforce, a department, a business unit or an entire corporation, putting together the best possible group of people for the job, and getting them to work concertedly as a team, is a key leadership task. Leaders need to take individuals and forge them into units that are more than the sum of the parts. This means influencing people to give up part of their autonomy and individual identity to become an integral part of a larger whole. Building a highly effective team involves more than only selecting the most knowledgeable and skilled individuals, and getting them to work side-by-side. As every sports coach knows, 'all-star teams' often get beat by squads that work together as well-oiled machines.

Achieving the right organisational composition starts with striving towards a shared goal – no unit without unity of mission. But to really pull together as a team, people need to also embrace common values, share a common worldview, speak a common language, adhere to common rules and work according to common practices. The more the team members are on the same wavelength, the easier it will be to communicate, cooperate and commit within the group. And the more tightly knit the culture, the stronger will be the feeling of belonging and the sense of shared destiny. Collins and Porras (1994) even propagate pursuing 'cult-like cultures' as a way of getting organisations that are 'built to last'.

Yet, besides unity, leaders will also want to have enough diversity of ideas, experiences and practices on board to fuel discussion and renewal. There is no innovation without diversity. IBM found out the hard way that having a 'big blue' monoculture led to groupthink and complacency in responding to changes in the outside world. It took an outside-CEO, Lou Gerstner (2005), and a shake-up of the entire top management team to bring in the requisite variety of views, values and visions to restore IBM's ability to renew itself.

In balancing unity and diversity, leaders that lean over to the side of unity can be said to have an *integrative leadership style*. These leaders tend to recruit a group of like-minded people and quickly align them into a tightly knit team with a strong sense of shared identity. Leaders that lean over to the side of diversity have a *federative leadership style*. These leaders select people that are not only of different backgrounds, but also have different worldviews. They allow for a more loosely knit culture, in which there is more autonomy and debate, but necessarily also more misunderstandings and conflicts.

Organisational decision making: The paradox of direction and participation

Leading also entails getting decisions made. Without decisions, organisations keep on marching on a pre-set path, or succumb to paralysis, becoming incapable of doing anything at all. Yet, while leaders need to ensure that decisions are taken, the question is whether they always need to make the choices themselves. Instead of making top-down decisions and commanding the way forward, they can also mobilise bottom-up participation in the decision making process (Vroom & Jago, 1988).

The advantage of a top-down approach is speed, consistency and clarity. When leaders call the shots, they can be fast, avoiding extensive consultation, deliberation and procrastination; they can be consistent, avoiding unaligned decisions and compromises; and they can be clear, limiting the 'wiggle room' for people to do their own thing. Moreover, by setting the direction of the organisation themselves, leaders explicitly take responsibility for the choices and the consequences. This too creates clarity, about who is the boss and who can be held accountable. Many followers appreciate this clear differentiation of roles, often also because they trust the judgment of the leader more than they trust their own opinion or the views of the group.

Yet, getting others to participate in decision making can be highly beneficial in a number of ways. First, broader participation can improve the quality of decision making. Leaders are not all-knowing and their judgment is not infallible, and therefore it is often indispensable to get the input from people with another expertise or with different experiences. Moreover, to look at an issue from various angles, to generate new ideas, to critically evaluate opportunities and to understand the implementation consequences, all works better if a variety of people are involved in the process. A second advantage of broader participation is that people generally feel more commitment to decisions to which they have contributed than to decisions that land on their desk. Employees can feel more appreciated and therefore more motivated, leading to more support for implementing the decision taken. This in turn can lead to faster implementation, even if the decision making itself took a bit longer. And thirdly, by participating in decision making, people understand the background of the choices made, learn about the assumptions and trade-offs, grow as individuals and become more flexible if a decision needs to be revised or changed.

As leaders balance between being directive and inviting participation, they often exhibit a natural tendency to feel more comfortable leaning over to one side or the other. Where they gravitate towards making decisions themselves, they can be said to have an *autocratic leadership style*. These leaders tend to prefer clear lines of authority and accountability, and take upon themselves the responsibility of making the tough choices, expecting others to respect and execute the decisions made. Where leaders are more inclined towards encouraging participation, they are said to have a *democratic leadership style*. These leaders tend to harness the power of the team, getting people to contribute to the emergence of a decision by bringing in their expertise, ideas and goodwill.

Strategic leadership

Strategic leadership deals with the role of leaders in the process of formulating and implementing strategy (Canella & Monroe, 1997; De Wit & Meyer, 2010). As leadership is about getting people to move in a certain direction, setting the strategic course of action is a crucial aspect of a leader's role. Leaders need to be intimately involved in the process of making strategic choices and mobilising people to realise the intended strategy.

Guiding the strategy process presents leaders with many challenges, but two stand out in particular. Firstly, leaders need to determine what type of strategic aims needs to be given to direct others. Leaders must choose how ambitious and specific the strategic goals they want to set should be. This task is referred to as *strategic goal-setting*. Secondly, leaders need to determine what type of strategic focus they should give others to ensure organisational continuity. Leaders must decide what kind of priorities need to be set to safeguard the sustainability of the organisation – this is the task of *strategic priority-setting*.

Strategic goal-setting: The paradox of idealism and realism

The task of strategic goal-setting is all about the classic leadership question: 'Where are we going?'. To get people to move in a certain direction, they will want to know where it is they are headed. But in setting a goal, the leader needs to consider that objectives can serve two different psychological needs of followers. On the one hand, most people want to have something to aspire to. Strategic goals are about ambitions – what would we like to become? We set strategic goals to challenge ourselves to rise above what we currently are capable of doing, to reach a higher level. As such, strategic goals are ideals, creating a stretch to become better or even the best. They can light a fire that mobilises the entire organisation to work hard over an extended period of time to achieve the shared dream.

On the other hand, many people also want to have certainty. They would like to know, with as much clarity and assurance as possible, where the organisation is headed and that these objectives are feasible. Even more tangibly, they would like to know what is expected of them personally and they need to feel confident that they will be capable of meeting these expectations. As such, strategic goals that are perceived as realistic can create a sense of security and organisational stability. They can help to establish a shared conviction that the organisation is capable of dealing with the challenges at hand and is in control of its future. This confidence can mobilise the entire organisation to work hard to reach the strategic goals as planned.

Yet, strategic goals that are ambitious and stretching will not score high on security and stability, and vice versa. Bullish objectives that stimulate people to rise above themselves don't fit well with the desire to have the assurance of specific and attainable aims. We refer to this tension between inspirational and feasible strategic goals as the *paradox of idealism and realism*.

As it seems impossible to be fully idealistic and realistic at the same time, in practice leaders tend to lean over to one side or the other, resulting in different leadership styles. Those that emphasise idealism have a *visionary leadership style*, as they outline an inspirational and challenging long-term vision, far beyond the organisation's current capabilities. Having set such a BOLD goal – broad, optimistic, long-term, and daring – such leaders tend to encourage people to find innovative ways of making it happen. Leaders emphasising realism over idealism have a *pragmatic leadership style*, as they communicate to others exactly what they want. They tend to set SMART goals – specific, measurable, acceptable, realistic and time-bound – focusing on the period for which they can plan.

Strategic priority-setting: The paradox of exploitation and exploration

Putting it crudely, the task of strategic priority setting is about whether the leader should be conserving the organisation or undermining it. The question is whether it should be the priority of the leader to maintain the status quo, creating stability and reaping as much value as possible from the current organisation, or whether the leader should challenge the status quo, accepting the short-term turmoil, but sowing potential future value, to be harvested at a later moment.

In the long run, all firms need to renew themselves, as their markets change and their products become commoditised. They need to search for new opportunities, serve new clients and provide new offerings. The required innovation can even call the existing business model into question. This strategic exploration, just as in the oil industry, is essential to keep the pipeline of new business opportunities filled – sometimes running just to stand still.

Yet, strategic exploration can be difficult and disconcerting. Innovation is a financially costly process, that is complex to manage and with results that are tricky to predict. At the same time, to be able to innovate means challenging the established way of doing things in the firm, upsetting existing practice and potentially creating cannibalistic products that could destroy the current business. Involving people in exploration means taking their attention away from current customers and current activities, on a potential wild goose chase of finding something new. The required experimentation can create unrest, inefficiency and lower customer satisfaction. This while the same attention and money could be invested in optimising the current business, making incremental improvements to existing processes. This exploitation of the present business is more predictable and manageable, while giving results in the short run.

Organisations might need a bit of both exploitation and exploration, but to a large extent the two are at odds with one another (March, 1991; Gupta et al., 2006). The money and attention can only be invested once, requiring leaders to set priorities. Moreover, it is difficult for leaders to send two messages at the same time ('let's shake things up' and 'let's focus on fine-tuning') without getting stuck in the middle and not being successful at either. Therefore, this tension truly is the *paradox of exploitation and exploration*.

Leaders who emphasise the importance of exploitation over exploration have an *executive leadership style*, as they focus on getting results. They concentrate on the efficient and effective functioning of the organisation by using, maintaining and extending the organisation's existing capabilities, infrastructure and client base. Leaders that give more priority to exploration have an *entrepreneurial leadership style*, as they see themselves as the driver of the entrepreneurial process within the organisation. As intrapreneurs ('inside entrepreneurs'), they concentrate on constantly rejuvenating the organisation by getting people to challenge the existing business model and search for pioneering ideas and approaches.

Leadership and mission

Knowing how to lead is important, but knowing why to lead is essential. If leadership is a choice, why do you want to choose this role? What is your mission? Which fundamental drivers will sustain you during the long hours of hard work, give you the strength to deal with uncertainty, bolster your courage to take on opponents and fortify your resolve to overcome setbacks? What will give meaning to your work and make it all worthwhile? Knowing your purpose as leader can make you stronger as a person, but also more capable of using your sense of mission to mobilise others.

Leaders can have many reasons why they want to lead, but there are two key questions that always come to the foreground; what does the leader ultimately want to achieve (*values-setting*) and whose interests does the leader want to serve (*interests-setting*)?

Values-setting: The paradox of wealth and health

People's core values are what they find fundamentally important. When deciding what to do and where to go, people's core values drive their choices. They provide the basic criteria for determining which options should be more highly regarded than the others. They constitute the gauge against which the goodness of a decision can be measured.

In the context of business, one of the core values needs to be the creation of economic value. Business leaders need to be focused on creating wealth, otherwise the life span of their firm will be extremely short. Without profit, they will not be able to invest and without an economically viable business model they won't be able to pay the bills. Therefore, leaders need to be driven by the desire to create economic value-added, by satisfying customer needs better than rival firms and by running an efficient organisation. They need to direct their people towards both market effectiveness and organisational efficiency, getting them to embrace the importance of winning the competitive game and making money.

Besides the 'money' side of organisational life, leaders also need to pay attention to the 'meaning' side (Fry, 2003; Reave, 2005). Firms are more than only economic machines; they are social environments in which people spend a large part of their waking lives. Many people don't feel fulfilled by only creating wealth, they want to strive towards a higher goal. They don't only want to do well (*welfare*), they want to do good (*well-being*). Some place a high value on their personal health and development, physically, emotionally and socially, while others want to contribute to the well-being of particular groups, society or the environment. Leaders, too, need to consider what will make them feel sound of body and mind. Which aspects of personal, social and environmental health should they value most?

The popular phrase 'people, planet, profit' suggests that it is possible to strive for wealth and health at the same time, but in practice there is a tension between the two that is not easily resolved, necessitating leaders to lean over to one side or the other. Moreover, many leaders just don't award equal importance to both wealth and health. Leaders who place more emphasis on wealth have a *value-driven leadership style*. They are in the business game to create material prosperity for clients, employees and/or themselves, focusing on achieving a strong competitive position and a sustainable level of profitability. Leaders gravitating more to the health-side of the balance have a *virtue-driven leadership style*. To them, money is a means, not an end. They need to run an economically viable business to survive, but the true purpose is to achieve a higher virtue – achieving personal development, contributing to science, alleviating regional unemployment, curing the ill or saving the rainforest, to name just a few examples.

Interests-setting: The paradox of self-actualization and service

Leaders also need to determine in whose interest they want to lead. Cui bono? Who should benefit from the act of leading, the leader or the followers? To some extent the leader needs to benefit, otherwise there would be no motivation to become a leader. Leaders need to understand their own needs and make sure that these needs are fulfilled. As Maslow already pointed out decades ago, these needs can range from a desire for money and power, to a craving for recognition and acceptance, to a longing for personal development and the achievement of a dream. With a wink to Maslow, we can label the fulfilment of any set of personal needs by a leader as self-actualization – the leader becomes what she/he wants to become.

Besides serving their own interests, leaders also need to serve the interests of the followers, otherwise there would be no motivation to follow. Different followers can have widely differing needs, varying from a sense of security and monetary gain, to acknowledgement, support, respect, advice, approval, challenge and meaning. Followers can also have their own dreams and personal development ambitions. To a certain extent the leader will need to be of service to the followers to be able to get people to move in a certain direction.

Yet, in balancing between self-actualization and service, leaders often exhibit a tendency to favour one side over the other. Leaders emphasising their own interests over those of the followers have a *sovereign leadership style*. They have become leaders because of their strong desire to fulfil their own dreams and they attempt to recruit people who are willing to help. They are the masters of their own destiny, who find followers willing to support them in their endeavour. Leaders emphasising service over self-actualization have a *servant leadership style* (Greenleaf, 1977; Sendjaya & Sarros 2002). They have become leaders because of their strong desire to help others and to work towards the success of the team.

Leadership and self

The previous eight dimensions have all dealt with the ways in which leaders try to influence others. But leaders also have a big impact by who they are. It is not only how they try to lead that sways others, but also what type of person they are and how they normally behave. How leaders listen, talk, sit, walk, look and gesture are all registered by potential followers. How they seem to think, how they show emotions, how they engage in conversation, how they react to stress and whether they actually practice what they preach; it is all picked up. Even characteristics such as personality, age, appearance, education, organisational position, social standing, nationality and beliefs can be significant. The identity of leaders, in all its aspects, is an integral part of the influence they have.

More precisely, it is the perception of the leader's identity in the eyes of potential followers that is of importance. It is the image that leaders have that wins the confidence of others. Therefore, leaders need to be concerned with both who they are and how others view them. Leaders can work on their self, improving their skills, changing their outlook, living the behaviour they expect from others and adjusting themselves to situational needs. But leaders also need to work on their 'personal branding', positioning themselves towards stakeholders, deciding which characteristics to emphasise and what to reveal of themselves.

There are many style differences due to the specific identity/image of leaders. One could even argue that all leaders have their own unique style. Yet, there are two key dimensions along which the basic behaviour of leaders strongly shapes how they are perceived by the potential followers around them. These two issues are how leaders approach leadership issues (*leadership problem-solving*) and how they adjust to their leadership environment (*leadership attunement*).

Leadership problem-solving: The paradox of thought and action

When confronted with any type of leadership issue, leaders need to think and act. Whether the challenge is in the market or in the organisation, and whether it is an opportunity or a threat, leaders need to reflect on the situation and take initiatives to deal with it.

Of course, thinking about leadership challenges is very valuable. Taking the time to thoroughly reflect on the situation can provide useful insights into the real concerns behind the issue. Taking a step back to carefully put things into perspective and to gain an overview of what's going on can help the leader to avoid jumping to conclusions. Proper analysis and some good mulling over can give the leader a range of possible options and a well-reasoned view on the advantages and risks of the various alternatives. Similarly, acting on leadership challenges is crucial. Taking the initiative to get things moving is the only way to achieve a result. Seizing the bull by the horns and mobilising people to help make things happen is how outcomes are realised.

Yet, in balancing thinking and acting, leaders don't always place equal emphasis on both. Nor do they always prefer to do thinking and acting in the same order. Leaders with a preference to think thoroughly before they act have a *reflective leadership style*. Instead of shooting from the hip, they take a disciplined response to external challenges, first letting the situation sink in, before formulating a response and then moving to action. Leaders favouring action over thought have a *proactive leadership style*. It is not that they don't think, but they don't wait to finish the thinking before they act. To them, thinking and acting go hand in hand, as most leadership issues can only be resolved by taking them on and figuring out how to proceed along the way. Instead of researching issues to death, proactive leaders believe in getting things moving, trusting that solutions will present themselves as the situation unfolds. Just do it, and apologise if you were wrong.

Leadership attunement: The paradox of authenticity and adjustment

As leadership requires followership, it has become widely accepted that leaders need to adjust themselves to the requirements of followers (e.g. Fielder, 1967;

Hersey & Blanchard, 1977; Yukl, 1989). Such 'situational leadership' demands that leaders understand the capabilities of their followers and the nature of the followers' work, so that these leaders can optimally attune their approach to the given situation. Yet, many other factors can come into play, requiring leaders to adjust. Followers can have different psychological needs, cultural backgrounds, interests, ambitions, cognitive abilities, prejudices and personal histories. Teams can have different compositions, personal relationships, unwritten rules and joint experiences. Not to mention the differences between functional areas, companies, industries and countries that can have an impact. Without the ability to adjust one's 'self' to the outside world, leaders would hardly be able to function.

At the same time, the need to be authentic is also widely accepted (Avolio & Gardner, 2005; George, 2003). To not be seen as a fake, merely 'playing' a leadership role, one needs to 'be' a leader, as close as possible to one's true self. Potential followers will quickly sniff out whether someone is bona fide in actions and intent, or just mouthing the words taught in a leadership course. Moreover, being genuine is easier to keep up in the long run and allows leaders to build on their core strengths, instead of attempting to do something for which they have no talents.

With the need for authenticity and adjustment so widely accepted, it is surprising to note how few people have acknowledged the tension between them. The two truly form a paradox, in which we would like to have both, while they seem the conflicting opposites of each other. Leaders favouring authenticity over adjustment have a *consistent leadership style*. Coming from the inside, the way they lead is highly consistent wherever they are and whoever they lead. Their character, beliefs, values and strengths shape their approach, more or less irrespective of the circumstances they are in. To them 'it doesn't all depend', but rather 'what you see is what you get'. Leaders favouring adaptation over authenticity have a *responsive leadership style*. Being highly sensitive to the needs and expectations of those around them, they tailor their approach to each specific situation they are in. To them it makes no sense to get everyone to 'read your manual', while you can provide a user-friendly interface. For the responsive leader it is not only a matter of effectiveness to adjust to the specific circumstances, but also a matter of respect – who do you think you are as a leader making everyone adapt to you?

Leadership and learnership

This is a good point at which to go back to the leadership style profiler in Table 1.2 and to check whether your first quick and dirty profile accurately portrays your current leadership styles. Where you feel that you cover a range of styles, feel free to circle more than one number. When you're finished, go through it a second time, circling the numbers representing the styles you would like to have in a few years' time. Take into consideration how you would like to develop as a person, what your career ambitions are, what your strengths are and where you see your organisation headed (or the circumstances in the organisation where you would like to work). If you want to keep the same style, but get better at it, you can make the circle a different colour. If you want to 'stretch' your style repertoire, circle some numbers representing styles you have difficulty putting into practice.

You now have your leadership development objectives set for the coming years. Without needing to aspire to become the next Richard Branson or Elon Musk, you can still work towards becoming a more effective leader. Your challenge is to work on the leadership style dimensions you have chosen, but without a simple blueprint telling you what to do. You need to experiment to find out what works for you, then practice and repeat until you feel you're getting it. Just as no great chef learnt haute cuisine from a cookbook, you too are on your own.

Well, not entirely. It's actually a good idea to share your objectives with people around you, in particular the ones you want to lead, for instance your direct reports, your colleagues and your boss. Recruiting your followers to be your teachers might seem counterintuitive and feel a bit awkward, but showing this vulnerability, openness and willingness to learn will tickle their interest, earn you a lot of respect and give them a stake in your development. As John F. Kennedy said four decades ago: 'Leadership and learnership are indispensable to one another' – giving the great example of learnership is a sure way to improve your leadership in more ways than one.

References

Avolio, B. J., & Gardner, W. L. (2005). Authentic leadership development: Getting to the root of positive forms of leadership. *Leadership Quarterly, 16*(3), 315–338.

Blake, R. R., & Mouton, J. S. (1964). *The managerial grid*. Houston, TX: Gulf Publishing.

Cannella, A. A. Jr., & Monroe, M. J. (1997). Contrasting perspectives on strategic leaders: Toward a more realistic view of top managers. *Journal of Management, 23*(3), 213–237.

Collins, J. C., & Porras, J. I. (1994). *Built to last: Successful habits of visionary companies*. New York: Harper Business.

De Wit, B., & Meyer, R. (2010). *Strategy synthesis: Resolving strategy paradoxes to create competitive advantage* (3rd ed.). London: Cengage.

Fiedler, F. E. (1967). *A theory of leadership effectiveness*. New York: McGraw-Hill.

Fry, L. W. (2003). Toward a theory of spiritual leadership. *Leadership Quarterly, 14*(6), 693–727.

George, B. (2003). *Authentic leadership: Rediscovering the secrets to creating lasting value*. San Francisco, CA: Jossey-Bass.

Gerstner, L. V. (2005). *Who says elephants can't dance: Inside IBM's historic turnaround*. New York: Harper Collins.

Greenleaf, R. K. (1977). *Servant leadership: A journey into the nature of legitimate power and greatness*. Mahwah, NJ: Paulist Press.

Gupta, A. K., Smith, K. G., & Shalley, C. E. (2006). The interplay between exploration and exploitation. *Academy of Management Journal, 49*(4), 693–706.

Hersey, P., & Blanchard, K. H. (1977). *The management of organizational behavior* (3rd ed.). Englewood Cliffs, NJ: Prentice Hall.

March, J. (1991). Exploration and exploitation in organizational learning. *Organization Science, 2*(1), 71–87.

Reave, L. (2005). Spiritual values and practices related to leadership effectiveness. *Leadership Quarterly, 16*(5), 655–688.

Sendjaya, S., & Sarros, J. C. (2002). Servant leadership: Its origin, development, and application in organizations. *Journal of Leadership & Organizational Studies, 9*(2), 57–64.

Vroom, V. H., & Jago, A. G. (1988). *The new leadership: Managing participation in organizations.* Englewood Cliffs, NJ: Prentice Hall.

Yukl, G. (1989). *Leadership in organizations* (2nd ed.). Englewood Cliffs, NJ: Prentice Hall.

Yukl, G., & Fu, P. (1999). Determinants of delegation and consultation By managers. *Journal of Organizational Behavior, 20*(2), 219–232.

2

Perspective

Reframing leadership

Why what you search for will determine what you find

Darren Dalcher

How should we think about leadership in projects? Indeed, which aspects should we focus on when trying to improve our success rates for project delivery?

The first chapter recognised that every project is unique and may require different approaches to leadership. Such diversity in options implies a plurality of contexts and interpretations. In this chapter we proceed to reframe some of the key issues related to leaders, leading and leadership.

Improved leadership is increasingly proposed as the answer to project delivery shortfalls. Yet, emphasising leadership can lead to a host of additional questions: What is the relationship between project management and leadership? Should we focus on the psychology and behavioural traits of the people labelled as leaders, or consider the groups that they belong to? Will the dynamics of the teams make a difference? If leadership is essential to project success, what is the role of followers? Do good followers make a leader effective?

Practitioners seek pragmatic answers, yet it is important to have a precise idea about what questions are being asked before we begin to seek appealing solutions. Ultimately, the questions we ask determine the approaches we utilise whilst looking for answers and therefore directly impact the answers we develop.

Starting with perspective

Perspective plays a key part in how we frame situations and contexts. The Oxford Dictionary defines perspective as: 'a particular attitude towards or a way of regarding something; a point of view'. The Cambridge Dictionary regards it as 'a particular way of viewing things that depends on one's experience and personality'. The Collins Dictionary views it as 'a particular way of thinking about something', while the Merriam-Webster Dictionary refers to it as 'a mental view or prospect'.

Perspective can therefore be summarised as a specific point of view, an attitude towards or a defined manner of viewing, thinking and considering something that is the focus of attention. In short, it is the mental image or prospect that we create in order to make sense of, categorise or rationalise about a particular issue, phenomenon or object of interest.

Einstein famously opined that 'it is the theory which decides what we can observe'. The mental image or accepted framing has a similar effect on how we view something and what actions or possibilities we consider as feasible with regard to influencing that something. Over time, particular ways of viewing become fixed and entrenched, resisting any efforts to dislodge, challenge or replace them.

Building a mental image

Voltaire delineates an idea as 'the image that paints itself onto the brain'. Once we develop a mental representation of the external world, we simplify and begin to operate on that mental representation rather than the world itself. Such simplification has crucial implications to future actions.

'The meaning that agents give to themselves, their products, their competitors, their customers, and all the relevant others in their world determine their space of our possible actions – and to a large extent, how they act' (Lane & Maxfield, 1995: p. 17).

Legrenzi, Girotto and Johnson-Laird (1994) affirm that many aspects of thinking, reasoning and decision making depend on the construction of mental models. Subjects form a mental image of a situation expressed in a premise and derive a tentative conclusion by examining the model (Baron, 2007). Mental images accordingly influence both how we understand the world and how we take action (Senge, 1990).

> At the first level, human beings understand the world by constructing working models of it in their minds. Since these models are incomplete, they are simpler than the entities they represent. In consequence, models contain elements that are merely imitations of reality – there is no working model of how their counterparts in the world operate, but only procedures that mimic their behaviour.
>
> (Johnson-Laird, 1983: p. 10)

Mental imagery and models underpin individual thinking processes, but more importantly, they also enable organisational sensemaking through the creation of images that permit the organisation to communicate and operate. Mental models, lenses, frames or images are thus used and shared in defining, understanding and negotiating a particular territory.

> Metaphors and other mental models provide a means for individuals and, ultimately, organisations to create and share understanding. These mental models establish images, names and an understanding of how things fit together. They articulate what is important and unimportant depending on underlying shared interests and common understandings.
>
> (Hill, 1995: p. 1059)

Morgan asserts that 'all theories of organization and management are based on implicit images or metaphors that lead us to see, understand, and manage organizations in distinct yet partial ways' (2006: p. 4). Such metaphors frame our understanding, producing limited, one-sided insights. Highlighting a particular interpretation inevitably side-lines alternative views and perspectives.

Mental models are used to explain situations, environments and processes. While they serve to clarify and distil understanding through simplification and abstraction, they also carry the seeds of destruction by limiting the situation to what can be pictured and included within the model. In that respect, they can also impede learning (Senge, 1990), and restrict effective performance.

Deconstructing the elephant

> Weick noted that 'organisations have a major hand in creating the realities which they then view as 'facts' to which they must accommodate.
>
> (Weick, 1979: p. 13)

The well-known parable of the blind men and the elephant can be used to illustrate how mental images are created as representations of the real world based on partial observations and accidental impressions, before they become immutable and incontestable 'facts'.

In a distant and remote village lived six blind men. One day the village was humming with the news that an elephant would be on display in the market square.

Having never encountered an elephant, the blind men decided to walk down to the centre of the village together to discover what an elephant is. Upon arrival the blind men were given permission to approach the animal one at a time.

The first blind man approached the animal with great trepidation, and stumbling against its broad and sturdy side, he concluded that an elephant is like a giant wall.

The second sauntered towards the animal and upon finding its tusk, determined that the elephant is like an enormous spear.

The third man came across the moving trunk and retreated in haste from what he could only imagine was just like a giant snake.

The fourth, moving confidently towards the animal, discovered a leg, and surmised that the elephant is like a colossal column.

The fifth man took his turn and on finding the flapping ear, deduced that the elephant resembles a giant fan.

The sixth man finally got to move forward and inspect the animal. As he did so he came upon the swinging tail and duly decided that an elephant is just like a rope.

When the six blind men were finally re-united, they tried to discuss their recent experience, but their experiences of a wall, spear, snake, column, fan and rope were at odds. They were confused, each insisting that their interaction captured the true nature of the animal. Surely an elephant could not be all these things at once?

A wise person who happened to be passing by heard the commotion and came forward to find out what was going on. The blind men complained that they could not agree on what the elephant was like and asked him to settle their argument and tell them which of their deductions was correct. The wise person explained that they were all correct as each one had encountered a particular facet and had simplified and generalised from it what the entire animal might be like.

Whilst all the individual positions based on specific features observed by the different participants were correct, they were also in the wrong as the totality of 'elephantness' is not encompassed nor encapsulated by any of the metaphors or likenesses that had been identified. In fact, none of the individual views captured the essence of the object being studied.

The parable calls attention to the subjectivity of experiences and the limitations in creating models emphasising a particular facet. The six participants had different perspectives based on their individual experiences and viewpoints. Engaging with any single facet of a situation may not address the totality of perspectives and experiences. Mental models represent idealised abstractions and simplifications. The absolute truth may thus elude participants who are only able to focus on a limited perspective or a partial experience. In reality, our constructions and frames are always potentially subject to the partial blindness that comes from only having a single point of view, a limited understanding, or partial and limited access to wider and more encompassing phenomena.

Reframing

Deconstruction seems to offer a limited focus and a partial view of reality. Complex situations often need to be considered from a variety of perspectives and viewpoints to derive a richer interpretation, however, the individual viewpoints do not aggregate into a bigger and more comprehensive single version of the truth.

Einstein memorably observed that it would be impossible to solve problems by using the same kind of thinking that created them in the first place. Having multiple frames or perspectives makes it possible to reframe problems and situations in order to gain additional clarity and insights, generate alternative options or uncover innovative strategies.

In his influential book *Images of Organization*, Gareth Morgan concedes that metaphors and images are inherently paradoxical as they create powerful insights and are a great way of seeing, but inevitably they also become a way of not seeing (2006: p. 5).

> Yet when we recognise this we can begin to mobilize the true power of metaphor and its role in management. In recognizing theory as a metaphor

we quickly appreciate that no single theory will ever give us a perfect or all-purpose point of view. We realize that the challenge is to become skilled in the art of using metaphor: to find fresh ways of seeing, understanding and shaping the situations that we want to organize and manage.
(Morgan, 2006: pp. 5–6)

Morgan (2006) identifies eight basic metaphors or perspectives on organisations:

- Organisations as machines;
- Organisations as organisms;
- Organisations as brains;
- Organisations as cultures;
- Organisations as political systems;
- Organisations as psychic prisons;
- Organisations as flux and transformation; and
- Organisations as instruments of domination.

Metaphors convey the complexity of organisations. They also embody the multiple facets of reality and create ways of seeing and shaping organisational life. Different metaphors have the capacity to explore and highlight alternative dimensions of a situation and thereby emphasise different features of the organisation, object or 'the elephant' being studied. While any one analogy is limited, 'a switch of metaphor can ... transform radically one's judgments and evaluations' (Wheeler, 1987: p. 227). A plurality of metaphors and the ability to shift between them can thus be engaged to foster richer understanding, novel thinking and inspired problem solving.

Bolman and Deal advocate the idea of reframing, or viewing the same situation from different perspectives, in order to sort through the multiplicity of voices competing for managers' attention (2017: p. 12). Each frame has its own image of reality (ibid.: p. 15), which may appeal or make particular sense at certain times or in specific contexts. Applying multiple frames can have a significant impact on the ability to understand a particular context, while the ability to use multiple frames is typically associated with greater effectiveness for both managers and leaders (ibid.: p. 16). Recognising that there are multiple ways to respond to problems and dilemmas can prove to be liberating: 'Managers are imprisoned only to the extent that their palette of ideas is impoverished' (ibid.: p. 17).

Bolman and Deal propose a four-frame mapping that shows that each frame develops its own image of reality (see Table 2.1). Each frame utilises central concepts to develop an image consistent with its metaphor, and each is then concerned with a different set of key issues and identifies with a basic leadership challenge.

While we may often find ourselves with little control over a particular situation, we are probably able to control the perspective by shifting the image.

Table 2.1 Overview of the four-frame model (adapted from Bolman & Deal; p. 16)

Frame:	Metaphor for organisation	Central concepts	Image of leadership	Basic leadership challenge
Structural	Factory or machine	Rules, roles, policies, technology, environment	Social architecture	Attune structure to task, technology, environment
Human resource	Family	Needs, skills, relationships	Empowerment	Align organisational and human needs
Political	Jungle	Power, conflict, competition, organisational politics	Advocacy	Develop agenda and power base
Symbolic	Carnival, temple, theatre	Culture, meaning, metaphor, ritual, ceremony, stories, heroes	Inspiration	Create faith, beauty, meaning

Alternative perspectives and images can prove to be essential in focusing on key aspects of a position and identifying major challenges. Table 2.1 identifies the fundamental leadership challenge that is derived from each set of logic and thinking approaches associated with four different thinking frames. It is notable that each perspective results in a different focus leading to different concerns, emphasis and fundamental questions revolving around leadership.

Rethinking leadership

It is often said that leadership is like beauty; it is difficult to define, but we know it when we see it. However, if leadership is in the eye of the beholder, and different stakeholders and participants engage with situations from their own unique stance, viewpoint and position, then the accumulation of perceptions and insights may only offer partial and highly subjective descriptions of parts that cannot add up to 'elephantness' – an integrated view that captures the essence of the different facets that make up the elephant. A partial perspective may be useful in isolation, especially if we seek to deconstruct the elephant, but such partial understanding when applied to leadership may only account for the contradictions and multiplicity of perspectives that are related to leaders and leadership.

Surely, there must be a better way to make sense of leadership in practice. Bolden, Witzel and Linacre (2016) reason that leadership must be difficult as is evidenced through a seemingly endless stream of leadership failures in organisations and a relentless search for guidance. They point out that while there is no universal definition of leadership, what is written about it is often ridden by paradoxes, defying any logical analysis. Instead, they propose taking a closer look at some of the contradictions, utilising the paradoxes that emerge as 'provocations and catalysts for further enquiry' (ibid.: p. 8).

The next contribution in this chapter first appeared in the book *Leadership Paradoxes: Rethinking Leadership for an Uncertain World*, edited by Richard Bolden, Morgen Witzel and Nigel Linacre and published by Routledge. Richard Bolden explores the paradoxes faced when researching leaders, leading and leadership. He draws on his experience of studying leadership in a range of different contexts to highlight the limitations of traditional perspectives on leadership and to offer alternative ways and approaches.

Bolden's work seeks to enhance leadership practice. By asking difficult questions and looking across different domains, he is able to consider some of the foundational concerns and interests. His critical gaze encompasses heroic, as well as toxic leaders, and relational alongside distributed modes of leadership. His work uncovers three crucial paradoxes that question the basis and form, and more importantly, the overarching role of leadership. As we increasingly engage with rising complexity, major projects and programmes, and increasing levels of uncertainty surrounding our undertakings, projects and change initiatives, many of the questions posed require fundamental rethinking.

The questions and reflections encouraged by Bolden are both timely and essential. The start of an impending intellectual revolution may well rely on asking some of the important questions that no one else is willing or able to voice. Recognising the paradoxical and messy nature of leadership has never been more critical, not least in a world inhabited by temporary organisations, agile delivery modes and rapidly changing technologies. In such a flatter and more closely coupled and networked world, new notions and ways of operating are required in order to succeed and endure. As we increasingly rely on groups and networks, it is important to ask if leadership resides in the individual or the collective group. When we adopt methods that give teams autonomy, we need to consider the overall impact on the delivery of strategic vision, intentions and expectations. Moreover, as we engage with wider and more diverse communities, and as we require them to use our products and artefacts in order to deliver the intended benefits and resulting value to wider society, we must seek improved understanding of the impacts, dimensions and potential of leadership to enhance, underpin and deliver enduring prosperity.

References

Baron, J. (2007). *Thinking and deciding* (4th ed.). Cambridge: Cambridge University Press.

Bolden, R. (2016). Paradoxes of perspective: Leaders, leading and leadership, in Bolden, R., Witzel, M., & Linacre, N. (Eds.). *Leadership paradoxes: Rethinking leadership for an uncertain world*. Abingdon: Routledge.

Bolden, R., Witzel, M., & Linacre, N. (Eds.). (2016). *Leadership paradoxes: Rethinking leadership for an uncertain world*. Abingdon: Routledge.

Bolman, L. G., & Deal, T. E. (2017). *Reframing organizations: Artistry, choice, and leadership* (6th ed.). San Francisco: John Wiley & Sons.

Hill, R. C., & Levenhagen, M. (1995). Metaphors and mental models: Sensemaking and sensegiving in innovative and entrepreneurial activities. *Journal of Management, 21*(6), 1057–1074.

Johnson-Laird, P. (1983). *Mental models.* Cambridge: Cambridge University Press.

Lane, D., & Maxfield, R. (1995, September). *Foresight, complexity, and strategy.* Working paper, New Mexico: Santa Fe Institute.

Legrenzi, P., Girotto, V., & Johnson-Laird, P. N. (1994). Focusing in reasoning and decision making, in Johnson-Laird, P. N., & Shafir, E. (Eds.). (1994). *Reasoning and decision making.* London: Blackwell.

Morgan, G. (2006). *Images of organization.* Thousand Oaks, CA: Sage.

Senge, P. (1990). *The fifth discipline: The art and science of the learning organization.* New York: Currency Doubleday.

Wheeler, C. J. (1987). The magic of metaphor: A perspective on reality construction. *Metaphor and Symbol, 2*(4), 223–237.

Paradoxes of perspective
Leaders, leading and leadership

Richard Bolden

Introduction

Questions of leadership have been at the heart of business and society for thousands of years, yet the challenges of the new millennium have prompted substantial shifts in both the theory and practice of leadership that challenge traditional accounts of influence and agency[1].

Concepts of distributed and shared leadership, for example, have become increasingly popular, as have approaches based on complexity science[2] and identity. Despite these developments the more we discover about leadership, the more elusive, ambiguous and contested it seems to become.

Leadership is a truly interdisciplinary subject and one that touches on many of the most important issues and questions of our times. This, of course, is what also makes it a frustrating and challenging topic of enquiry. Everyone has their own opinion on leadership and research insights are often partial, fleeting or ambiguous. As Meindl, Ehrlich and Dukerich (1985) observed, there is a romance to the concept of leadership that makes it difficult to pin down:

> It has become apparent that, after years of trying, we have been unable to generate an understanding of leadership that is both intellectually compelling and emotionally satisfying. The concept of leadership remains elusive and enigmatic.

> (ibid.: p. 78)

Rather than being a problem to be solved, I suggest that engaging with the elusive and enigmatic qualities of leadership is key to understanding what it is and to enhancing leadership practice and its development. As Socrates famously proclaimed: 'the only true wisdom is in knowing you know nothing!'

In this chapter I use the concept of paradox to highlight the limitations of traditional perspectives on leadership and to offer some alternatives. A paradox is defined as 'a statement or proposition that seems self-contradictory or absurd but in reality expresses a possible truth' or 'an opinion or statement contrary to commonly accepted opinion' (dictionary.com, 2015). It is different from the notion of a 'dilemma' or 'conundrum' in that it does not suggest the need to make a decision between two or more alternatives and nor does it suggest the possibility of finding a resolution.

A paradox requires us to accept that multiple truths may co-exist simultaneously – something that we in the West can struggle with. As the American Theatre Director Shellen Lubin noted:

> Living with contradiction may be nothing new to humans, but acknowledging it, and accepting it are. Even the dictionary has trouble accepting a paradox, calling it 'two things that seem to be contradictory but may possibly be true'. But that's not a real paradox—a real paradox IS contradictory and IS true.
>
> (goodreads.com, 2015)

In this chapter I will highlight three paradoxes that have been revealed through my own work and explore their implications for leadership theory, practice and development. In particular, these paradoxes focus on the tensions between individual and shared perspectives on leadership.

The enduring allure of heroic leadership

A quick search on Google Images throws up lots of pictures where we see some figure, usually masculine in appearance, boldly showing the way whilst their faceless minions obediently follow. We're bombarded by these kinds of messages all the time be it on television programmes such as *The Apprentice* or *Dragons' Den* – where young hopefuls desperately try to impress some authoritarian figure – or in the news – where our political leaders compete to be regarded as the most inspiring, authentic and dependable leader of the people[3].

I have no doubt that, on reflection, most of us realise that such simplistic views of leadership are nonsense, yet, in the Western World at least, they are hard-wired into us from an early age. I had the opportunity to test this out for myself a couple of years ago when I asked my children, then eight and six, two questions. The first of these was 'what is a leader?' and, almost immediately my daughter piped up 'the person at the front of the line'. My second question, 'what is leadership?' was rather trickier and, after an uncomfortable moment's silence, my son suggested 'the ship at the front of the line'.

Such views that suggest that leadership is all about leaders are referred to as leader-centric or 'heroic' approaches and they have a long history in both the scholarship and practice of leadership. The Scottish writer Thomas Carlyle (1840: p. 34) suggested: 'the history of the world is but the biography of great men'. This has become known as the 'Great Man Theory of Leadership' and despite extensive critique the idea has been difficult to dislodge.

In more recent years we have thankfully acknowledged the exceptional leadership of women as well as men, however, there remains a popular fascination with the personal stories of people who have achieved greatness... or increasingly it seems just some form of notoriety or celebrity.

There is no consistent scientific evidence, however, to suggest that leaders with particular traits or qualities are more likely to be successful than those with other traits, yet organisations of all kinds continue to develop and promote competency frameworks to measure and assess leadership capability.

A little over ten years ago my colleague Jonathan Gosling and I did some research to support the development of the National Occupational Standards in Leadership and Management[4] which underpin the National Vocational Qualifications Framework and which have subsequently been adopted by professional accreditation bodies such as the Chartered Management Institute.

In this work we compared the qualities identified in 30 of the most widely used leadership and management frameworks with characteristics identified as important to leadership and society by mid to senior leaders attending programmes at the Windsor Leadership Trust[5]. As you might expect, there were some significant areas of difference. Most notable was that, despite the importance attributed to them by the practicing leaders, around two thirds of the frameworks made no explicit reference to trust, ethics, inspiration, adaptability or resilience; and fewer than a fifth made reference to personal beliefs, courage, humility, reflection, work–life balance or an ability to cope with complexity (Bolden & Gosling, 2006).

Amongst the articles that we wrote based on this work was one entitled 'Is the NHS Leadership Qualities Framework Missing the Wood for the Trees?' (Bolden, Wood & Gosling, 2006). In brief, the answer was 'yes' – in that we suggested the focus on measurable individual behaviours largely overlooked the inherently relational, emotional and ethical nature of leadership and management in a healthcare context.

By attempting to boil leadership down to its basic ingredients the National Health Service (NHS) and the many other organisations whose frameworks we analysed were in danger of missing the point – leadership is not simply the sum of its parts! Much like concepts such as love, beauty and creativity, leadership has an aesthetic quality that cannot be sub-divided and which defies purely rational analysis.

This brings us to the first of the paradoxes:

Paradox 1 – *in attempting to identify and measure the essence of leadership we may inadvertently lose sight of the very thing we are seeking to capture.*

To draw parallels to biology, a focus on leadership traits and qualities is rather like trying to understand a rare species of bird by capturing, killing and dissecting it. There are certainly things to be learnt but all we're left with at the end of the day is a pile of feathers, bone and flesh and little opportunity for further enquiry. If, however, we seek to understand the bird's behaviour, appreciate its beauty or understand the part it plays in the wider ecosystem we need to take a somewhat different approach. We need to find ways to observe it in its natural surroundings – to watch it in flight, in interaction with other members of its species and to carefully study the environment in which it lives.

Towards a relational perspective on leadership

Recent years have seen increased calls for greater inclusion and participation in leadership and decision making that shift the perspective from 'who' is leading to 'how' leadership is accomplished. This approach regards leadership as 'a social influence process through which emergent coordination (i.e. evolving social order) and change (i.e. new values, attitudes, approaches, behaviours, ideologies, etc.) are constructed and produced' (Uhl-Bien, 2006: p. 668) – no longer an attribute of individuals themselves but a property of the system… or paradoxically perhaps both.

My opportunity to explore the relational nature of leadership arose through a project I undertook for the British Council, along with my colleague Phil Kirk. This project took us to sub-Saharan Africa to explore and evaluate the process and impacts of a Pan-African leadership development programme called 'Interaction'. At the heart of this programme was the simple belief that anyone with some motivation and a willingness to engage in leadership could have an immense impact. The programme, delivered over a period of six months to a cohort of 300 participants from 19 African nations, sought to catalyse people's engagement with their communities both locally and more widely across the continent.

These remarkable people came from all walks of life. There were bankers, doctors, students, teachers, lawyers, administrators and many more – each of whom had responded to an advert inviting them to apply if they were passionate about Africa and wanted to make a positive difference. The programme itself did little more than bring people together, to encourage them to embrace a few simple principles and to engage in dialogue. Much of the time on the programme involved them working with a local organisation – such as a children's home, a community project or a school – to help mobilise leadership amongst those they met.

I had the pleasure of both spending time with the participants and the communities they had visited and was struck by the way in which this initiative facilitated a shift in perspective from 'leaders' to 'leadership' – from the idea that leadership is something possessed by the few to leadership as a shared responsibility in which everyone has a part to play (Bolden and Kirk, 2006; Bolden and Kirk, 2009).

In analysing findings we used a systemic framework for leadership development and suggested that the programme give participants the opportunity to walk, talk and see new possibilities for leadership together (Bolden and Kirk, 2011). It wasn't a case of learning complex theories and models or of developing specific skills or competencies – but rather of coming to recognise a sense of profound connection to others and the wider environment in which we are located; what theorists such as George Herbert Mead (1934) call the 'relational self'.

We concluded the paper by suggesting that: 'leadership is the mobilization of human effort in a collective enterprise' (ibid.: p. 33). This is not a romantic ideal, but an endeavour that is accomplished in the midst of contradictions, inequalities, conflicts, hopes and disappointments – as illustrated by the story of a Tanzanian grandmother's attempts to propagate and plant trees in the face of poverty and drought. When asked how it was that an elderly woman could undertake this feat she dismissed the question saying that if one was alive one could do it!

A concept that I discovered whilst in Africa, and which I've continued to explore ever since, is that of 'ubuntu'. A Zulu word, with parallels in many other African languages, ubuntu is commonly translated into English with the phrase 'I am because we are'. It is best described as a philosophy of social interdependence, founded on principles of care and community, harmony and hospitality, respect and responsiveness. There is an associated saying that goes 'it takes a village to raise a child', which conveys a need for diversity and shared responsibility (Bolden, 2014).

In South Africa, ubuntu was a fundamental pillar of the Truth and Reconciliation Commission chaired by Archbishop Desmond Tutu in the late 1990s that sought to document, bear witness and on occasion grant pardon for the wrong doings perpetrated under Apartheid. Tutu has called ubuntu 'the gift that Africa will give the world' and, amongst others, including Bill Clinton, has called for its wider adoption beyond Africa (see Mangaliso, 2001; Lutz, 2009).

Ubuntu and the concept of the relational self, described earlier, hold some interesting implications for the notions of heroic and individualistic leadership that continue to dominate thinking in most countries.

If, indeed, we are highly dependent on others for both our sense of who we are and what we can accomplish, then the common distinction between 'leaders' and 'followers' may be unhelpful in that it creates a false dichotomy between the roles played by members of a group.

The dysfunctional effects of this way of thinking were highlighted in a seminal paper by Gemmill and Oakley (1992) where they described leadership as 'an alienating social myth' that 'functions as a social defence whose central aim is to repress uncomfortable needs, emotions and wishes that emerge when people work together' (ibid.: p. 114). In idealising the leader, they argue, members detach themselves from their own visions and emotions and become complicit in maintaining the status quo.

We need only look at the Banking industry over the past few years to get a sense of the importance of being able to challenge dysfunctional leadership (see Hutton, 2014 for a review), yet this is not easy. In the opening paragraph of her book titled *The Allure of Toxic Leaders*, Jean Lipman–Blumen (2005) says:

> Toxic leaders cast their spell broadly. Most of us claim we abhor them. Yet we frequently follow – or at least tolerate – them, be they our employers, our CEOs, our senators, our clergy, or our teachers. When toxic leaders don't appear on their own, we often seek them out. On occasion, we even create them by pushing good leaders over the toxic line. That paradox of ambivalence ticks at the core of this book. Exploring that paradox, plus the strategies we might use to recognize, avoid, reform, overthrow, or escape from destructive and corrupt leaders, is the challenge of the *Allure of Toxic Leaders*.
>
> (ibid.: p. ix)

As early as the 1940s, Mary Parker Follett argued for recognition of leadership as a reciprocal relationship between leaders and followers, and in 1954 the Australian psychologist C. A. Gibb suggested: 'leadership is probably best conceived as a group quality, as a set of functions which must be carried out by the group' (Gibb, 1954: p. 884).

It has, however, taken a long time for the rest of the world to catch up with them and it is only really since the turn of the millennium that concerted efforts have been made to develop and extend robust theory and research on shared and distributed leadership that put the collective and relational nature of leadership at their heart (see Bolden, 2011 for a review).

This then takes us to the second paradox:

> **Paradox 2** – *to better understand leadership we should spend less time studying 'leaders'.*

What I mean here is that, in organisations and other spheres of life, people carry roles and responsibilities that, to a certain degree, dictate the ways in which they will interact with others. A Chief Executive, for example, has a formal responsibility for the running of an organisation; a parent or teacher has different obligations from a child; yet none can accomplish outcomes alone and all operate within a set of norms and structures. They are also all subject to reciprocal influence, in that there are times when roles are flipped – for example when a child leads the parent or a staff member leads their manager.

We all experience this at some point but it's surprising how rarely it's acknowledged – that all leaders need to be able to follow and the best followers are those that can lead. Leading and following are two sides of the same coin and most of us are very skilled at switching between them – at taking turns as 'leader' and 'follower' and, on occasion, both or neither.

The American academic Joanne Ciulla (1998: p. 1) says that: 'leadership is not a person or a position. It is a complex moral relationship between people, based on trust, obligation, commitment, emotion, and a shared vision of the good'. And the British leadership scholar, Keith Grint, concludes:

Leadership... is not just a theoretical arena but one with critical implications for us all and the limits of leadership – what leaders can do and what followers should allow them to do – are foundational aspects of this arena. Leadership, in effect, is too important to be left to leaders.

(Grint, 2005a: p. 4)

Leadership as a distributed process

So if we need to broaden our perspective beyond 'leaders' where should we look and where do we draw the line between leadership, management and other processes?

One concept that I've found useful in addressing these questions is that of 'distributed leadership', which suggests that:

1 Leadership is an emergent property of a group or network of interacting individuals;
2 There is openness to the boundaries of leadership; and
3 Varieties of expertise are distributed across the many, not the few (Bennett et al., 2003: p. 7).

Much of the original research on distributed leadership was done in the school sector and it is now firmly embedded in teacher training and development and even the regulatory framework of organisations such as Ofsted in the UK.

In my own work I've explored the application of these ideas to the higher education sector. Whilst studying leadership in your own sector can at times seem a little too close to home, I've found universities to be a very interesting context in which to explore questions of leadership, influence and identity.

A cartoon that was published in the *Times Higher Education Supplement* alongside an article summarising the findings of a study we conducted called 'Developing Collective Leadership in Higher Education' (Bolden, Petrov & Gosling, 2008) nicely captures some of the ambiguity around leadership in universities. It shows an alien who has landed on a university campus being told by an academic 'we don't have a leader to take you to'.

The idea that there is an absence of leadership in higher education and that leading academics is like herding cats of course speaks to popular stereotypes but is somewhat misleading. At the risk of spoiling the joke I'd like to suggest that the academic might go on to explain his response by saying '... because there are many leaders, contributing to different aspects of the academic enterprise, and who serve different functions for different communities'.

The idea that leadership takes many forms and that it is the combination of these influences that matters was brought home particularly strongly in a more recent study by the Leadership Foundation for Higher Education (Bolden et al., 2012).

Figure 2.1 Word cloud of most influential persons (Bolden et al., 2012: p. 18). Reproduced with the permission of the Leadership Foundation for Higher Education.

Whilst recent years have seen increasing emphasis and investment on leadership in universities, most of this has focused on people with formal management responsibilities and has framed leadership in terms of organisational goals and objectives. Our project, however, explored the leadership of academic work from the perspective of those being led.

Through a combination of methods we explored where and when academics look for leadership and found that, in most cases, the greatest influence comes from people who are not in formal authority relationships with them.

The word cloud in Figure 2.1 shows the descriptions our respondents gave when identifying people who exerted the most influence over their academic work. Out of over 400 responses only one person made direct reference to anyone in the senior executive team of the university. This, of course, is not to say that they are unimportant but does highlight the significance of informal leadership, much of which comes from people outside the respondent's own department or institution.

In the interviews, when we began asking about academic leadership, in most cases people went to long lengths to explain that it is not 'academic management'. Findings suggested that academics across the sector tended to recognise leadership in actions that (a) provide and protect an environment that enables productive academic work, (b) support and develop a sense of shared academic values and identity and (c) accomplish boundary spanning on behalf of individuals and work groups (ibid.).

One of my favourite quotes from the interviews was from a lecturer who, when asked, 'who do you look to for leadership?' replied:

People I've never met, mostly – some of them dead.... And my supervisor of my doctorate degree as well.... As a more mature academic, I've enjoyed working with collaborators. But that's not leadership. I really dislike this concept of leadership, because once you're grown up, you don't want to be led, you want to work as a member of a team.

(Bolden et al., 2012: p. 30)

This quote says quite a lot about leadership and followership in universities. Firstly, that we choose our leaders, and that they may not necessarily be aware of their influence on us. Secondly, that there are times in our career, particularly when we are developing our professional practice, where people such as PhD supervisors and line managers can play a very important developmental leadership role (even if it is not often described as such). And thirdly, that much of the time we do not actually want to be led by someone else, but would rather be able to lead ourselves in relation to what the work requires.

Figure 2.2 shows a diagram we developed to try to capture the distinction between academic leadership, academic management and self-leadership that was being made by participants in this study.

We call it the 'sailing ship' model and it suggests that an effective environment for academic work requires a balance between 'academic leadership', which shapes values and identities, and 'academic management', which focuses on the allocation and completion of tasks and processes. Where these are

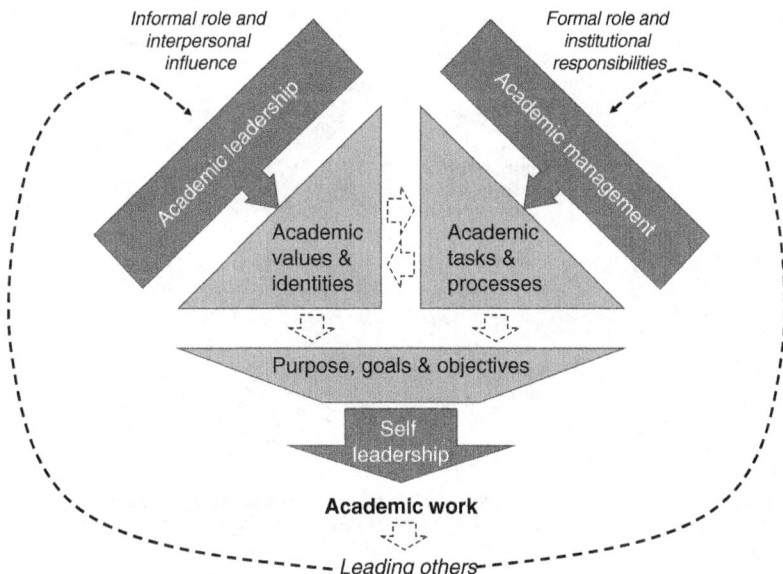

Figure 2.2 The 'sailing ship' model of academic leadership (Bolden et al., 2012: p. 35). Reproduced with the permission of the Leadership Foundation for Higher Education.

aligned they create a coherent sense of academic purpose, goals and objectives that are then accomplished through 'self-leadership' by academic professionals.

Much as we liked the sailing ship model, however, we felt that it was rather too neat and too static to capture the sense of dissonance many people expressed about leadership and management in their own institutions. So we developed this second diagram – the 'sinking ship' (Figure 2.3).

This research was conducted in 2011 when English universities were negotiating a significant increase in student fees, preparing for the forthcoming national research assessment process and introducing changes to pensions and contracts. It was a time of substantial change and uncertainty about the purpose and future of UK higher education.

As you can see from Figure 2.3, there was a suggestion that competition for students and funding is driving a corporate leadership approach within institutions that is based on market principles and is implemented through formal management processes. In such a context, it was suggested 'academic leadership' might become fragmented, side-lined or go underground.

An example of this in our study was a junior lecturer in one university who campaigned to keep the university bookstore open following a campus redevelopment. Whilst this might be seen as resistance by the organisation itself, to academic colleagues it was perceived as leadership as it involved making a stand about important academic values[6].

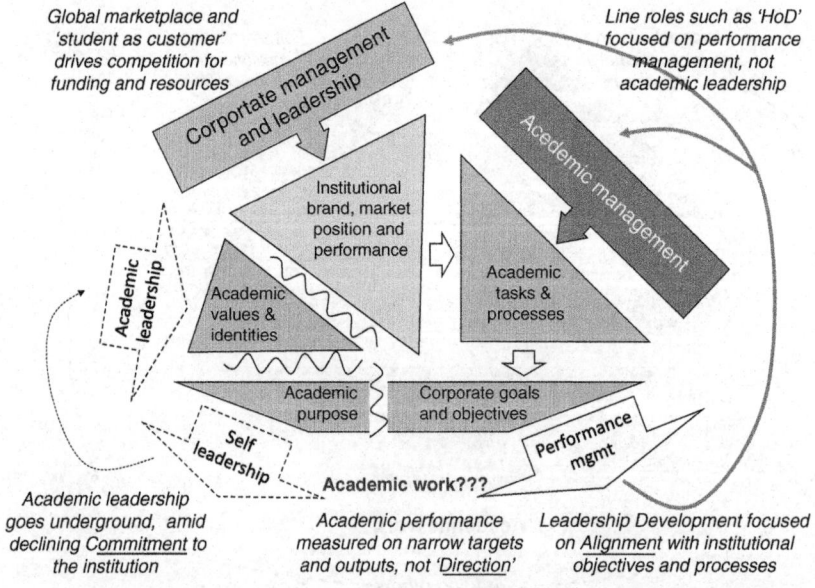

Figure 2.3 The 'sinking ship' model of academic leadership (Bolden et al., 2012: p. 37). Reproduced with the permission of the Leadership Foundation for Higher Education.

Whilst it is important to stress that the 'sinking ship' diagram is based on perceptions rather than objective reality, it has some important implications for how institutions promote and facilitate leadership. In particular, it highlights the risks of disengagement. As one of the participants in our study said:

> I think the tendency all over the country is to get more and more managerialist... I think, especially at universities, managers have to hold their nerve and trust their staff... looking around, I think most of us are engaged. There's a few who aren't, who've either burnt out or become extremely cynical, but I'd say most of us are engaged but we're engaged with the role and with our students, not necessarily with the university. So I think leaders have to work on that because there are times when I was almost alienated from the university and that is not a good thing.
>
> (Bolden et al., 2012: p. 33)

Within our research we were frequently struck by a strong commitment to the ideals of higher education from our participants yet frequent ambivalence, and occasional hostility, towards their own employer.

The tension that such a situation can present for those who take on formal management and leadership roles is expressed well by the Critical Management scholar Martin Parker in his autobiographical paper titled 'Becoming manager: Or, the werewolf looks anxiously in the mirror, checking for unusual facial hair', in which he describes his experience of taking on the role of Head of Department in a university where he had worked for some time.

The paper highlights the anxieties that arise when acquiring apparently conflicting roles and identities. Whilst it's perhaps inevitable that a person who has spent much of his professional life critiquing management will experience a degree of discomfort as he comes to terms with his new managerial role, the need to work through competing and sometimes contradictory identities is not unusual. Parker sums it up well when he says:

> I think that the most important distinction to be made is that I am a manager with an alternate 'professional' identity. Like other professionals in large organizations (doctors, engineers, lawyers) I have a somewhat divided series of identifications, some of which have little to do with my employer as such.
>
> (Parker, 2004: p. 56)

Despite the idiosyncrasies of the higher education sector, we have found that our findings have resonated in a wide range of industries and well beyond the UK. With the rapid growth of professional and knowledge-intensive work rather than being an anomaly of higher education, these issues are likely to become increasingly common across many sectors and occupations[7].

This takes me to the third and final paradox:

Paradox 3 − *the most effective leadership is where 'leadership' is not required.*

In perhaps the first ever book on leadership, written in the 5th century BC, Lao Tzu, the founder of Daoism, said:

> A leader is best
> When people barely know he exists
> Not so good when people obey and acclaim him
> Worse when they despise him
> But of a good leader, who talks little,
> When his work is done, his aim fulfilled,
> They will say:
> We did it ourselves.
>
> (Lao Tzu, cited in Manz and Sims, 1991: p. 35)

It is ironic, therefore, that in most of our organisations it continues to be those who shout the loudest who tend to reap the greatest rewards and that most people's promotion opportunities depend on them highlighting how they, rather than others, achieved particular outcomes.

New leadership for new times

As I suggested at the start of this chapter, questions of leadership have long been of concern but it's really only been in the last 50–60 years that people have tried to systemically study and analyse leadership and only really in the last 20–25 years that a global leadership development industry has emerged.

Whilst this has undoubtedly contributed to our knowledge about leadership and the availability of leadership training and development, I'm less convinced that it has had an equivalent impact on our understanding of leadership and, in particular, an understanding that will help us tackle the challenges we will face throughout the rest of this century.

Most of the leadership and management concepts and practices used in our organisations have their origins in an Industrial Era view of the world − where the centralisation of power and resources was important to support advances in manufacturing and production (Staron, Jasinski & Weatherley, 2006).

In more recent years, particularly with the growth of computers and communications technology, we have moved towards a more networked view of organisations and alongside this we've seen a shift in emphasis from management and administration to leadership − from control to influence.

The changes since the turn of the millennium, however, have come at such a rate that it's been hard for both theory and practice to keep up. In reflecting on the changes that have happened since the publication of his book *The World is Flat* in 2005, Thomas Freidman noted:

When I said the world is flat, Facebook didn't exist. Or for most people it didn't exist. Twitter was a sound. The Cloud was in the sky. 4G was a parking place. LinkedIn was a prison. Applications were something you sent to college. And, for most people, Skype was a typo. That all happened in the last seven years. And what it has done is taken the world from connected to hyper-connected. And that's been a huge opportunity and a huge challenge.

(Freidman, 2012)

These, of course, are just the shifts in technology. In the past 15 years we've also seen the attack on the World Trade Centre in New York and the subsequent War on Terror and rise of Islamic fundamentalism. We've come to recognise the extent of global climate change and the huge consequences this will have for future generations. We've had the global financial crisis and the subsequent austerity drive that continues to shape the geo-political landscape. We've seen an increase in the world population from six to over seven billion, of whom around 20 percent now live in China. To paraphrase the Chinese proverb – we do indeed live in interesting times!

In the late 1990s, the US Army War College developed the acronym 'VUCA' to refer to the volatile, uncertain, complex and ambiguous nature of the challenges facing nations in the post-cold war era (Stiehm, 2010). In recent years the term has been applied to business, management and leadership (Johansen, 2009). Organisations in the public, private and third sector are increasingly recognising the challenges they face as 'wicked'[8] and in need of a collaborative response. In such situations the work of leadership is far less about providing answers than asking the right questions and ensuring the right people are engaged in developing a solution (Grint, 2005b; 2008).

In a VUCA world, established approaches to strategy, planning and control often accentuate rather than alleviate the problem. Turbulent times highlight all too quickly the limits of traditional models of leadership and leadership development that focus almost exclusively on what is happening at the top of the organisation. Whilst the CEO, Chairman and other members of the senior leadership team are clearly important, the factors that contribute towards organisational adaptability, innovation and performance are far more widely distributed. Context, both internal and external to the organisation, ultimately determines what works… but often in ways that could not have been anticipated in advance.

So to return to the notion of paradox – much as quantum physicists such as Paul Callaghan and Niels Bohr have embraced a science of uncertainty to rethink the nature of our physical world, I believe that similar advances are required in our understanding of the social world.

There is, indeed, an emerging area of study within the field of leadership around the application of a complexity approach (Stacey, 2010; Obolensky, 2010; Uhl-Bien, Marion & McKelvey, 2007) and a number of organisations that are championing this within the field of leadership development. Flinn and Mowles (2014) summarise the implications as follows:

> From the perspective of complex responsive processes of relating, leading leadership development involves encouraging radical doubt, enquiry and reflexivity as a way of developing the capacity of leaders to manage in circumstances of high uncertainty and ideological and political contestation. However, radical doubt does not mean throwing everything up in the air at once. It means learning how to navigate between the poles of absolute certainty and absolute doubt, while persisting in seeing the world as more complex than it is portrayed in the dominant discourse.
>
> (ibid.: p. 19)

Conclusion

In this chapter I've suggested that there are a number of paradoxes that emerge when researching, practising and developing leadership. Many of these relate to the tensions between traditional perspectives that tend to present leadership as an individual quality, competence or behaviour, and shared perspectives, that regard leadership as a reciprocal process of influence.

I suggest that in an interdependent and networked society an ability to embrace and work with paradox and complexity is a key part of effective leadership. Rather than providing direction, control and decision making, leaders increasingly influence through sensemaking, boundary spanning and providing a compelling narrative. Leadership, however, is ultimately a group process and, as this chapter argues, we would do well to rethink the leader–follower relationship in order to find ways of mobilising the collective capacity of individuals, groups, organisations and communities.

Barker (1997: p. 352) describes leadership as 'a process of change where the ethics of individuals are integrated into the mores of a community'. From this perspective, leadership development is an important forum for negotiating shared values and purposes and is ultimately a process of community development.

Notes

1   The term 'agency' is used to express the degree of free-choice a person has (or believes him/herself to have) when deciding how to act within a particular context/situation.

2   A complexity approach suggests that rather than viewing organisations as rational, bounded systems that can be managed in predictable and controlled ways, they are better conceived of as 'patterns of human interaction constantly emerging in both predictable and unpredictable ways in the living present, mostly through conversational activity' (Flinn and Mowles, 2014: p. 2).

3   See, for example, the BBC Election Debate 2015, http://tiny.cc/bbc-election-debate-2015

4   http://www.management-standards.org/standards/standards

5   The Windsor Leadership Trust describes itself as 'a charity that provides transformational leadership development programmes, for senior leaders from all sectors of society', http://www.windsorleadership.org.uk
6   Some authors now refer to this as 'resistance leadership' (Zoller and Fairhurst, 2007).
7   Indeed, evidence suggests that a sense of autonomy, mastery and purpose are the strongest motivational drivers for people in all kinds of work and have a significant positive impact on health and well-being (Pink, 2009).
8   A 'wicked' problem is complex, intractable and cannot be resolved through the application of prior knowledge.

References

Barker, R. A. (1997). How can we train leaders if we do not know what leadership is? *Human Relations, 50*(4): 343–362.

Bennett, N., Wise, C., Woods, P. A., & Harvey, J. A. (2003). *Distributed leadership.* Nottingham: National College of School Leadership.

Bolden, R. (2011). Distributed leadership in organizations: A review of theory and research, *International Journal of Management Reviews, 13*(3), 251–269.

Bolden, R. (2014). Ubuntu. In D. Coghlan & M. Brydon-Miller (Eds.), *The SAGE Encyclopedia of Action Research.* London: Sage Publications, pp. 799–802.

Bolden, R., & Gosling, J. (2006). Leadership competencies: Time to change the tune? *Leadership, 2*(2), 147–163.

Bolden, R., Gosling, J., O'Brien, A., Peters, K., Ryan, M., & Haslam, S. A. (2012). *Academic leadership: Changing conceptions, identities and experiences in UK higher education.* London: Leadership Foundation for Higher Education.

Bolden, R., & Kirk, P. (2006). From 'leaders' to 'leadership'. *Effective Executive, 8*(10), 27–33.

Bolden, R., & Kirk, P. (2009). African leadership: Surfacing new understandings through leadership development. *International Journal of Cross Cultural Management, 9*(1), 69–86.

Bolden, R., & Kirk, P. (2011). Leadership development as a catalyst for social change: Lessons from a Pan-African programme. In S. Turnbull, P. Case G. Edwards D. Schedlitzki & P. Simpson (Eds.), *Worldly leadership: Alternative wisdoms for a complex world.* Basingstoke: Palgrave Macmillan, pp. 32–51.

Bolden, R., Petrov, G., & Gosling, J. (2008). *Developing collective leadership in higher education: Final report.* London: Leadership Foundation for Higher Education.

Bolden, R., Wood, M., & Gosling, J. (2006). Is the NHS leadership qualities framework missing the wood for the trees? In A. Casebeer, A. Harrison & A. L. Mark (Eds.), *Innovations in health care: A reality check.* New York: Palgrave Macmillan, pp. 17–29.

Carlyle, T. (1840). *On heroes, hero-worship, and the heroic in history.* London: Chapman and Hall.

Ciulla, J. (1998). *Ethics: The heart of leadership.* Westport, CT: Praeger.

Dictionary.com (2015). Paradox. http://dictionary.reference.com/browse/paradox, accessed 15 April 2015.

Flinn, K., & Mowles, C (2014). *A complexity approach to leadership development: Developing practical judgement.* LFHE Stimulus Paper, London: Leadership Foundation for Higher Education.

Follett, M. P. (1942/2003). *Dynamic administration: The collected papers of Mary Parker Follett.* London: Routledge.

Freidman, T. L. (2005). *The world is flat: A brief history of the globalized world in the twenty-first century.* London: Allen Lane.

Freidman, T. L. (2012). On 'connected to hyperconnected'. *Huffington Post*, 28 September 2012, http://huff.to/1CNx3HW, accessed 14 December 2018.

Gemmill, G., & Oakley, J. (1992). Leadership: An alienating social myth? *Human Relations*, 45(2), 113–129.

Gibb, C. A. (1954). Leadership. In G. Lindzey (Ed.), *Handbook of social psychology*, Vol. 2. Reading, MA: Addison-Wesley, pp. 877–917.

Goodreads.com (2015). Shellen Lubin: Quotes, http://bit.ly/1FdGfbd, accessed 05 March 2015.

Grint, K. (2005a). *Leadership: Limits and possibilities*. Basingstoke: Palgrave Macmillan.

Grint, K. (2005b). Problems, problems, problems: The social construction of 'leadership'. *Human Relations*, 58(11), 1467–1494.

Grint, K. (2008). Wicked problems and clumsy solutions: The role of leadership. *Clinical Leader*, 1(2), http://bit.ly/1HqT8CH, accessed 14 December 2018.

Hutton, W. (2014). Banking is changing, slowly, but its culture is still corrupt. *The Guardian*, 16 November 2014, http://tiny.cc/hutton-banking, accessed 14 December 2018.

Johansen, B. (2009). *Leaders make the future*. San Francisco, CA: Berrett-Koehler.

Ladkin, D. (2010). *Rethinking leadership: A new look at old leadership questions*. Cheltenham: Edward Elgar.

Lipman-Blumen, J. (2005). *The allure of toxic leaders*. New York: Oxford University Press.

Lutz, D. W. (2009). African ubuntu philosophy and global management. *Journal of Business Ethics*, 84:313–328.

Mangaliso, M. P. (2001). Building competitive advantage from ubuntu: Management lessons from South Africa. *Academy of Management Executive*, 15(3), 23–33.

Manz, C. C., & Sims, H. P. (1991). Superleadership: Beyond the myth of heroic leadership. *Organizational Dynamics*, Spring, 18–35.

Mead, G. H. (1934). *Mind, self, and society: From the standpoint of a social behaviorist*. Chicago: University of Chicago Press.

Meindl, J. R., Ehrlich, S. B., & Dukerich, J. M. (1985). The Romance of Leadership. *Administrative Science Quarterly*, 30(1), 78–102.

Obolensky, N. (2010). *Complex adaptive leadership: Embracing paradox and uncertainty*. Farnham: Gower.

Parker, M. (2004). Becoming manager: Or, the werewolf looks anxiously in the mirror, checking for unusual facial hair. *Management Learning*, 35(1), 45–59.

Pink, D. H. (2009). *Drive: The surprising truth about what motivates us*. New York: Penguin-Riverhead.

Stacey, R. D. (2010). *Complexity and organizational reality* (2nd ed.). London: Routledge.

Staron, M., Jasinski, M, & Weatherley, R. (2006). *Life based learning: A strength based approach for capability development in vocational and technical education*. Darlinghurst, NSW: TAFE NSW International Centre for VET.

Stiehm, J. H. (2010). *U.S. Army War College: Military education in a democracy*. Philadelphia: Temple University Press.

Uhl-Bien, M., Marion, R., & McKelvey, B. (2007). Complexity leadership theory: Shifting leadership from the industrial age to the knowledge era. *The Leadership Quarterly*, 18(4), 298–318.

Zoller, H., & Fairhurst, G. (2007). Resistance leadership: The overlooked potential in critical organization and leadership studies. *Human Relations*, 60(9): 1331–1360.

3

Teams

Team dynamics and the perils of agreement

Darren Dalcher

Project managers are accustomed to avoiding and overcoming disagreements inside the team, amongst stakeholders, with suppliers and with others senior managers, sponsors and leaders. Indeed, the abilities to remove or resolve conflict and deal with contradictions are highly prized in leaders in most domains.

Project management has followed a similar set of traditions and assumptions. The 6th edition of the APM Body of Knowledge focuses on the seven crucial interpersonal skills, which include conflict resolution, alongside communication, delegation, influencing, leadership, negotiation and teamwork. Similarly, The 6th edition of PMI's *A Guide to the Project Management Body of Knowledge* makes multiple references to conflict management, before addressing it as a key area under the Project Resource Management knowledge area, identifying it as a key interpersonal and team skill, alongside decision making, emotional intelligence, influencing and leadership. IPMA's Individual Competence Baseline also makes a reference to the area of 'conflict and crisis' under the people section, given the need to moderate or solve conflicts and crises.

> Conflict can be defined as different objectives and attitudes between two or more parties. Conflict management is the process of identifying and addressing differences that, if left unresolved, could affect objectives.
>
> > (APM, 2012: p. 56)

> The success of project managers in managing their project often depends on their ability to resolve conflict.
>
> > (PMI, 2017: p. 348)

> The potential means of resolving conflicts involve collaboration, compromise, prevention or the use of power.
>
> > (IPMA, 2015: p. 86)

The Oxford Dictionary defines conflict as: a serious disagreement or argument, typically a protracted one; a prolonged armed struggle; or, a serious incompatibility between two or more opinions, principles or interests. Given the implication of disagreement between ideas, beliefs or perspectives, it is only natural that managers and leaders try to minimise disagreements and maintain harmony and balance.

But what if the core of our problems stems from agreement rather than conflict?

The real problem with agreement

Variation is highly cherished, especially in teams, in order to avoid homogenous thinking and problem resolution. Nature also favours variation as a mechanism for infusing diversity, resilience and flexibility. Design is often informed by the creativity that emerges from the conflict between ideas, needs and perspectives.

Project teams bring together a diversity of opinions, views and team members encouraging a wider spectrum of approaches designed to avoid the uniformity and conformity of groupthink and encourage diversity through challenge. And yet, project managers often seek to banish conflict in order to simplify decision making, reach consensus and limit the potential for disagreements and blockages in systems, plans and the execution of initiatives.

The approaches for addressing the harmful impacts of excessive conflict are well featured in the literature, but what about the harmful impact of violent (or perhaps, silent) agreement? Can agreement, which after all seems to be the outcome of effective conflict resolution, become powerful enough to undermine a good project or destabilise a good team? Can absolute agreement derail success?

A journey to Abilene

US management scholar Jerry B. Harvey (1974) captured the risks of agreement in the following tale.

On an extremely hot July afternoon, a couple is visiting the wife's parents in Coleman, Texas. The temperature of 104 degrees combines with a persistent wind that re-distributes the topsoil throughout the house to make being outdoors unpleasant. But as they settle on the back porch, the family has an old-fashioned fan, cold lemonade and is becoming engrossed in a game of dominoes. This has the makings of an agreeable, if slightly lazy afternoon in Coleman, until the father-in-law suggests that they take a trip to Abilene, 53 miles north, to have dinner in the cafeteria.

The husband is concerned about making the journey, given the heat and dust storm, and the need to travel 53 miles each way in a non-air-conditioned 1958 Buick.

However, when his wife retorts 'sounds like a great idea. I'd like to go. How about you, Jerry', he fears being out of step with the others, promptly replying, 'Sounds good to me', before adding a final opt out clause, 'I just hope your mother wants to go'.

The mother-in-law also appears to be up to the task, responding with 'Of course I want to go, I haven't been to Abilene in a long time'.

The drive turns out to be long, dusty and very uncomfortable. The food in the cafeteria is extremely disappointing, described by Jerry as fit for a 'first rate prop in an antacid commercial'. Four hours later they return to Coleman, hot, bothered and exhausted, as they all collapse in front of the fan on the porch.

To break the silence one of them dishonestly says: 'It was a great trip, wasn't it?'. The mother-in-law angrily retorts that she would rather have stayed at home, but was swayed by the enthusiasm of the other participants, as she felt pressured to join in.

The husband questions the version of events, stating: 'I wasn't delighted to be doing what we were doing. I only went to satisfy the rest of you'. The wife responds, 'I just went along to keep you happy. I would have had to be crazy to want to go out in the heat like that'. Finally the father-in-law confirms that he only suggested the excursion because he thought the others might be bored, and because the visits are seldom, he wanted everyone to enjoy the day. Personally, he explains, he would have preferred another game of dominoes on the porch and eating the leftovers from the icebox.

The group then sits back in silence, reflecting on the 106-mile trip through the desert that nobody wanted, and the food that no one enjoyed.

While each participant would have preferred to sit comfortably and relax on the porch, the entire group travelled to Abilene and back under terrible conditions, in the mistaken assumption that they were doing it for the sake of the rest of the group.

Many groups and organisations take their own Abilene journeys... Jerry B. Harvey summarises it thus: 'When organizations blunder into the Abilene Paradox, they take actions in contradiction to what they really want to do and therefore defeat the very purposes they are trying to achieve' (ibid.: p. 18).

Managing agreement

Organisations often find themselves embarking on unnecessary and counter-productive journeys to their own version of Abilene. Lewis asserts that while many theorists advocate the development of conflict resolution approaches in the belief that the management of conflict is a key concern, the real challenge faced by most organisations is actually the need to manage agreement!

> Inability to manage agreement may be the major source of organization dysfunction.
>
> (ibid.: p. 18)

The characteristics of being in an Abilene Paradox (ibid.: pp. 18–19) can be paraphrased as follows:

1   Individual members agree in private about the nature of the problem or situation;
2   Members agree in private about what steps are needed to cope with the situation or problem;
3   Members fail to accurately communicate their desires and beliefs; in fact they do the exact opposite, leading one another to misperceive the collective reality;
4   Invalid assumptions and inaccurate information lead the team to take actions contrary to their wishes and desires, and counterproductive to the organisation's intent and purposes;
5   Members experience frustration, anger and dissatisfaction as a result of the counterproductive actions; this may lead to the formation of subversive subgroups that blame others and complain about the leaders and other groups; and
6   If members do not deal with the chronic inability to manage agreement, the cycle is likely to repeat with greater intensity and stronger emotions and dissatisfaction.

The key feature of 'going to Abilene' is that individuals seem to act against their own preferences and against their own interest, and are aware of it and seem resentful of the sacrifice and the wrong outcome. In contrast, members of teams engaged in groupthink appear to conform to the preferred thinking patterns of the group but do not act against their own interests. Inability to express views and preferences – or to manage agreement – may thus condemn groups and organisations to actions that seem contrary to their preferences, well-being, and even to the success of the individual and the collective.

Team dynamics and high-stakes leadership

The Abilene Paradox depicts a particular type of group dynamic, where a wish for social conformity and social influence may result in individuals acting contrary to their own preferences in what is, mistakenly, assumed to be the inclination of the wider community. Teams are subject to a host of other influences and complex dynamics that occur within the group and between its participants. The chapter by Dr. Constance Dierickx focuses on some of the invisible traps in project teams that can lead to crises. It is derived from the book *High-Stakes Leadership: Leading through Crisis with Courage, Judgment and Fortitude*, published by Bibliomotion, part of the Taylor & Francis Group.

Dierickx's work (2017) emphasises the attributes that enable leaders to address and overcome crises. Her work is important in drawing attention to the needs of teams in uncertain, ambiguous and difficult times. Recognising that leaders are tasked with the difficult decisions, especially in times of crisis, she focuses on the three key elements that make leaders great:

- *Courage* as the ability to act with clarity and focus, identify important information and eschew habit;
- *Judgment* as a way of testing ideas using reason and demanding improvements and corrections; and
- *Fortitude* as the renewable source of energy needed to inspire and accomplish great tasks

The resulting three-part model can be utilised to illuminate the mindsets, strategies and tactics that leaders must employ to resolve problematic situations and make difficult decisions. Her work also identifies three major psychological barriers, which she describes as decision traps that get in the way of recognising and responding to crisis. The chapter presents the three principal decision traps of overconfidence, groupthink and anxiety avoidance and explores their role and impact in compromising decisions, complicating action and derailing initiatives.

Dierickx does a good job of offering pragmatic advice that helps leaders and organisations to act decisively; test ideas and challenge perspectives using reason; and be resolute and inspire others to continue, even in the face of severe challenges.

Conflict and agreement: A reprise

Sometimes the problem may be lack of conflict or of evidence of what the common opinion is. Journeys to Abilene represent an organisational drift towards dysfunction through a series of small, yet reversible, steps.

How does one get all the way to Abilene?
One inch at a time…

The drift occurs as opportunities to identify the lack of communication are ignored, until the team finally finds itself eating that unwanted meal (perhaps disguised as an effective prop for an antacid in a commercial) in the cafeteria at Abilene. And then the team will still have to face the journey back…

It is normally recognised in politics that an agreement cannot be the result of imposition, but it can be equally perilous to simply assume that everyone is always on board. Agreement becomes a problem when we are unable to communicate and confirm it.

Mexican spiritualist Don Miguel Ruiz offers a simple recipe:

Don't Make Assumptions. Find the courage to ask questions and to express what you really want. Communicate with others as clearly as you can to avoid misunderstandings, sadness and drama. With just this one agreement, you can completely transform your life.

Patrick Lencioni (2006) identified fear of conflict as the second dysfunction of teams, which is fed by a desire to preserve artificial harmony that stifles the occurrence of productive, passionate and ideological debate. Where team members are unable to express their opinions, the quality of the resulting decisions is inferior. In contrast, he observed that

> on great teams – the kind where people trust each other, engage in open conflict, and then commit to decisions – team members have the courage and confidence to confront one another when they see something that isn't serving the team.
>
> (ibid.: p. 56)

Successful teams need the trust, courage and judgment to determine if everyone is on board for the journey. Even if they appear to be, there is always one more chance to question the purpose of the journey…

US business executive Alfred P. Sloane wryly summarised,

> If we are all in agreement on the decision – then I propose we postpone further discussion of this matter until our next meeting to give ourselves time to develop disagreement and perhaps gain some understanding of what the decision is all about.

Whilst we may acknowledge the role of conflict management in team dynamics and organisational settings, there is ample room to improve our ability to identify and define agreement. The words that are left unspoken and the feelings and preferences that remain unshared can also carry the abject seeds of failure and underachievement. Managing agreement is largely concerned with avoiding unnecessary and unwanted excursions to Abilene. In order to begin to challenge such unnecessary explorations, we may need to learn to listen to the silence that troubled Alfred P. Sloane and endeavour to challenge its basis and continuing presence.

References

APM (2012). *APM Body of Knowledge* (6th ed.). Princes Risborough: Association of Project Management.

Dierickx, C. (2017). *High-stakes leadership: Leading through crisis with courage, judgment, and fortitude.* New York: Bibliomotion.

Harvey, J. B. (1974). The Abilene paradox: The management of agreement. *Organizational Dynamics, 3*(1), 63–80.

IPMA (2015). *Individual competence baseline for project, programme & portfolio management,* version 4. Zurich: IPMA.

Lencioni, P. (2006). *The five dysfunctions of a team.* New York: John Wiley & Sons.

PMI (2017). *A guide to the project management body of knowledge* (PMBOK Guide) (6th ed.). Newtown Square, PA: Project Management Institute.

Invisible traps in project management lead to crisis

Constance Dierickx

When we think of great project management, most of us imagine very smart people, tight processes and rigour to spare. Calendars, charts, metrics all skilfully employed by people with project management credentials. Yet, things go wrong. Sometimes resulting in disaster. Why? Because projects require humans to create the project, do the project and monitor it. Even smart people have cognitive limitations and emotions that influence their thinking. Even project managers of great experience, skill and intellect are subject to these influences. In my book, *High-Stakes Leadership*, I talk about the three aspects that make a leader great when ambiguity and risk are both high. These are the same attributes that enable leaders to move through crisis and often avoid it in the first place. They are: courage, judgment and fortitude. Even when leaders have these qualities in abundance, invisible decision traps can get in the way of even the most intelligent people.

What are the things that get in our way? The top three:

1 Overconfidence;
2 Groupthink; and
3 Anxiety avoidance

Who me? Overconfident?

Regardless of how rational we think we are and no matter how objective we believe our assessment of our abilities, most people are overconfident. Surprisingly, more education doesn't improve this. Fortunately, it doesn't make it any worse either. Research by Russo and Schoemaker shows us that executives and undergraduates are equally likely to be overconfident. Neither experience nor recent advanced education creates immunity. This surprises almost everyone.

Russo and Schoemaker devised a very clever test of overconfidence and permitted me to update it for my book. I have used this test with executives for over 15 years and it never fails to yield the same result. What result is that? Surprise. Disbelief. Argument. Regardless of how smart and experienced we are, humans are overconfident. Since the research on this is clear, what should we do?

First, answer the questions in Table 3.1. Provide both low and high answers for each such that you are 90 percent sure the correct answer falls between the two. Then, check your answers with those that appear at the end of this chapter. If your answers were all correct or nine of ten were correct, ask yourself, 'How did I do that? What method was I using?' This sort of reflection is essential to learning so don't rush! Think about whether or not the approach you used for the test can be applied elsewhere.

If you are like most people, you missed several questions. What might you learn from this? Whether your answers were mostly right or not, thinking about your own thinking is worth doing, especially if you can keep the need to be right tucked away.

When I was a stockbroker I had several clients who were sure they had 'the answer', they knew 'the secret' to making money. No matter how poorly their investments did, some of them still managed to hold tight to their blatantly ineffective methods. I watched a very arrogant college professor lose a lot of money using an algorithm he developed and thought was 'the answer', a 66 year-old woman close her account and give all her money to her son-in-law who was opening a retail store and a woman in her 80s beg to trade options (the firm wouldn't approve her for an options account – whew!) Each of these examples was either a crisis in the making or it actually became one. Everyone was fuelled by overconfidence.

It seems that poor results would call into question what we are doing. Yet, often it takes too many data points before we stop doing what is causing bad outcomes. Why? People are not just overconfident about what *will* happen, they tend to remember events and outcomes that have already happened if the events support what they believe. That's right, we see what we believe, not the other way around. The confirmation bias is a well-known phenomenon and you can see it everywhere if you look. If you are honest with yourself, you'll

Table 3.1 Overconfidence test

	Low	High
1. John F. Kennedy's age at death		
2. Height of Mt. Kilimanjaro		
3. Number of countries in Africa		
4. Area of California in square miles		
5. Diameter of the earth (in miles)		
6. Year of the *Challenger* shuttle disaster		
7. Year the Mona Lisa was painted		
8. Average weight of an Asian elephant		
9. Distance from New York to Berlin		
10. Deepest point of the ocean (in feet)		

see it in your own life. Really good project management utilises tools and feedback loops to tell us when things aren't going right. Good project management avoids crisis by subjecting the tools to scrutiny and the data gathered with these tools to even greater examination. Yet, people misinterpret data, explain it away and ascribe cause, erroneously. Further, someone (a human being) has to set up the check-points in the first place.

What are my options? If you are a normal, well-meaning person who wants to do well and create value for yourself and others, you summon courage. You keep in mind that as talented, smart and experienced as you may be, you are fallible. Richard Feynman, a Nobel Laureate in Physics, famously wrote, 'The first principle is that you must not fool yourself and you are the easiest person to fool'. It takes someone of Feynman's stature to say this for us to consider it rather than push the idea aside. I have found that the research on how cognitive biases and emotion affect our thinking and decisions is helpful and supports Feynman's statement. Though not a cognitive scientist, Feynman had a tremendous knack for observation. He was especially adept at spotting false beliefs, foolish habits and useless protocols.

These are the questions you need to answer if your efforts are to have superior value.

1 Am I clear on the objective? I'm talking about the organisational objective.
2 Do I know how the leaders will determine success?
3 Do I understand why making a change matters? To whom?
4 Is the value (why it matters) clear and compelling?

   a To whom?
   b By what measures?

I'm independent

A phenomenon that many are loath to accept applies to them is groupthink.

Groupthink is a psychological process that many of us learn about in an introductory psychology course. It means exactly what it sounds like, even if the name is new to you. It is the name for a group dynamic in which the people in a group think alike. What's wrong with that? The feeling of agreement and even camaraderie can be very rewarding. It's nice to agree. Sure, but what are the consequences when agreement is achieved at the expense of a beneficial outcome?

A few crises where groupthink no doubt played a role:

- US Navy leaders' belief that they would 'not be caught napping' days before the attack on Pearl Harbor.
- The executives and board of Enron creating and then going along with illegal financial arrangements that ultimately took the company down and the life savings of thousands with it.

- The data breach at Equifax in the fall of 2017, months after a supplier of software made them aware of a problem.
- Encyclopedia Britannica failing to move its content to digital media when the value of doing so was high, instead selling the company for a low price years later.
- Wells-Fargo retail executives knowingly tolerating practices that were illegal so they could make their goals.
- Volkswagen engineers scheming to rig the testing for diesel engines to meet a standard they couldn't figure out how to meet otherwise.

We like to think that in the face of a bad decision, we would speak up. If we see or become aware of a bad actor, vulnerability or a blatant wrong, we would say something. Sometimes people do, but it isn't as easy as it sounds. The social costs of going against the group are real undercurrents that are like undertows threatening to take us down.

When a project is led by someone who demonstrates low tolerance for 'going along to get along' and mistakes are obscured, this creates the atmosphere for everyone involved to speak up when there is cause to do so. A project manager needs to set the standards for the technical aspects of the work and, equally important, for the human processes. Ignoring the latter because it seems 'too squishy' will eventually undermine your best technical performance. If the human processes are ignored and nothing does go wrong, the bad practice will be reinforced and repeated, not only strengthening the practice with the project manager but also modelling it for many others. This is how a seemingly small thing becomes a systemic weakness of huge proportion.

Go fever

If ever there were big projects, with many levels of project management, it's in the space program. The crew involved in the Challenger launch had reason to be fatigued, frustrated and anxious. Delays in launches are very frustrating and they happen in public. Thousands of people and the media gather near Cape Canaveral and the surrounding towns to watch. The project teams can't escape their own frustration by going home. It's in the news, the locals talk about it and the tension amongst visitors, who come to watch, is palpable. The engineers, managers and even the astronauts themselves experience the tension that rises higher and higher with delays and also understand that their decisions can either prevent or cause a crisis.

The explosion of the Challenger was a bona fide crisis. Its cause, in part, was 'go fever'. The people involved are smart, experienced and take it from me, a former beach kid who grew up very close by, everyone takes their responsibilities seriously. Smart, successful people are still human and especially when there are delays and mounting frustration, emotion can distort our perception and have more sway in decisions than we care to admit.

Most of us aren't managing rocket launches but the work we do carries various risks nonetheless. We may endure long meetings, lose sleep and eat bad food in the belief that we are 'getting the work done'. Tension mounts when things go wrong or deadlines loom that we fear won't be met. People do things to reduce tension, some of which relieve anxiety but are bad for the project and may lead to a crisis. Procrastination, anger at others, seeking more data and analysis when it isn't needed, self-medicating and working harder (even if it isn't effective) can be attempts to reduce tension. Project managers are human and when the pressure of their work environment is extreme and they become exhausted, judgment suffers and the crisis that might have been avoided becomes more likely.

What do we do instead? Two things. First, leaders shouldn't model this type of behaviour – working themselves and others beyond the point where they are effective. Second, we need to learn about the human system. We talk about people, organisations, families, corporations, etc. as systems for good reason. Leaders need to think systemically to reduce unintended and negative consequences. Sometimes this means using a clutch to shift rather than push-ing, pushing and pushing forward using the same methods.

Daniel Kahneman writes about the kind of thinking we need when a task is complex. In these cases, we need the type of thinking that is more effortful, what he calls System Two. People can resist this because it feels like a waste of time to slow down and be more deliberate. It is as if you are deciding what to have for lunch. Yet, we tend to use rules of thumb too often when the task doesn't lend itself to quick judgments. When we fail, it's easy to think it is an aberration because the pattern is hard to see for oneself.

Methodology doesn't equal outcome

In project management and in any area where people become skilled in a par-ticular approach or method, they can become over-reliant on the processes, tools and, dare I say it, rituals to keep things moving. Tools and common practices are necessary and useful. That said, the brilliant project manager is one who is thinking all along the way and looking at the obvious and what is below the surface. The brilliant project manager has his or her eye on the *outcome* and not the *methodology*.

Brilliant project managers do this:

1 Clarify objectives.
2 Establish metrics that matter.
3 Know why what they are doing matters and to whom.
4 Attract other brilliant people.
5 Help people grow to brilliance.
6 Do not wait until their feet are wet to tell them the tide is in.
7 Ask 'what if we are wrong?'

8 Have a working clutch. They shift from fast, auto-pilot thinking and decision making to a slower, more deliberate approach when there is complexity.
9 When anxiety creeps in, they look for the cause, not the band-aid.

It has been my privilege to know and work with some very talented leaders who possess the qualities that enable them to guide, inspire and teach others. Project managers are leaders, at least the good ones. As a student of leadership for most of my life, I have been captivated by leaders in many situations and observed what they have in common. They have in common courage, judgment and fortitude, which are the very things a project manager needs to be brilliant.

Lead on!

Answers:

1 46
2 19,431 feet
3 54
4 163,695
5 7,917.5
6 1986
7 1507
8 Male – 12,000 lbs Female – 6,000 lbs
9 3.965
10 36,200

References

Kahneman, D. (2001). *Thinking fast and slow*. New York: Farrar, Straus and Giroux.
Russo, J. E., & Schoemaker, P. J. H. (2001). *Winning decisions: Getting it right the first time*. New York: Doubleday.

4

Culture

Why culture really matters

Darren Dalcher

According to the Merriam Webster Dictionary, acculturation is defined as the cultural modification of an individual, group or people by adapting to or borrowing traits from another culture. The phenomenon refers to the cultural change that stems from intentional blending between cultures, which aims to alter a pre-existing perspective, approach or way of thinking and replace it with a preferred, and more highly valued alternative response pattern.

A 'giant' new kid on the block

The 1984 breakup of AT&T in the US resulted in the creation of seven independent telecoms companies that were formed from the original 22 AT&T controlled members of the Bell system. Pacific Bell, controlled by the holding group Pacific Telesis Group, was considered by many to be the weakest of the emerging new organisations.

> Of all the Bell regional holding companies, Pacific Telephone holds the most risk for investors. The company's record of poor earnings and its long-running feud with the California Public Utilities Commission make it a risky investment at best.
>
> *New York Times*, 1985

Finding itself within the new and fiercely competitive Californian telecommunications marketplace, Pacific Bell had to reform itself into a savvy and successful organisation, much removed from its Bell origins. Pacific Bell launched aggressive marketing campaigns to capture a significant share of the burgeoning market. However, the company quickly found itself enmeshed in controversy for selling unneeded telephone services to non-English speaking customers who did not understand what they were buying. As tales of the dubious sales tactics of the company became public knowledge, morale within the organisation plummeted and its reputation, increasingly on par with that of a dubious used car dealership, also took a hit (Kirp, 1989).

Pacific Bell decided to turn its attention to transforming the organisation into a modern and efficient conglomerate. Modernising the company would require the shaking up of its massive workforce of 62,000 workers and drastically reshuffling the rigidly hierarchical structure, described as a steep pyramid with 14 very precisely delineated levels.

In search of a new culture

More crucially, management also targeted the total transformation of the culture within the organisation. They were worried that Pacific Bell did not have the right culture and competitive attitude and concerned that employees were not sufficiently entrepreneurial for the corporation to be able to succeed in its new environment.

Looking for direction, they turned to a well-known, local Californian recluse and organisational development consultant, Charles Krone. Years earlier, Krone made his fame as an internal specialist within the Proctor & Gamble soap division, for which he set up a liquid detergent plant in Lima, Ohio, that outperformed every other soap plant in the company (Rose, 1990). His counterpart, Herb Stokes, who had since become a corporate consultant and rancher in Abilene, Texas — led a similarly successful effort at a P&G paper products plant he organised in Albany, Georgia. Krone's methodology was based on a mélange of systems theory, socio-tech thinking, sufi mysticism and the writing of 20th-century Armenian Mystic George I. Gurdieff, who believed that most humans spent their days in 'waking sleep' and that is only by shedding ingrained habits of thinking that individuals could liberate their inner potential.

Krone's work was supposed to teach people to think more precisely, but it was jargon-laden and off-putting (Rose, 1990). Pacific Bell contracted with two associates of Charles Krone for $40 million worth of leadership development and personal-growth training (Kirp, 1989) to acculturate the workforce and embed the new culture. Some reports suggest that the full figure was closer to $147 million. Staff at Pacific Bell were instructed in new concepts such as 'the law of three' (a thinking framework that helps to identify the quality of mental energy that people have) and discovered the importance of 'alignment', 'intentionality' and 'end-state visions' (Spicer, 2017).

> This new vocabulary was designed to awaken employees from their bureaucratic doze and open their eyes to new higher-level consciousness… But it had some unfortunate side effects. First, according to one former middle manager, it was virtually impossible for anyone outside the company to understand [it]. Second, the manager said, this new language led to a lot more meetings, and the amount of time wasted nurturing this higher consciousness meant that everything took twice as long.
>
> (Spicer, 2017)

While the acculturation effort was packaged in the New Age language of psychic liberation, the training was backed by all the normal threats of an authoritarian corporation (Spicer, 2017). Managers were regularly summoned to the offices of their superiors, following the traditional hierarchical structures, to quell rebellion and ensure their underlings followed instruction.

The idea behind the system was that certain words help employees to communicate better, improving the health of the entire organisation. The approach backfired massively. Instead of opening up communication, it sharpened divisions between the few adherents and the rest of the organisation (Kirp, 1989). Instead of easing relations with the California utility regulator, the controversial corporate expenditure triggered a public inquiry and ultimately resulted in the issuing of a 'cease and desist' recommendation, which Pacific Bell decided to ignore.

While attendance at the 'Krone sessions' was supposed to be voluntary, those who resisted were left with the impression their careers would be jeopardised (Rose, 1990). Eschewing the organised opportunity to 'care more about their work and express themselves more clearly', several Pacific Bell employees wrote to their congressmen with allegations of mind control, sparking a public outcry.

On 30 October 1987, Pacific Bell finally announced the abandonment of its costly leadership development programme in favour of a more mainstream employee-training programme.

> We tried to do too much too fast', President Philip Quigley conceded in announcing an end to the program… 'With all the challenges posed by the changing nature of our business, we found we were moving too quickly.
>
> (Keppel, 1987)

The role of culture

Organisational theory, organisational behaviourists and change experts have long recognised the fundamental role of culture and its impact on the success and failure of organisations and their endeavours.

Failure is a great and dear teacher. As we have seen, organised attempts at engineering an appropriate culture, underpinned by agreed and acquired attitudes, norms and emotions, can cause significant industrial and emotional upheaval, spectacularly achieving the exact opposite of the harmony and growth originally intended. The consultants working for Pacific Bell failed to recognise the need to reconcile the proposed new methodology with the existing culture within the organisation, thereby feeding an ongoing clash between cultures.

MIT Professor, Edgar Schein, who has made his reputation and academic career in the area of organisational culture, has observed that 'organizational learning, development and planned change cannot be understood without considering culture as the primary source of resistance to change' (Schein, 2016).

Schein noted the central role of culture:

> the bottom line for leaders is that if they do not become conscious of the cultures in which they are embedded, those cultures will manage them. Cultural understanding is desirable for all of us, but it is essential for leaders if they are to lead.
>
> (Schein, 2016)

Schein developed a detailed organisational culture model to make culture more visible within the organisation by dividing organisational culture into three levels:

- Artefacts: Artefacts and symbols that mark the surface of the organisation and include any tangible, overt or verbally identifiable elements in an organisation: Logos, architecture, furniture, dress code, office jokes. Artefacts are the visible elements in a culture and they can be recognised by people not part of the culture.
- Espoused values: Stated standards, values and rules of behaviour
- Assumptions: Basic underlying assumptions and values; deeply embedded ideas, taken-for-granted behaviours which are usually unconscious, but constitute the essence of culture. These assumptions are typically so well integrated in the office dynamic that they are difficult to discern from within.

The three layers of culture are sometimes described as the onion layers of culture, with the outer layer representing the visible and identifiable artefacts, with inner layers made of espoused values, further underpinned by hidden assumptions. The model can easily explain why making external changes at one level, such as the company logo, will fail to address internal priorities, issues and values and thus will fail to embed and anchor a wider change in culture.

Culture invades project management

Now, what would happen if we turned the lens of culture onto our very own profession?

The chapter, authored by Gabrielle O'Donovan, examines the creation of a culture of partnership between project management and change management. It is extracted from her book *Making Organizational Change Stick: How to Create a Culture of Partnership between Project and Change Management*, published by Routledge. Gabrielle takes issue with the poor results of organisational change initiatives and wonders whether the disconnect between the cultures of project management and change management plays a key part in embedding the gap between the different disciplines and stopping the bridging of cultures which should surely lead to a better track record in delivering organisationally ready change initiatives.

O'Donovan's work (2018) makes a case for establishing a productive partnership between the professions of change management and project management and she sets about to determine what such a partnership might look like. Her model focuses on culture as a common link between the professions and she utilises it to ascertain why the new culture is essential for business benefits realisation and utilises it in the development of life cycle integration and improvement across the different domains. The work proposes strategy, structures and processes that are informed by the cultures of both disciplines and which are able to integrate the strengths of both areas and develop a sustainable and commercially powerful and meaningful business change.

O'Donovan also extends existing ideas within cultural theory to develop new and heightened understanding of the impact of culture in projects. More critically, she is able to utilise such models to surface ideas regarding the common culture needed to underpin the integrated perspective of change and projects. She is also able to offer specific mechanisms for developing the joint culture through shared artefacts, life cycles and perspectives that can enrich both disciplines. Following the proposals made in the work can enrich the development and management perspectives and offer the common ground needed to build a supportive new culture capable of supporting new understanding and insights.

When culture strikes back

Management professor Adam Grant observed that 'The culture of a workplace – an organization's values, norms and practices – has a huge impact on our happiness and success'.

Yet, one of the key problems is in seeing how cultures can work together and look across the divide to build on what is already commonly in place.

French philosopher Pierre Bourdieu noted, 'the point of my work is to show that culture and education aren't simply hobbies or minor influences. They are hugely important in the affirmation of differences between groups and social classes and in the reproduction of those differences'.

Culture continues to provide an immutable barrier to communication and problem resolution.

The imposition of the new change regime at Pacific Bell created difficult conditions for tens of thousands of internal employees. Amongst them was a young computer programmer struggling to make sense of the shifting new work culture. During the difficult transition period, the young programmer started to draw a cartoon that mercilessly mocked the new management-speak and strange culture that invaded his workspace and impacted his life. The comic strip featured a hapless and micromanaged office drone, his disaffected colleagues, his evil boss, and an even more evil management consultant who was intent on making everyone's life a misery (Spicer, 2017).

The cartoon became an instant hit, syndicated in newspapers all over the world. The programmer's name was Scott Adams and the series of cartoons he created was *Dilbert*.

The consultant's brand of 'kroning' methodology, as it became known, barely lasted a couple of years. However, in a bitter twist of irony, the humour that emerged from the pain of dealing the vagaries of management speak and ill-conceived acculturation continues to entertain new generations of workers and managers. Indeed, the longest lasting legacy of the Pacific Bell educational programme experiment, which cost at least $40 million, is the series of cartoons celebrating its folly... *Dilbert* has won multiple awards and is now recognised as one of the best international comic strips as it continues to share the lessons of poor management and flawed culture. It is only by paying attention to culture and its deeper impact that we can begin to address the anthropological side of bringing people on board and the social and personal aspects of embedding and delivering meaningful change.

References

Keppel, B. (1987). Pacific Bell calls halt to disputed training plan. *Los Angeles Times*, 30 October 1987.

Kirp, D. L. (1989). Uncommon decency: Pacific Bell responds to AIDS. *Harvard Business Review*, May–June 1989.

O'Donovan, G. (2018). *Making organizational change stick: How to create a culture of partnership between project and change management*. Abingdon: Routledge.

Rose, F. (1990). A new age for business? *Fortune*, 8, 1990.

Schein, E. H. (2016). *Organizational culture and leadership* (6th ed.). New York: John Wiley & Sons.

Spicer, A. (2017). From inboxing to thought showers: How business bullshit took over. *Guardian*, 23 November, 2017.

Creating a culture of partnership between project management and change management

Gabrielle O'Donovan

The dismal results achieved by organisational change initiatives over the past decades drive home the need for a step change in how we deliver projects. We can no longer be satisfied to hop along with a 'one-legged approach', where only project management methodologies are used or, alternatively, limp along with project management in the driving seat and change management playing second fiddle. Rather, a firm-footed 'two-legged approach' to project delivery, that employs both project management and change management methodologies and expertise, will enable projects to stride forward in confidence and derive business benefits. Achieving this requires the thoughtful integration of project management and change management methodologies throughout the end-to-end project life cycle, and *the cultivation of a culture of partnership* between project managers and change managers – a 21st-century solution to a 21st-century problem.

The current disconnect between project management and change management feeds the well-documented projects' failure rate (40–70 percent), and the laying of many a dud egg. While much work has been done in recent times to try to address this issue, cross-discipline integration efforts thus far have only touched the tip of the iceberg (policies, practices and processes), ignoring that below-the-surface subterranean cultural components can divide or unite project teams. An effective joint value proposition between project management and change management must incorporate both perspectives. By way of an example, on any given project team shared assumptions drive the expression of shared attitudes and behaviours. These in turn impact what gets done and what doesn't, and cultural assumptions at play are reflected in project outcomes and results. For instance, if the project team holds a shared assumption that successful measurement of project delivery is simply 'on time, on scope and on budget', they will not appreciate the need to secure end-user adoption of new ways of working, and are likely to see the work of change managers early on in the project cycle as little more than interference and a distraction. They may rationalise this mind-set by saying, 'If we don't have a system, we won't need users to be on board'. Where this assumption is in action below the surface, strategies and plans that involve project managers' cooperation with change managers early in the project cycle (e.g. to agree how the end user will be impacted) may prove very difficult to implement, and undermine business benefits realisation.

Making culture explicit and measurable

Because mapping any given culture could be a never-ending task, it is essential to define the parameters of such work. Context is one such parameter and the context here is 'the integration of project management and change management methodologies for projects'. The other parameter I am employing is a three-part framework designed by Edgar Schein, Professor Emeritus, MIT, on those universal 'problems' or challenges that organisations face:

1 Deepest assumptions about universal macro issues.
2 The second part of the framework considers those challenges that the organisation faces as it adapts to its external environment. My new additions supplementing Schein's original list include getting consensus on the 'shared approach to problem solving', and 'shared approach to risks and issues resolution' – challenges that are in the forefront for project leaders and teams.
3 The third part of the framework considers those universal problems that the organisation faces in terms of internal integration. Newly identified challenges added to Schein's original list include getting consensus on 'maximizing problem solving capability' and 'openness to feedback'.

These problems are as relevant to change projects as they are to business-as-usual. The project is, after all, an organisation, albeit a temporary one. While leaders may give considered thought to some or even all of the problems above when considering the larger organisational context, they rarely give these problems due attention in the temporary projects environment – and certainly not in terms of how they can define a network of cultural assumptions that will help resolve these issues. Therefore, these challenges are an excellent reference point for doing just that, as they add a structured level of detail to that higher-level parameter of 'Change Management/Project Management integration'.

Below, the first category, 'Deepest Assumptions about Macro Issues Affecting the Project,' is expanded upon by way of illustration. To learn about the second and third categories, and how project managers and change managers can cooperate on a daily basis to bring this culture of partnership to life and ensure that change is not only implemented, but embedded, read *Making Organizational Change Stick* (O'Donovan, 2018).

Deepest assumptions about macro issues affecting the project

Universal macro issues to be resolved for project teams relate not just to their project environment, but also to the organisational and broader context that informs the workplace culture. These are fundamental issues that any group needs to agree on in order for the group to function. Macro-related issues that the project team needs to reach consensus on include:

1   How life and change unfold in general, and in the project's environment;
2   The nature of the project;
3   How the project relates to its environment beyond the immediate project environment;
4   How change management and project management will contribute to delivery;
5   How the change manager and the project manager will cooperate;
6   The roles of the change manager and project manager as separate to the core team who will report into these two key roles;
7   Respecting differences in ways of thinking about project concepts, based on occupational subcultures and finding common ground;
8   The nature and value of masculine versus feminine reasoning for managing organisational change; and
9   The nature and value of gender roles and what it means for project delivery.

In Table 4.1, cultural assumptions relating to each of these nine problems or challenges are presented on with an X indicating the optimal assumption for each. From there, each taken optimal assumption is presented in italics and discussed, alongside alternative, and less constructive, assumptions.

The nature of life

Life is messy and projects are messy too.
    The essential nature of life is that of renewal, brought about by evolutionary, transitional and transformational change. Some of that change is predictable, but a lot of it is not, making life a rather messy business with many a twist and turn. Projects are messy for this and other reasons too; they are typically a melting pot of employees, consultants and contractors and, as temporary environments, projects are perhaps more vulnerable than business-as-usual to political shifts, weak governance and poor general management practices. Take the following real-life examples:

• Project/programme management overly dependent on a particular project management consultancy that used this power to hinder the best efforts of perceived competitors who were project team members;
• The new project manager who pushed out existing project team members, instated those of his own choosing and received back-handers from the recruitment agency that he was colluding with;
• Programme directors taking Friday afternoons off to play golf, with project team members sneaking out to the pub during their absence en masse;

Table 4.1 Project and change partnership cultural assumptions continuum: macro issues (O'Donovan, 2018)

The Nature of Life

_____X____

| Tidy | Messy |

The Nature of the Project

_____X_____

| Concrete set of linear tasks | Both | Series of activities arising from the needs of people and business |

The Nature of the Relationship between the Project and the Organisation

_____X____

| Separate from organisational realities | Inter-linked |

The Nature of the Change Management/Project Management Relationship

_____X_____

| Independent | Inter-dependent | Dependent |

The Nature of the Change Manager/ Project Manager Relationship

_____X_____

| Independent | Inter-dependent | Dependent |

The Role of the Project Manager/Change Manager as Separate to the Core Team

_____X_____

| Getting plan and sticking to it | Both | Team leaders and integrating force |

The Nature and Value of Masculine versus Feminine Ways of Reasoning for Managing Organizational Change

_____X_____

| Masculine Reasoning Superior | Equal Value | Feminine Reasoning Superior |

The Nature and Value of Gender Roles

_____X_

| Stereotypical | Non-stereotypical |

_____X_____

| Male input more valued | Equally valued | Female input more valued |

The Nature of Change Management and Project Management Epistemic Cultures

X

| Essentially Different | A Strong Degree of Sameness | Essentially the Same |

- The project sponsor who signed off the project Statement of Work without consulting his direct reports, and had his plans for organisational structure change derailed as a result;
- The operations director who responded, 'We don't care; employees will do what they're told' when advised that a tiny change management team reporting into business as usual (BAU) could not support a global workforce for a technology project;
- The project director who went abroad on holiday during a critical and external stakeholder facing project activity because he feared it would fail (the change manager led the activity, although it was new to her too, and it was a resounding success);
- The employee who had never managed a project, project senior stakeholders or a Steering Committee before and was given the role of project manager for a global deployment as a 'stretch assignment'; and
- High project turnover among female team members, due to a culture of bullying, which went unnoticed in a constantly changing environment.

Any seasoned veteran in the projects space is likely to raise a wry smile and may even have some more examples to add. Yet, project and programme management literature, for the most part, seems to operate on the assumption that projects are neat and tidy, and come across as sanitised and academic. Such literature does not reflect the real world. Projects are messy environments indeed and, although addressing general management practices such as those listed above is beyond the scope of this chapter, it is worth bearing in mind that all members of the team –from both project management and change management disciplines –will have varying levels of general management skills that will impact teamwork. The same goes for project support partners working in business-as-usual. Behaviours in the projects space need to be subject to the same controls and good governance one would expect in the business-as-usual space, and it is for leaders to set the tone.

The nature of the project

The project is a series of linear and non-linear tasks and activities arising from the needs of the business.

This cultural assumption recognises both the consecutive and the emergent nature of project tasks and activities, while emphasising the relationship between the product of the project and end users. In a study on masculine and feminine logic systems in the projects environment, Thomas and Buckle-Henning (2007) found that the masculine way of thinking sees the project as a 'concrete linear set of tasks with a clear start and finish' and 'separate the project from its context'. The feminine way of thinking sees projects as 'a series of activities deeply embedded in a goal arising from the needs of the company's people and business' and emphasises 'connectedness' and 'interdependence'.

The recommended optimal assumption captures both these views to create common ground.

The nature of the relationship between the project and the organisation

Projects don't exist in a vacuum; they emerge, exist and die in their host organisations.

The relationship between the project and the organisation has been the subject of much research. Grabher (2002) illustrates it by describing its different facets, which can be summarised as follows:

1 Projects are vehicles for introducing change and achieving organisational goals.
2 Projects are often hard to decompose into constituent tasks and such a (commonly agreed) decomposition is only possible when stakeholders interrelate with each other continually.
3 The contractor is the lynchpin on whom trust is focused (for our purposes, the contract will be the project manager and the change manager cooperating to bring change to the organisation). The role of the manager is particularly important in projects on which team members do not have the time to get to know each other well.
4 The contractor is also the wielder of organisational authority as far as the project is concerned. He or she is, in this sense, a representative of the organisation – a person whose presence underlines the fact that the project exists to achieve specified organisational goals.
5 The final deadline of a project culminates in the termination of the project and serves as a connector with the rest of the organisation. As the project team disbands, the outputs of the project disperse into the wider organisation.
6 Projects draw on organisational resources.
7 Organisational culture plays a role in determining how projects are governed, managed and run.
8 The project can serve as the lynchpin for strategic partnerships.
9 The organisation hosts a range of processes that are needed to organise and run a project.
10 Projects present the opportunity to enhance organisational learning. However, as projects are typically high-pressure environments, there is little time for documenting knowledge.

Additional facets of the relationship between the project and the organisation include the political landscape and organisational climate. Project progress, coordination and control are often hindered by organisational politics, and all the more so when project leadership is lacklustre and stakeholders in the business are not united behind a common purpose and objectives. Poor employee engagement in the larger organisation can create a sense of inertia that can only increase the challenge faced by the project. All of the points above support the operating assumption that the project and the organisation are interlinked. However, it can be tempting for project managers to choose to operate from the alternative assumption that the project is isolated from its environment and not subject to organisational controls. With this mind-set, relationships and politics are seen as external to the project and problems relating to coordination and control are simpler to manage. The project team works, for the most part, in isolation to the host organisation. My strongest first-hand experience of this assumption in action was when I worked as change manager for a successful M&A project where a firm was acquired by another. Our project team was located on a secure floor of the head office building and access to the floor was strictly limited. As we were dealing with highly sensitive information and liaising with legal advisers on a daily basis, we worked largely in isolation from the rest of the organisation where there were, not untypically, strongly divided views on the best way forward. Politics could not but impact the project and the team members whose rewards and punishments were influenced not only by those who were for the change but also by those who were against it. In the real world, it is unrealistic to suppose that the project can operate in a vacuum and not be subject to organisational controls.

The nature of the change management and project management relationship

Project management and change management are separate, but interdependent, disciplines.

Project management is concerned with end-to-end delivery of the change, with change management concerned about bringing stakeholders on the journey and ensuring that change meets the needs of the organisation and is embedded. Each has its own distinctive service proposition and toolkit. When the project team operates on the assumption that one of the disciplines is dependent on the other, or to be assimilated by it, it is typically project management tools that dominate with the change management toolkit being used to a lesser degree. Alternatively, when the project team operates on the assumption that project management and change management disciplines are independent, they can overlook opportunities for synergies and the need to incorporate change management processes into project plans. An interdependent approach will reap the best results.

The nature of the change manager/project manager relationship

The project manager and change manager develop the plan, lead the team to deliver the plan and work with stakeholders to integrate diverse perspectives.

Traditionally, the project manager has been the central axis of project delivery. Carrying the weight of the responsibility, it is easy to see activities such as team leadership and interfacing with the organisation being neglected as the demand to deal with technical matters presses. Where the project manager and change manager work together to develop a joint plan, co-lead with the team on delivery and utilise their respective strengths to manage the stakeholder equation, synergies are created and the burden is shared. Note that while the change manager will have facilitation and team-building skills, it is not the job of the change manager to make up for any weaknesses the project manager may have in terms of those tasks traditionally associated with female roles, e.g. people management and performance management, as suggested in some quarters.

The nature of the project manager and change manager relationship

The project manager and change manager are interdependent partners who together can implement – and embed – change.

When the project team operates on the assumption that one of the managers/teams is dependent on the other, it is typically the project manager who wins out on the power-sharing agreement, and the change management team takes on a secondary and even administrative support role. Alternatively, when the project team operates on the assumption that the project manager and change manager best work independently, they miss important opportunities for synergies, and the results work in parallel to project team organisational structure, rather than in unison.

The nature and value of masculine versus feminine ways of reasoning for managing organisational change

Neither masculine nor feminine ways of reasoning are inherently superior to the other (Thomas and Buckle-Henning, 2007).

In their study of masculine and feminine logic systems at work in project management, Thomas and Buckle-Henning describe the masculine way of thinking 'field independent' (detached from the individuals and situations they seek to understand), 'objective', 'impersonal', 'independent' and 'analytical', presenting in behaviours such as 'competitive', 'decisive', 'assertive', 'task-orientated' and 'directive'. Decisions are made with a preference to conforming to predetermined project realities and tasks preferably executed according to predetermined views, regardless of the context. Feminine reasoning is described as 'field dependent', conceiving tasks and plans through emerging realities, relationships and information, and presenting in behaviours such as 'power sharing', 'collaborative sensemaking and working styles', 'information sharing' and 'empathy'. Thomas and Buckle-Henning argue that, as healthy adult life involves moving towards wholeness, both male and female project managers need to understand the differences inherent in masculine and feminine reasoning and ways of managing projects. They assert that 'neither style is the domain or liability of males or females' and that 'both sets of capacities are present in any healthy individual'. However, society still tends to view masculine behaviour as inappropriate for women and feminine behaviour as inappropriate for men. Wholeness and strength can be achieved for the individual, the organisation (including the project organisation) and society when both males and females claim the strengths of both approaches. In their research, Thomas and Buckle-Henning found that in the PMBOK® 'hard masculine logic systems exert considerable influence on the "best practice" outlined in the PMBOK®. Softer feminine logic systems appear less influential and presumably less valued or trusted in the profession'. In essence, the culture of project management is inherently masculine and dominated by power relationships and task orientation. This has serious implications for change management and successful change adoption, as feminine reasoning and behaviours that focus on interpersonal relationships and process orientation are integral to the work of change managers who build stakeholder buy-in and embed change in the business.

The nature and value of gender roles

Male and female roles are not bound by stereotypes that are harmful to both, but to women in particular.

Gender stereotypes stem from traditional male and female roles, depicting women as more communal (nurturing, relationships-focused and interdependent) and men as more agentic (ambitious, task-orientated and self-reliant). These stereotypes create expectations about how women should behave and how men should and should not behave, and they have shifted little, despite the growth of women in the workforce. Studies have shown that both males and females experience backlash when displaying non-stereotypical behaviour. But females face additional challenges and punitive behaviours. Rudman and Phelan (2008) conducted research on this topic and found that:

> because women are perceived to be less competent, ambitious, and competitive (i.e., less agentic) than men, they may be overlooked for leadership positions unless they present themselves as atypical women. However, the prescriptive nature of gender stereotypes can result in negative reactions to female agency and authority (i.e., backlash). This dilemma has serious consequences for gender parity, as it undermines women at every stage of their careers. It also has consequences for organizations, as it likely contributes to female managers' higher rates of job disaffection and turnover, relative to male counterparts.

The male and female contributions to the project are equally appreciated and respected. It will be no surprise to readers that often a macho culture reigns on projects. The project's environment is typically male-dominated, although this can vary in degree depending on the nature of the project (e.g. HR projects can have more female project managers than other types of projects), and how intergender relations present in the organisational and national culture. In *The Culture Code*, author Clotaire Raphialle provides perspective on the role of national culture on intergender relationships. Commenting on male bonding, and English culture in particular, Clotaire has this to say:

> The English men have a remarkably strong bond with one another, per-
> haps stronger than the relationship between men in any other culture.
> Because they truly believe that only other men can understand their feel-
> ings, all of their meaningful friendships are with other men ... this under-
> standably leads to a real disconnection from English women, who feel left
> out of the party.

The dominance of male versus female project managers (70 percent to 30 percent, respectively) suggests that more projects are run by men with more females playing a support role. Yet studies on gender in the projects environment strongly suggest that feminine reasoning is essential to the management of change. Author Charles Handy (1994) even goes as far as to say:

> They [organizations] want people who can juggle with several tasks and
> assignments at one time, who are more interested in making things happen
> than in what title or office they hold, more concerned with power and
> influence than status. They want people who value instinct and rational,
> who can be tough but also tender, focused but friendly, people who can
> cope with these necessary contradictions. They want, therefore, as many
> women as they can get.

The nature of change management and project management epistemic cultures

Project management and change management epistemic cultures fundamentally differ, attracting students and practitioners with different, but complementary, interests and talents.

Different thought worlds can lead to conflict over goals and methods, impending the collective action required to implement and embed successful change. As observed by Lehmann (2010), a huge gap exists between conceptualisations in change management and project management. Lehmann highlights the tendency for project management practitioners to focus on planning, control, processes and methodologies, while change management practitioners are more interested in 'change's objects and underlying mechanisms' and the behavioural aspects. Bresnen (2006) sees the two fields as representing two different approaches to the mechanisms of knowing, with project management bringing projects to the foreground (obscuring understanding of how projects dovetail with the wider organisational context), unlike change management which brings the organisational context to the fore. Differences in epistemic cultures become more rigid and entrenched if the change project is subject to external threat or failure and high stress levels prevail, as project managers and change managers will default to known behaviour that they are comfortable with.

In summary, universal macro issues that the project team needs to achieve consensus on include issues such as the relationship between the project and its broader environment, the nature of the change management and project management relationship, and the nature of the relationship between the change manager and the project manager.

Those leaders who create a culture of partnership between project management and change management will benefit from the unique value that these interdependent disciplines bring to project delivery. It is they who will drive up project success rates, laying golden eggs and securing business benefits.

References

Bresnen, M. (2006). Conflicting and conflated discourses? Project management, organisational change and learning, in Hodgson, D. & Cicmil S. (Eds.) *Making projects critical*. Basingstoke: Palgrave, pp. 68–89.

Grabher, G. (2002). Cool projects, boring institutions: Temporary collaboration in the social context. *Regional Studies, 36*(3), 205–214.

Handy, C. (1994). *The empty raincoat: Making sense of the future*. New York: Random House.

Lehmann, V. (2010). Connecting changes to projects using a historical perspective: Towards some new canvases for researchers. *International Journal of Project Management, 28*(4), 328–338.

O'Donovan, G. (2018). *Making organizational change stick: How to create a culture of partnership between project and change management*. Abingdon: Routledge.

Raphialle, C. (2006). *The Culture Code*. New York: Random House.

Rudman, L. A., & Phelan, J. E. (2008). Backlash effects for disconfirming gender stereotypes in organizations. *Research in Organizational Behavior, 28*, 61–79.

Thomas, J. L., & Buckle-Henning, P. (2007). Dancing in the white spaces: Exploring gendered assumptions in successful project managers. *International Journal of Project Management, 25*(6), 552–559.

5

Strategy

Strategy as learning to discover the way forward

Darren Dalcher

The term *strategy* appears to be amongst the 1,000 most commonly used words in the English language (EF, 2017), particularly in a business context; yet it can still have a multitude of alternative meanings. The Oxford English Dictionary defines strategy as: 'a plan of action designed to achieve a long-term or overall aim'; whilst also offering an alternative definition as 'the art of planning and directing overall military operations and movements in a war or battle'. The Cambridge English Dictionary meanwhile offers a single, more all-encompassing definition in the form of 'a detailed plan for achieving success in situations such as war, politics, business, industry, or sport, or the skill of planning for such situations'.

The most iconic definitions of strategy found in the literature include the following:

> The determination of the basic long-term goals and objectives of an enterprise, and the adoption of courses of action and the allocation of resources necessary for those goals.
>
> (Chandler, 1962: p. 13)

> Essentially, developing a competitive strategy is developing a broad formula for how a business is going to compete, what its goals should be, and what policies will be needed to carry out those goals.
>
> (Porter, 1980: p. xvi)

The definitions above, while emerging almost two decades apart, point to a few essential themes:

- Strategies focus on the (long-term) future and the goals that can be reached as part of that future;
- Strategies determine the goals and objectives that will be pursued;
- The key concern is around the achievement of these goals;
- Resources are therefore allocated, and actions carried out, specifically in order to enable the actions required to facilitate the goals;

- Business environments are competitive, implying that some organisations will fare better, while others may not succeed; and
- Consequently, given the focus, long-term impact and competitiveness, determining the strategies is a critically important and defining function of top management.

The term strategy has been in use for centuries. Bracker (1980: p. 219) identifies the etymological origin of the word, from the Greek *Strategos*, 'a general', which in turn, comes from roots meaning 'army' and 'lead', as befitting the second definition offered by the Oxford Dictionary.

> The Greek verb *stratego* means to 'plan the destruction of one's enemies through effective use of resources'. The concept of strategy in a military or political context has remained prominent throughout history, and has been discussed by such major writers as Shakespeare, Montesquieu, Kant, Mill, Hegel, Calusewitz, Liddell Hart and Tolstoy.
>
> (ibid.)

Carter, Clegg and Kornberger (2010: p. 2) observe that the idea of strategy can be traced back to the early writings on military strategy by Sun Tzu, whose work, *The Art of War*, is often said to mark the birth of the discipline. Other military tacticians expanded on the idea of the strategy of war.

> Strategy is the employment of the battle to gain the end of the War; it must therefore give an aim to the whole military action; in other words, Strategy forms the plan of the War, and to this end it links together the series of acts which are to lead to the final decision, that, is to say, it makes the plans for the separate campaigns and regulates the combats to be fought in each.
>
> (Von Clausewitz, 1940: p. 79)

Given the competitive nature of the business environment and the need to succeed in the long term, business schools appear to have extended the war analogy and adopted the notion of competitive strategy, replacing the adversarial enemy with the seemingly less sinister, yet equally cunning, cold and calculating entity known as business competition.

Strategy from the top down

Cummings and Wilson (2003: p. 14) concede that because corporate strategy was conceived in the middle of the 20th century, it was fashioned around the prevailing images and understanding of science typical of that era. They caution that Chandler's classic definition of strategy – see above – is premised upon his hierarchical view of the organisation as composed of successive layers of top management, middle management, lower management, supervisors and so forth.

The prevailing approach resulting from Chandler's position is that strategy formation is about achieving the essential fit between internal strengths and weaknesses and external threats and opportunities (Lampel et al., 2014: p. 21). Indeed, according to Chandler, strategy is the result of smart decisions that seek to achieve a fit between market opportunities and organisational structure, with the detailed analysis resulting in a new conceptual object – 'the strategic plan that drives, dominates and determines organizational structure' (Carter, Clegg & Kornberger, 2008: p. 22). In other words, strategy takes primacy: Having defined the best possible strategy, companies could then determine the most appropriate organisational structure to achieve it (Crainer, 2000).

> To this day strategy is subsequently seen by textbooks as management at the highest, overriding and most detached level 'the planning, directing, organizing and controlling of a company's strategy related (i.e. higher level and longer term) decisions. The geometrical image upon which this view was based was fleshed out by Igor Ansoff.
>
> (Cummings & Wilson, 2003: p. 14)

Igor Ansoff authored the first complete book dedicated to corporate strategy (1965) and is considered to be the father of modern strategic thinking (Hindle, 2008: p. 215). Strategic planning was therefore further enacted through Ansoff's rational planning approach, predicated on the gap analysis, identifying the mismatch between where you are and where you would like to find yourself. He also formalised the process through detailed analysis of copious amounts of data about the past in order to predict the future. Ansoff developed an elaborate model that ultimately led to claims of 'paralysis by analysis' and incidents of strategic planning failure.

The long-term impacts of hierarchical organising

Ansoff himself subsequently reflected that:

> In retrospect, the incidence of strategic planning failure should not have been surprising. After all, it was a practical invention designed by staffs in business firms as a solution to a problem which was poorly understood, and in the absence of a theory which could have guided design.
>
> (reported in Crainer, 2000: p. 128)

Nonetheless, in Ansoff's view (1965, 1968, 1987), strategic action was concerned with controlling the relationship with the environment. Top management would therefore become primarily concerned with the formal process of planning, controlling and monitoring of the correct realisation of strategic plans.

(Ansoff) advocated a classic rational planning approach to strategy. It was to have a strong influence in areas such as project management in the construction industry and the large-scale engineering and exploration projects in the oil industry. It contributed directly to the canon of the project management body of knowledge. In this respect it follows on from the direction that F.W. Taylor set at the birth of management.

(Carter, Clegg and Kornberger, 2010: p. 24)

The writings of Ansoff and Chandler reflect a classical view that enshrines a linear-hierarchical dimension concerned with developing a rational, accurate and objective depiction of the environment. This is meant to allow for careful positioning of the organisation to maximise efficiency and determine specific strategic moves and directions. The view accounts for the growing popularity of steep hierarchies which began to appear in the 1880s and 1890s as railroad and telegraph companies required extended management structures to account for the growing geographical spans covered by their companies (Chandler & Daems, 1980: p. 3). Indeed, in these companies, 'the visible hand of managerial direction has replaced the invisible hand of market mechanisms ... in coordinating flows and allocating resources in major modern industries' (ibid.: p. 9).

To achieve economies of scale, the firms organised their management ranks to coordinate high volume production with national and international distribution (Savage, 1996). As the firms expanded, they employed medium- and top-level managers to optimise their operations. With work divided amongst the different functions, different sub-sections became specialised with new policies, procedures and routines created by the cadre of new managers that had to be recruited to maintain and control the individual silos. An ironic side effect of this growth was 'a division and subdivision of management that paralleled Adam Smith's earlier concept of division and subdivision of labour, especially with respect to two key features: sequential work and narrowly defined tasks' (Savage, 1996: p. 149).

The division into distinct areas made it easier to control and monitor the capital resources of the firm, albeit in a functional fashion. However, it also required new mechanisms and systems to support the resulting differentiation of the functions and the need for integration in order to manage and direct linked and strategic activities. Structure often becomes a key-integrating stimulus, or need, across an organisation. Accordingly, the division also reinforced the need to manage portfolios of critical strategic initiatives at an enterprise level across the entire organisation, and the necessity for more complex cross-functional integration in programmes and major change initiatives, which span and impact multiple turfs and jurisdictions.

As noted above, Chandler's and Ansoff's hierarchical structures were deeply influenced by Taylor's direction. Fredric Taylor's conception of scientific management posited that in order to improve efficiency, managers were required to do all the thinking related to the planning and design of work, leaving workers with the task of implementation, resulting in a clear separation between planning and doing (Dalcher, 2017: p. 4). The principle of separating the planning and design from execution, and the intended desire of freeing the workers from the need to think, flow naturally from the desire to simplify tasks, improve efficiency and throughput, reduce waste and increase monitoring and control. They are also responsible for many of the dysfunctional aspects of life cycles and work schemes that we still encounter nowadays. One side effect of Taylor's approach was the replacement of skilled craftspeople, with unskilled workers only trained to do specific tasks in prescribed ways (ibid.: p. 5) resulting in the loss of valuable expertise, motivation, responsibility and professional judgment.

> Ansoff's influence is echoed in modern management thinking that understands those at the top as the strategic thinkers of the organization, seeing their task as defining the big picture, steering the organization with a strong grasp, whereas the lower levels of the hierarchy realize and implement what they have been told but which they could never see – because they are outside the corporate elites who set the strategic vision.
>
> (Carter, Clegg and Kornberger, 2010: p. 24)

At a micro-level, the tendency to separate the layers of management and move the strategic planning upstream left project managers devoid of strategic insight and wisdom and bereft of involvement in the early phases of the project. This would account for the apparent separation and isolation of project management as reflected in the more traditional bodies of knowledge. Such bodies were thus able to rely on the appearance of pre-defined chunks of work that could be operationalised through the allocation to project managers to complete the delivery aspects of the project.

So what might be the residual impact of upfront, hierarchical planning, the division of management and the separation of thinking and doing? Moreover, given the identified changes, what kind of models and images might be needed to control and manage such environments?

Getting lost without a compass?

Karl Weick (1987, 1995) tells a powerful story about a Hungarian military detachment stranded on manoeuvres in the Alps, which is paraphrased below:

The Young Lieutenant in charge of the detachment, orders a reconnaissance unit into the icy wilderness beyond their camp. Immediately, as the unit departs, it begins to snow, with a significant snowstorm continuing unabated for a further two days.

The unit fails to return and no further contact is established, leading the young officer to regret that he may have condemned his own soldiers to their death.

However, on the third day, the unit returns to the camp leading to many questions: What has happened? Where had they been? How did they survive? How did they make it back?

The soldiers report that they considered themselves lost and waited for the end. They did not have any maps, compasses or any other equipment with which to ascertain their current position. The constant heavy snow made it impossible to retrace their steps, identify any landmarks, or plot a potential route back.

However, as they were preparing themselves for their unhappy demise, one of them reached into a seldom-used inner pocket and discovered an old crumpled map.

The discovery calmed them down and they quickly started to pitch a shelter, with the knowledge that they could now return to base. After the storm, they took out the map and discovered their bearings.

The map did not quite fit the terrain, but they were able to establish their position. They followed the map down the mountain and after taking a few wrong turns and retracing some of their steps, they made their way back to camp.

After the initial action comes further introspection: When the lieutenant examined the map more closely, he discovered to his astonishment that it was not a map of the Alps, but of the Pyrenees.

The story's appeal makes it extremely popular in courses that deal with strategy. Cummings and Wilson (2003: p. 1) note that the analogy is immediately recognisable as the value of the map comes not just from the detail that it encompasses, but also from its ability to focus minds and help people commit to a particular course of action. The vignette has been criticised by Mintzberg, Ahlstrand and Lampel (1998), pointing out that navigation in mountain regions is considerably more difficult than the story implies, and by Basbøll and Graham (2006) for adding further embellishments and failing to recognise the original sources of the tale, including Holub's (1977) poem about the young Lieutenant. Nonetheless, Weick (2006: p. 193) retorts that the story is a powerful allegory, offering an example 'that minimal structures, when trusted, updated and acted on attentively, tended to generate data that improved problem solving'.

While the unit may have been lucky to survive by following the wrong map, the story emphasises the power of the process of *mapping*, as opposed to blindly following a map. Indeed, mapping and navigation provide the basis for a journey into less certain and less recognisable terrains, with a general goal or overarching purpose.

Strategy as emergent forward planning

The notion of rational planning may sound attractive at the surface level and yet, while we have to acknowledge that it clearly underpins a lot of the thinking approaches, frameworks and techniques that are utilised in classical project management, there are alternative approaches devised for planning for less well defined and more uncertain perspectives.

In some situations top-down thinking delivered through boxes and lines predicated through prescriptive control and influence triangles can become hazardous. Indeed, Raynor (2007) identifies a strategy paradox, an ever-present, if little understood trade-off: Most strategies are built on specific beliefs and assumptions about an unpredictable future. Yet, the current approaches for defining and implementing strategies demand a single strategic commitment, thereby constraining leaders to an inflexible and irreversible course of action. The trade-off between early commitment and latent uncertainty can bind organisations to a particular course of action, and stop them from adjusting and adapting to emerging circumstances.

Mintzberg (1994: p. 108) introduces a distinction between strategic planning – which has been practised as a form of strategic programming, the articulation and elaboration of strategies, or visions, that already exist with the support of analytical techniques – and strategic thinking. In his view, strategic planning models failed because they overemphasised quantitative analysis, whilst failing to offer an opportunity to synthesise experience, intuition and creativity. Strategic planning is therefore best suited to follow the more creative acts of strategic thinking and vision development. Mintzberg identifies three fallacies (ibid.: p. 110) which underline the fundamental shortcomings of strategic planning:

- **Prediction fallacy**: That *prediction is possible* (and by implication that the world holds still while we predict and plan; and that the past provides a good indication regarding the future);
- **Detachment fallacy**: That *strategists can be detached from the subjects of their strategies* (this talks to the idea that strategies are detached from operations, and thinkers are separate from doers, which might work in deep hierarchical silos, however, it is likely to fail in practice as managers seek additional autonomy), and, above all;
- **Formalisation fallacy**: That *the strategy making process can be formalised* (and thereby implying a rational, programmable sequence).

Undoubtedly, contingency also plays a part. Mintzberg (1990) offers a more organic view of organisations, pointing out that high complexity and fast rates of change necessitate emergent strategies. In contrast, relatively stable situations, with low levels of complexity and uncertainty, may benefit from a top-down approach. However, as the environment becomes messier, more turbulent and uncertain, the process of defining a strategy becomes more experimental and driven from the bottom up as new insights and learning emerge from interactions and discovery. Under such conditions strategy becomes more of a learning process than a pre-defined state. In recognising the existence of different schools and positions, Mintzberg (1994) therefore concludes that strategy can be either an emergent pattern or a deliberate perspective.

Returning to the world of military strategy and the writing of Von Clausewitz (1874/1940) reveals a similar sentiment:

> As these are all things which to a great extent can only be determined on conjectures some of which turn out incorrect, while a number of other arrangements pertaining to details cannot be made at all beforehand, it follows, as a matter of course, that Strategy must go with the Army to the field in order to arrange particulars on the spot, and to make the modifications in the general plan, which incessantly become necessary in War. Strategy can therefore never take its hand from the work for a moment.
>
> (ibid.: p. 79)

Yet, von Clausewitz appears less keen on the idea of separation between planning and doing:

> That this, however, has not always been the view taken is evident from the former custom of keeping Strategy in the cabinet and not with the Army, a thing only allowable if the cabinet is so near to the Army that it can be taken for the chief head-quarters of the Army.
>
> (ibid.)

The writing appears to acknowledge the role of bottom-up emergence of strategic details through learning, adjustment and sensemaking. Undeniably, this idea chimes with Mintzberg's findings that the interaction critical to strategy occurs between the operational base of the organisation and the environment, rather than between senior executives and the outside world. Instead of coming from the top, a fair amount of real strategy emerges bottom-up.

Strategies, much like the map used by the lost Hungarian military unit, can provide a means of orientation, and a basis for making decisions and taking action. They also appear to provide added confidence and perhaps an early glimpse of the future orientation needed for any successful journey.

Going on a strategy journey

This contribution by David Booth is based on his book *Strategy Journeys: A Guide to Effective Strategic Planning*, published by Routledge. David recognises that strategic planning can invoke a variety of different responses, including the potential for angst, apprehension and fear. Whilst acknowledging that strategic planning suffers from bad press, he also reflects on the prominence of strategy courses in the most prestigious MBAs and business schools, thereby identifying a mismatch between the perceived value and the practical application. Despite the plethora of courses and resources related to strategic planning, many organisations still seem to struggle with the concept.

Booth's approach is to develop a much-needed pragmatic resource concerned with demystifying the strategy journey. The journey image recognises the exploration and discovery features as organisations endeavour to make sense of their position. Rather than promote standard methods and processes, the journey recognises that each organisation starts at a different starting point along an individual path to develop and improve. The journey allows each organisation to initiate its own exploratory adventure as it begins to think, reason, decide, communicate and adapt.

Booth introduces much-needed reflection and pragmatism into the strategic planning space. He avoids the explicit prescription of methodologies and standards, preferring instead to familiarise and engage senior managers and executives. He is able to convey some of the more difficult aspects through an extremely effective use of diagrams and figures. The diagrams bring the life cycle of a strategic plan to life, allowing executives to assess the impacts of actions such as refreshing the plan, charting the realised versus the intended strategy and evaluating the impact of changing contexts.

The stance of the work recognises the contingency of each particular context, thereby allowing for deliberate as well as emerging approaches. The openness to contexts, situations and decisions enriches the discussion and enables executives to grasp a fuller set of potential circumstances and implications.

Overall, the work makes an important contribution to strategic planning, not least by focusing explicitly on the strategy journey. The latter part of the journey enables the strategy to inform the themes that lead to specific initiatives. Even more intriguingly, a change energy model is offered to identify the impact of change against the effort and the critical momentum needed in order to deliver the expected benefits. Engagement, stakeholders and culture also receive extensive coverage. The idea of a strategy journey provides a platform for action and offers an opening for beginning to address organisational learning in the context of strategic management and improvement.

Strategy reprised: In search of a revolution

Strategy requires learning, development and adaptation. Gary Hamel (1996) notes that unusual times call for unusual strategies. Recognising that incremental improvement appears to have reached the boundary of 'incrementalism' where additional investment no longer justifies the benefits, he instead agitates for revolutionary strategy, offering a set of ten principles that can help liberate its revolutionary spirit and dramatically increase its chances of discovering truly revolutionary strategies. The principles are paraphrased and augmented below (cf. ibid.: pp. 70–82):

1 **Strategic planning isn't strategic**: It needs to move from a reductionist calendar-driven ritual based on simple rules, to an exploration of the potential for revolution: Discovery and playful exploration are key.

2 **Strategy making must be subversive**: If there is a hope for revolution, there needs to be a challenge: always question what is taken for granted.

3 **The bottleneck is at the top of the bottle**: In most organisations it is senior managers who protect the old order and only have experience of the past: Replace the hierarchy of power with a hierarchy of imagination.

4 **Revolutionaries exist in every company**: Many middle managers strain against industrial orthodoxy, but their voices are often muffled by defensive layers of bureaucracy: Let them be heard: If they do not challenge the company from within, it will ultimately be challenged from the outside.

5 **Change is not the problem, engagement is**: change cannot be imposed on people: The objective is not to get people to support change but to empower revolutionaries and give them the responsibility for engendering change: Create a discourse about a potential future and encourage commitment.

6 **Strategy making must be democratic**: The capacity to think creatively about strategy is distributed widely in an enterprise: Be flexible, break norms, cast the net wide and include young people, outsiders and those on the margins: In order to create your own revolutionary measure of success, do something different; for example, learn something new from a 25 year old.

7 **Anyone can be a strategy activist**: Give revolutionaries a voice and the space to speak, involve the crowds and transform potential anarchists into passionate and energetic advocates.

8 **Perspective is worth 50 IQ points**: Look at the world in new ways to discover opportunities: Make people see with fresh eyes: Change perspective, lens or viewpoint.

9 **Top-down and bottom-up are not the alternatives**: It is not an either/or: top-down will achieve unity of purpose, bottom-up can offer diversity of perspective, so, the strategy-making process must involve a diagonal slice of the organisation that is both deep and wide.

10 **You cannot see the end from the beginning**: A process that involves a broad cross section, delves into the discontinuities and competencies, and encourages employees to escape typical conventions will almost inevitably reach surprising results: If you open a dialogue and ignore the outcome, you will poison the well: The new, participative and inclusive strategy creation process will follow new rules, uncover new options and lead to a future that cannot be foreseen as it unfolds when people begin to experiment and explore new avenues: It will also absolve the need to sell the strategy and result in buy-in and engagement.

Hamel's revolutionary ruminations are well over 20 years old, yet they seem even more apt nowadays, as we endeavour to adopt and embrace experimentation, agile principles, creativity concepts, responsive approaches and innovative leanings. The revolutionary principles offer guidelines for a new and exciting strategy journey that endeavours to take everyone on board. Inviting new voices, new perspectives and new conversations will enrich the range of options and make the journey more stimulating and informative. French post-imperialist painter Paul Cezanne quipped that 'the day is coming when a single carrot, freshly observed, will set off a revolution'. As we experiment, discover and engage in our revolutionary strategy journeys, we need to be able to break away from old habits and established coalitions, and instead engage a wider constituency in the continuous pursuit of fun experimentation, active curiosity, invited change and cherished improvement to the ultimate betterment of all.

References

Ansoff, H. I. (1965). *Corporate strategy: Business policy for growth and expansion*. New York: McGraw-Hill.

Ansoff, H. I. (1968). *Corporate strategy: Analytical approach to business policy*. London: Penguin.

Ansoff, H. I. (1987). *The concept of corporate strategy*. Homewood, IL: Irwin.

Basbøll, T., & Graham, H. (2006). Substitutes for strategy research: Notes on the source of Karl Weick's anecdote of the young lieutenant and the map of the Pyrenees. *ephemera*, 6(2), 194–204.

Booth, D. (2017). *Strategy journeys: A guide to effective strategic planning*. Abingdon: Routledge.

Bracker, J. (1980). The historical development of the strategic management concept. *Academy of Management Review*, 5(2), 219–224.

Carter, C., Clegg, S. R., & Kornberger, M. (2008). *A very short, fairly interesting and reasonably cheap book about studying strategy*. London: Sage.

Chandler, A. D. (1962). *Strategy and structure: Chapters in the history of the American enterprise*. Cambridge, MA: MIT Press.

Chandler, A. D., & Daems, H. (Eds.). (1980). *Managerial hierarchies: Comparative perspectives on the rise of the modern industrial enterprise* (Vol. 32). Cambridge, MA: Harvard University Press.

Crainer, S. (2000). *The management century: A critical review of 20th century thought and practice*. San Francisco, CA: Jossey-Bass.

Cummings, S., & Wilson, D. (2003). Images of strategy. In S. Cummings & D. Wilson (Eds.), *Images of strategy*. Oxford: Blackwell, pp. 1–40.

Dalcher, D. (2017). What has Taylor ever done for us?: Scientific and humane management reconsidered. *PM World Journal*, 6(4).

EF (2017). 1000 most common words in English. *Education First*, https://www.ef.co.uk/english-resources/english-vocabulary/top-1000-words/, accessed 27 January 2018.

Hamel, G. (1996). Strategy as revolution. *Harvard Business Review*, 74(4), 69–82.

Hindle, T. (2008). *Guide to management ideas and gurus*. London: The Economist.

Holub, M. (1977). 'Brief Thoughts on Maps', *Times Literary Supplement*, 4 February, p. 118.

Lampel, J., Mintzberg, H., Quinn, J.B., & Ghoshal, S. (2014). *The strategy process: Concepts, contexts, cases*. London: Pearson Education.

Mintzberg, H. (1990). The design school: Reconsidering the basic premises of strategic management. *Strategic Management Journal*, 11(3), 171–195.

Mintzberg, H. (1994). The fall and rise of strategic planning. *Harvard Business Review*, 72(1), 107–114.

Mintzberg, H., Ahlstrand, B. W., & Lampel, J. (1998). *Strategy safari: A guided tour through the wilds of strategic management*. New York: Free Press.

Porter, M. E. (1980). *Competitive strategy: Techniques for analyzing industries and competitors*. New York: Free Press.

Raynor, M. E. (2007). *The strategy paradox: Why committing to success leads to failure and what to do about It*. New York: Currency Doubleday.

Savage, C. M. (1996). *Fifth generation management: Co-creating through virtual enterprising, Dynamic teaming, and knowledge networking* (revised edition). Newton, MA: Butterworth-Heinemann.

Tzu, S. (2002). *The art of war*. New York: Deodand Publishing.

Von Clausewitz, C. (1874/1940). *On war* (translated). London: Jazzybee Verlag.

Weick, K. E. (1987). Substitutes for strategy.' In D. J. Teece (Ed.), *The Competitive challenge: Strategies for industrial innovation and renewal*. Cambridge, MA: Ballinger, pp. 222–233.

Weick, K. E. (1995). *Sensemaking in organizations*. London: Sage.

Weick, K. E. (2006). Dear editor: A reply to Basbøll and Graham. *ephemera*, 6(2), 193.

How strategy happens

David Booth

An introductory tale

The pressure was on. A major new division of a large international company had just been set up with great expectations, and as the new executive team got to work, the cry went up 'we need a strategic plan!'.

External help was sought, and a parade of management consultancies presented their recommendations for how the new organisation should go about developing this within the tight timescale set out in the brief: there were detailed project plans specifying what had to be achieved by when, with week by week deliverables, critical deadlines, templates and outline document formats – all very logical and thorough, and appropriately ambitious, and a stack of impressively prepared proposal documents built up in the file.

But one consultant walked into the boardroom with just a blank sheet of paper, sat down and asked, 'So what precisely do you want to achieve?' Out of the ensuing discussion came the realisation that – despite the agreed formal brief – those in the room had widely differing views about the new organisation. More talking, and some listening. Another blank piece of paper – this time flipchart-sized – and a marker pen. Discussion, clarification, different views. The 30 minutes 'credentials and presentation' slot became two hours of intense communication, at the end of which there was a simple sketched flipchart diagram mapping out how we were going to begin to address some of the issues. The organisation's strategy journey had started, not as a result of some detailed project plan, but from people talking and – importantly – listening, to achieve a common understanding of the challenges and how they were going to work together to address them.

The traditional 'textbook' approach to strategic planning is a structured process of working methodically through stages of analysis, consideration of strategy options and consequent decisions, and then the equally crucial challenge of implementation, setting up a programme of strategic projects ranging in nature from IT to organisational change – a linear, logical sequence by which an organisation determines its direction and intended destination and marshals its resources to achieve this. Such formal strategic planning processes were adopted widely in the 1970s, with organisations following a series of neatly defined steps to produce a detailed '5 Year Plan' which was then implemented through a structured project programme. But the world – industries, markets, businesses – has moved on since those days when relative stability meant that ambitions could be realised through sustained implementation projects delivered over extended periods; the increasing pace of change (a cliché perhaps, but its perceived veracity is sufficient to drive organisational attitudes) means that such a planned approach to developing and implementing strategies seems outmoded, a resource-intensive process whose determined outcomes are seldom delivered successfully before being overtaken by events.

The emphasis on rapid change has led to the adoption of a more dynamic approach to the development and implementation of strategy, with an emphasis on adaptability and organisational agility to react rapidly to changing circumstances or emerging opportunities (see, for example, Mintzberg, 1998).

Starting points and journeys

What prompts an organisation to develop a strategic plan? Every organisation's circumstances and rationale will be different. However, it might be helpful to consider two questions: a) what has prompted the decision to embark on that particular strategy journey, and b) what is determining the principal approach that is driving this?

To illustrate this, consider four scenarios:

A   Company A operates in a regulated industry. The regulatory body requires all companies to submit a strategic plan that meets defined criteria by a specified deadline. (One example of this occurred in the UK financial services industry in the early 2000s, when the then-regulator, the Financial Services Authority, required all providers of financial services to produce strategic plans that included financial projections including scenarios for varying economic and market conditions. A more recent example was in 2014, when Monitor, the regulatory body for NHS Foundation Trusts, introduced compulsory five-year strategic planning including issuing best practice guidelines and minimum requirement frameworks. One purpose for this was to be able to collate an overview of the NHS Foundation Trusts hospital sector at a time of severe NHS funding challenges, and assess the hospitals' capabilities and vulnerabilities within the sector.)

B   The new Board of Corporation B decide that they need to undertake a review of their operating Divisions and assess how each will fit strategically and contribute to the Corporation's ambitions; and they also want to test the capabilities of their Divisions' senior executive teams. A small Head Office team is set up to drive forward and coordinate the strategic planning process across the Divisions, setting out the process with specific requirements, timelines and formats for the resulting outputs. (Of course, much energy is expended here as the Divisional teams compete with each other to achieve all the milestones and demonstrate their abilities with sophisticated charts, glossy presentations and comprehensive appendices!)

C   After several years of steady sales growth supported by investment in marketing and manufacturing equipment to improve productivity and capacity, the future is looking less certain for Company C. One of their competitors has just been acquired by a US Group with a reputation for stripping out costs and low-cost production techniques, and people across Company C are beginning to worry about what might happen. The marketers are concerned about the consequences of a high volume/low price drive from their competitor for market share, the Financial Director is anxious about the impact on margins, and the Production team fears the consequence will ultimately be the transfer of manufacturing to low-cost factories in China. Meanwhile, Sales managers are talking up the risk of salespeople leaving to join the competitor as it builds its salesforce, although HR thinks this is just a ruse to increase salesforce remuneration. As the various concerns are raised more frequently and volubly it becomes apparent to all that there needs to be a more structured process to consider all the implications, and decide on how Company C should respond.

D   Entrepreneurial technology start-up D has evolved over five years to a medium-sized organisation spread over several sites. As the organisation has grown, some supporting infrastructure has been introduced, but working practices and bonus arrangements vary considerably across the different locations, and there are differing approaches to outsourcing or in-company resourcing of supporting technical and non-core services. Department heads have tabled several opportunities for future development of their product areas, ranging from acquisition of new technologies to scaling up manufacturing. Whilst people are still keen to promote their own views, a consensus gradually forms that D needs a collective process to consider all these issues and opportunities and decide on the next phase of its development.

Considering these examples from the perspective of the two questions posed earlier, in the case of both Company A and Company C it is *external* factors (the industry regulator and a threat from a competitor respectively) that have prompted their decisions to develop their strategic plans; whereas Corporation B and technology start-up D were driven by *internal* situations (a formal review of the future direction in the case of B and the need for a clear, cohesive and understood strategy across the organisation for D).

The principal approaches that are driving the process also differ in these examples (see Figure 5.1): A and B are adopting a *deliberate* approach to formulating their strategic plans, setting out clear parameters and a structured process; whereas in the cases of C and D their strategy journeys have *emerged* from a growing realisation that there was a need to find a collective way to address various issues.

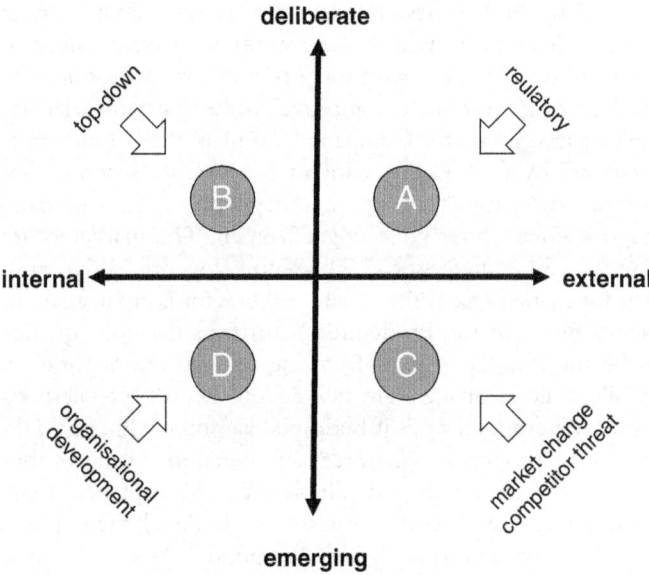

Figure 5.1 Drivers for developing a strategic plan.

These examples illustrate how the drivers for developing a strategic plan can differ according to an organisation's individual situation. There are important differences too in how these organisations' strategies might develop and be implemented: in the case of Company A there will be considerable input and monitoring from the industry regulator requiring formal responses, whereas it is the internal stakeholders of technology start-up D who are likely to be the most critical in determining whether that organisation's strategic plan has succeeded, as well as being instrumental in its implementation.

Both the examples above and the (true) story at the start of this chapter demonstrate how no single 'standard' strategic planning process can meet the needs of all organisations. Each has its unique set of circumstances, drivers, key issues and influences, and these are unique to a particular time; indeed, arguably the 'best practice' approach to strategic planning is to recognise this uniqueness. Hence my use of the term '*strategy journey*' to describe the process an organisation takes to assess its situation, develop its strategy (including evaluating realistic options), plan and organise how to implement this and then make it happen. This concept conveys a broader (and deeper) meaning than the traditional 'strategic planning as a project' approach. (In the introductory example, the 'strategy journey' of exploration, discovery, deliberation and debate that actually ensued as people – individually and collectively – tried to make sense of their organisation's situation highlighted the importance of this more fundamental approach compared to the 'standard process' proposals of the other management consultants.)

Changes

The concept of strategic planning as an organisation's strategy journey is useful also when we consider the life cycle of a strategic plan. The phase of developing a strategic plan is usually one of intense organisational focus and effort, carried forward with determination into the implementation phase (see Figure 5.2). This momentum dissipates in time as initiatives are progressed (or not, in some cases), changes become assimilated into 'business as usual' activity and new issues and opportunities arise that take up the attention of the organisation.

Radical changes (external or internal) can prompt the need to reconsider the organisation's current strategic plan; or it might be the case that the impetus of the current strategic plan has been lost, and the organisation would benefit from a reinvigoration of focus and energy through a renewal of the strategic plan (see Figure 5.3).

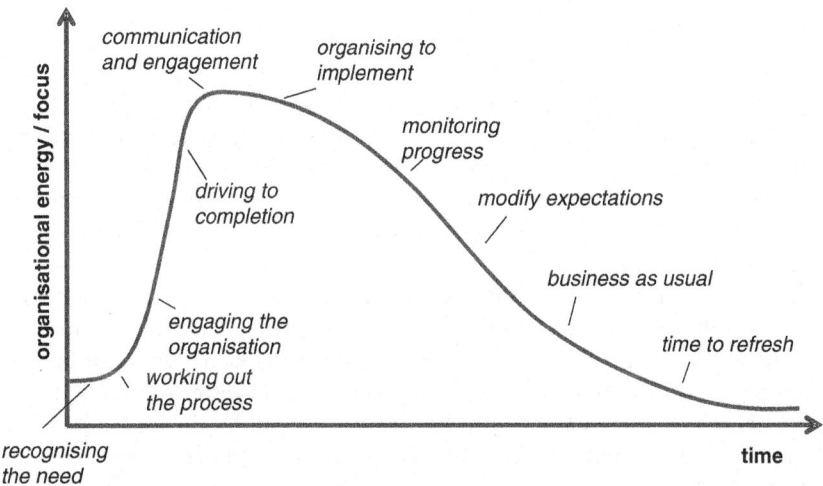

Figure 5.2 The lifecycle of a strategic plan.

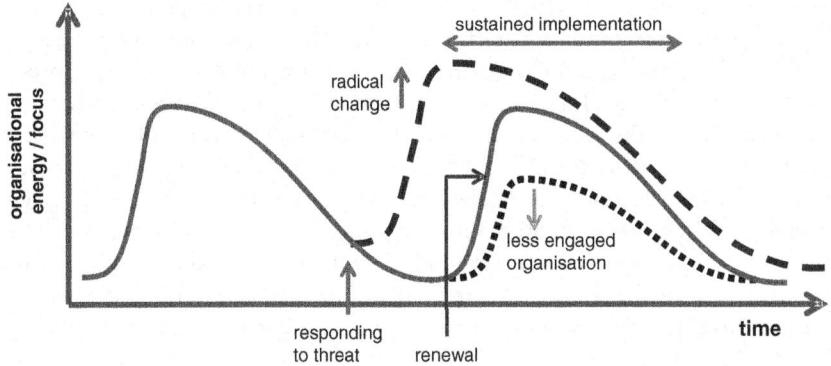

Figure 5.3 Refreshing the strategic plan.

In the case of organisations like Company A, where in a couple of years the main reason for undertaking a strategic planning process might be because it has become an established part of a regular planning cycle (whether internally or externally determined), if there have been no significant changes in the context for the organisation the process might focus on refreshing the plan and its implementation rather than reviewing the organisation's strategy. Company C, on the other hand, might be faced with significant new competitor threats or product innovations that are changing their market, in which case an urgent reassessment of their strategy is called for, possibly resulting in a change of direction.

All the best plans

Let us consider how the strategy journeys might map out for one organisation over the course of a few years.

The organisation's first strategic plan set a clear direction, and in the initial stages of implementation this intended strategy was being realised. But progress started to drift from this – initiatives faltered, new products didn't achieve the projected sales, assumptions used in financial planning turned out to be too optimistic given changes in the market, competitors increased their market share more than expected, technological innovations changed customers' requirements: any of the many ways that real life can turn out differently to what was anticipated.

Although there was increasing deviation from the original strategic plan, there was still sufficient recognition that the basic strategic direction remained relevant as a broad goal, even if the organisation had fallen somewhat behind its intended plan to implement this. The ambition still resonated with people in the organisation, and a rationale had been accepted by the Board for why the actual, realised strategic plan differed from the intended – even if some suspected that there were initiatives which hadn't been implemented as well as they should have been.

Towards the end of the second year of the strategic plan one of the organisation's competitors introduced a technological breakthrough that would change the market; it was apparent to all that this would undermine sales of several of the organisation's leading products. After initially trying to throw doubts on the efficacy of the innovation, when it became clear that consumers were switching to this new technology, the organisation reacted by exploring options to enable it to compete, including potential acquisition of manufacturers with the capability to replicate the innovation to stepping up its own research and development programme to find a patentable alternative. The efforts to respond to the new threat resulted in the organisation acquiring a different technology that offered other product benefits, and a strategy began to emerge about how this could be developed, including entry into new market segments (see Figure 5.4).

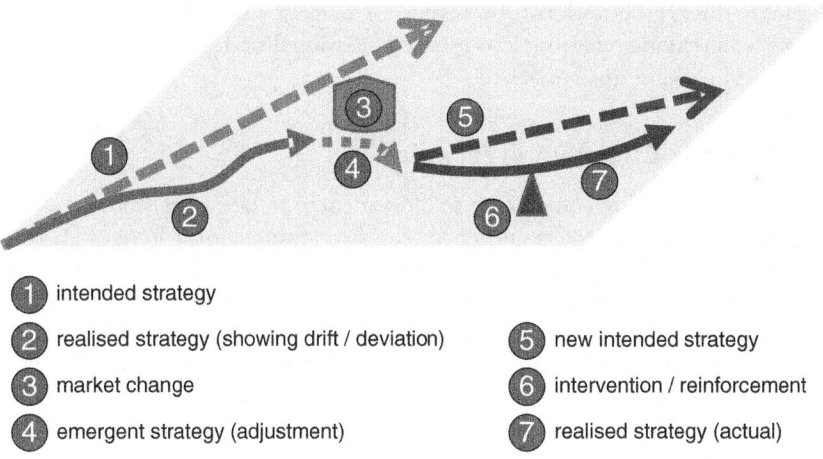

1 intended strategy

2 realised strategy (showing drift / deviation)   5 new intended strategy

3 market change   6 intervention / reinforcement

4 emergent strategy (adjustment)   7 realised strategy (actual)

Figure 5.4 Realised vs intended strategy.

The implications of this for the organisation needed to be considered, and a strategic plan was developed to work out what changes were needed to be able to support this new direction, including disinvesting in some activities and changing the structure of the organisation. However, several assumptions were made in the new intended strategic plan that turned out to be wide of the mark (understandable in a fast-changing market at the early stages of adopting new technologies, but not without some internal retributions) and within the first year it was apparent that the financial plan would not be achieved. A series of crisis discussions was convened, resulting in reducing operational overheads by closing down the manufacture of some less profitable products, and gradually financial performance improved and the organisation was able to begin to pull back towards its intended strategic plan.

This fictional example illustrates some of the strategy journeys that one organisation could experience over the course of a few years, including how events can make strategic plans no longer relevant, and the way in which strategies can emerge without a formal strategic planning process – and sometimes need to be developed rapidly in response to significant changes (for further exploration of how organisations adapt and apply a systems thinking approach, see Stacey, 2007). The fictional example also demonstrates the differences between *intended strategies* and *realised strategies*.

One very useful way of looking at this is to consider it as a series of changing contexts. There was one context when the organisation started its first strategic planning process; then there was a different context as a gap developed between this and what was happening. The market-changing competitor innovation was a significant new context that prompted the need to respond, although not by instigating a formal organisation-wide strategic planning process. At each stage there was a new context, and the organisation had to judge how best to address the key questions of assessing its current situation, considering its options and making decisions about where it wanted to go, then organising to do this and making this happen.

Conclusion: Effective strategies

Strategy-making is dynamic. The traditional interpretation of strategic planning as a defined project resulting in the development of a long-term plan is limiting; organisations need to be adaptable to changes in their situation and responsive to challenges and opportunities, both external and internal. Continually assessing where the organisation is on its strategy journey, what progress it is making, what it might face around the next corner, how it might overcome obstacles, whether it needs to change its route – all these are part of the art of effective strategic management in an agile organisation.

References

Mintzberg, H., Ahlstrand, B. W., & Lampel, J. (1998). *Strategy safari: A guided tour through the wilds of strategic management*. New York: Free Press.
Stacey, R. D. (2007). *Strategic management and organisational dynamics: The challenge of complexity to ways of thinking about organisations*. Harlow, Essex: Pearson Education.

6

Complexity

The map is not the territory

Darren Dalcher

In the previous chapter, we recognised the potential use of a map in enabling decisions and facilitating forward movement and progress, even in foggy or highly challenging contexts. The point made was that the process of mapping, as opposed to blindly following a map, enables reasoning and adjustments to emerge so that corrections can facilitate improved performance and a more purposeful journey.

> Indeed, mapping and navigation provide the basis for a journey into less certain and less recognisable terrains, with a general goal or overarching purpose.
>
> (Dalcher, 2018: p. 6)

This chapter explores the issues related to both maps and mapping in complex and unpredictable terrains.

So what is the problem with maps?

Maps have been in use for centuries. The Oxford Dictionary defines a map as a 'diagrammatic representation of an area of land or sea showing physical features, cities, roads, etc.', implying that they offer a depiction or a picture of the earth.

Maps are known to represent key facts, often extending beyond location information to feature temperature, rainfall, prosperity, education or any other pertinent facet or feature. Maps are thus utilised to emphasise particular relationships that the cartographers consider to be of interest. Consequently, it is important that the users recognise the intended purpose of a given map and select an appropriate type (e.g. physical, political, geological, climatic, relief, thematic, topographical, economic, resource, road, navigational chart), projection (cylindrical, pseudo-cylindrical, conic, azimuthal, gnomonic, etc.) and scale. In other words, the choice of a map needs to be fit for the observational or navigational purpose and the expected goal.

People utilise maps for many varied reasons, including (Hessler, 2015):

- To find their way;
- To assert ownership;
- To record human activity;
- To establish control;
- To encourage settlement;
- To plan military campaigns; and
- To demonstrate political power.

While maps have enabled humans to comprehend their surrounding environment, they have also played a critical part in labelling, establishing and claiming power across neighbours, regions and resources. Hessler's list of reasons seems to comprise only a single item focused on guiding the journey. Indeed, Rankin (2016) reasons that maps provide the means for governments to understand, manage and defend their territory, pointing out that during the two world wars maps were produced by the hundreds of millions. Barber and Harper (2010) note that maps use size and beauty to convey messages of status and power, while Monmonier (2010) observes that some maps control behaviour by providing the basis for regulating some activities and prohibiting others (for example, by designating residential zones and locating chemical plants outside cities).

Maps hold immense value, and are often taken to be a rational, unbiased and objective representation of reality. However, Wood and Fels (1992) assert that maps, like photographs, represent a subjective point of view. King (1996) concludes that there can be no such thing as an objective map reproducing a pre-existing reality, as powerful choices will always have to be made about what to represent and how, and what to exclude. Black (2000) affirms that maps are coloured by the political purposes of their makers, therefore arguing that map-making and map-using cannot be divorced from aspects of the politics of representation. Monmonier (2014) maintains that maps lie, and the choices that mapmakers make – either consciously or unconsciously – mean that a map, far from being objective, can present only one version out of the range of possible stories about the places it depicts.

> Why is Europe at the top half of maps and Africa at the bottom? Although we are accustomed to that convention, it is, in fact, a politically motivated, almost entirely subjective way of depicting a ball spinning in space. As *The Power of Projections* teaches us, maps do not portray reality, only interpretations of it. To begin with, they are two-dimensional projections of a three-dimensional, spherical Earth. Add to that the fact that every map is made for a purpose and its design tends to reflect that purpose. Finally, a map is often a psychological projection of the historical, political, and cultural values of the cartographer – or of the nation, person or organization for which the map was created.
>
> (Klinghoffer, 2006, back cover)

In addressing the more technical aspects of map-making, Snyder (1997) concedes that cartographers have been forced to grapple with making a flat representation of an ellipsoid world. The mismatch has resulted in the creation of hundreds of map projections full of beauty, ingenuity and innovation (Hessler, 2015), and yet, none of the representations has proved to be consistently accurate.

> As a result of these well-known distortions, many alternative projections to the Mercator projection have been proposed and presented. But none has succeeded perfectly; none is perfectly accurate. Every map is a compromise; each has its own distortions. Navigators must choose which distortion will least affect their travel and thus pose the least danger. Although I know of no mathematical proof that a perfect projection is impossible, 500 years of trying to develop a perfectly accurate projection have not led to success; instead they have led to the acceptance of imperfection – and some disasters – by the navigators of land, sea and air. So, rather than continuing to reject imperfect projections, which would leave us without any map whatever, the imperfect projections have been accepted; and when their use can be defended as better than nothing, they are used with the knowledge of their imperfection.
>
> (Hammond, 2007: p. 289)

Yet, maps exist precisely because they offer a basic and appealing representation mechanism. Moreover, maps are universal forms of communication, easily understood and appreciated regardless of culture or language (Akerman & Karrow, 2007).

Confusing the map with the territory

The Cambridge English Dictionary defines mapping as the 'activity or process of creating a picture or diagram that represents something'. The essence of making sense of mapping lies in understanding the distinction and complex relationship between reality and the human descriptions of the world. If indeed the descriptions of the world are simpler, or more abstract than the full scale of reality, processes of change, improvement and growth must acknowledge whether they are focusing on, acting on and endeavouring to change 'reality' itself, or a mere simplified, abstracted and limited representation of it.

The map-territory relation refers to the association between the map, as the representational output of the mapping process, and the object being studied, or the actual, physical territory. The distinction draws on the early work of Korzybski (1931; 1933) representing his view that a simplification or an abstraction derived from something is not the thing itself.

> A map is **not** the territory it represents, but, if correct, it has a **similar structure** to the territory, which accounts for its usefulness.
>
> (Korzybski, 1933: p. 58)

The position acknowledges that when we view a representation, it is far too easy to confuse the model of reality (the map) with the reality itself (the territory). Project managers and business analysts could similarly benefit from reflecting on their object of change. In other words, are we endeavouring to change reality or are we simply acting on our simplified model, whilst ignoring the actuality and complexity of our reality?

Over many generations, traditional maps had been accepted with very limited questioning; reflecting a scientific positivist view of the need to impart and share accepted knowledge. Cartography, the science and art of map-making, thus assumed a direct link between reality and its representation. Harley (1989: pp. 4–5) notes that the idea of a map as a 'mirror of nature' leads to some complications, including an assumption of highly confirmed knowledge; ignorance of alternative cultures and dismissal of the truthfulness and objectivity of their maps; and belief that measurement and standardisation lead to a 'true' and increasingly more detailed map.

Early writing by Lewis Carroll introduces the fictional character of a German professor to explain that the mapmakers of Germany had experimented with the use of increasingly larger-scale maps, until they reached near perfection:

> 'What a useful thing a pocket-map is! ' I remarked.
>
> 'That's another thing we've learned from your Nation', said Mein Herr, 'map-making. But we've carried it much further than you. What do you consider the largest map that would be really useful'?
>
> 'About six inches to the mile'.
>
> 'Only six inches'! exclaimed Mein Herr. 'We very soon got to six yards to the mile. Then we tried a hundred yards to the mile. And then came the grandest idea of all! We actually made a map of the country, on the scale of a mile to the mile'!
>
> 'Have you used it much'? I enquired.
>
> 'It has never been spread out, yet', said Mein Herr: 'the farmers objected: they said it would cover the whole country, and shut out the sunlight! So we now use the country itself, as its own map, and I assure you it does nearly as well'.
>
> (Carroll & Furniss, 1893: p. 169)

Whilst in the extreme, the most accurate map possible would be an exact match and replica of the territory that would clearly be both wasteful and pointless. Some of the implications emerging from the distinction between the artefact and reality, or the map and territory, can be summarised as follows:

- **Objectivity**: Maps are developed through the eye of the observer; they are not objective;
- **Relevance:** No map is value free; purpose, values, propaganda and ideology infuse many maps;

- **Limitation**: Maps only offer a partial and abstracted representation of reality;
- **Incompleteness**: A map extracts certain features from reality; it is a simplification and abstraction of reality and as such cannot encompass the full set of characteristics in terms of space, time and complexity of relationships and interactions;
- **Timeliness**: Traditional maps are temporal, while real life continues to evolve – indeed, if we only observe static snapshots in our maps, we can miss the actual flow of life;
- **Accuracy**: No map is completely true; indeed, Brooke-Hitching (2016) even shows that non-existent islands, mountain ranges and civilisations that were presented as facts in maps were patently wrong, or mere phantom data; and
- **Permanence**: Models, representations and maps decay with time, further loosening their fidelity and relationship to real life.

The direct implications for project managers are that we come equipped with less than perfect maps of reality; that different sides and stakeholder groups may have their own versions, interpretations and partial representations; and that the models we create and work with are likely to have serious limitations.

Consequently, two key points emerge:

- Firstly, the map is separate to reality; yet, it can still develop a life of its own outside it.
- Secondly, arguing around the map and scribbling all over it will not change the territory itself. Project managers can become attached to a particular favourite depiction of reality or a specific map, but the changes that they impose, and the new dynamics they introduce will impact the snapshot of the map rather than the territory itself.

Completeness versus understandability: Invoking Bonini's paradox

Reality is far too complex to be conceived as a whole. Maps are often used to capture and simplify the complexity of a real life that is too difficult to glimpse in its full context. Lewis Carroll's German mapmakers, introduced earlier in the chapter, observed the need to search for higher and higher fidelity in order to capture a true likeness to real life. However, their experience identified that developing models rich in detail and relations requires ever-bigger models that can rival real life in size and scale.

A model, or a map, is an abstraction of reality, with much of the detail of reality left out. It is some real or imagined thing or process, which behaves similarly to some other thing or process (Harré, 1984). The model represents certain aspects of interest taken from reality. Models and maps embody only the essential features of reality relevant to the investigation and are utilised in explanation, description or prediction.

> A model is an attempt to represent some segment of reality and explain, in a simplified manner, the way the segment operates.
>
> (Harrison, 1987: p. 95)

Reality is too complex for decision makers and managers to comprehend and replicate. Science proceeds by simplifying reality (Weizenbaum, 1976). The first step in this process of simplification is the abstraction of crucial details, which also entails leaving out the details or data which are not of interest or do not fit (i.e. stripping of the physical and non-essential features). The choice of aspect and level of detail is a function of the model builder's perspective, value system and purpose. The utility of a model or map, therefore, can only be assessed against these factors.

> The value of a model lies in its substitutability for the real system for achieving an intended purpose.
>
> (Cleland & King, 1975: p. 135)

Models and maps reproduce parts of reality that are deemed significant. The more detail included, the more difficult the conceptualisation. 'The aim of the model is of course not to reproduce reality in all its complexity. It is rather to capture in a vivid, often formal, way what is essential to understanding some aspect of its structure or behaviour' (Weizenbaum, 1976)]. Essential implies a purpose and the modeller's mental model is used to select the features of reality that are considered essential to that purpose.

> Abstraction is the crucial feature of ... knowledge, because in order to compare and to classify the immense variety of shapes, structures, and phenomena around us we cannot take all their features into account, but have to select a few significant ones. Thus, we construct an intellectual map of reality ... Because our representation of reality is so much easier to grasp than reality itself, we tend to confuse the two and to take our concepts and symbols for reality.
>
> (Capra, 1991)

Charles Bonini identifies an essential dilemma in constructing models that fully capture the workings of real life, which has become known as the Bonini Paradox:

> If our model is to be at all realistic, it will also need to be rather complex. It will in fact be too complex for easy handling by the traditional analytic measures, even after suitable simplifications.
>
> (Bonini, 1963: p. 11)

Complete and comprehensive models and maps are therefore extremely hard to construct and ascertain. Dutton and Starbuck (1971: p. 132) explain that 'as a model of a complex system becomes more complete, it becomes less understandable. Alternatively, as a model grows more realistic, it also becomes just as difficult to understand as the real world processes it represents'.

Put simply, a model cannot be both comprehensive and fully understandable. Paul Valéry (1937) expresses an analogous sentiment: 'everything simple is false. Everything which is complex is unusable'.

> It is of course desirable to work with manageable models which maximize generality, realism, and precision toward the overlapping but not identical goals of understanding, predicting, and modifying nature. But this cannot be done.
>
> (Levins, 1966: p. 422)

Maps and models provide a simplification and a partial distortion of reality. The distortion in the map can later become lazily accepted as a complete and exhaustive synonym of reality, unless we remain alert to the simplification and abstraction that have been utilised.

> The larger, more detailed and complex the model – the less abstract the abstraction – the smaller the number of people capable of understanding it and the longer it takes for its weaknesses and limitations to be found out.
>
> (Adams, 1995: p. 200)

The problems we increasingly attend to are complex and interdependent, requiring new types of approaches in order to make sense of them and engage with their features and characteristics in meaningful ways.

A dose of complexity: In search of simplicity

Mathematical and computational models offer limited value in devising improved ways of addressing the inherent complexity of systems that encompass the interaction of people, nature and technology. Indeed, scientific theory proffers limited insights into systems, people and their multiple interactions, connections and complex relationships. Yet, if the scientific principles and models are unable to address emergence, complex relations and interaction, where else might we turn to?

Complexity practitioners agitate for the adoption of an alternative worldview that sees the world as essentially interconnected, rich with a diversity of forms and emergent patterns. This chapter, written by David Bentley, draws on his book, *Choosing to Change: An Alternative Understanding of Change Management*, published by Routledge. David has been reflecting on his practice as a change practitioner and on the apparent disconnect between change and unpredictability on the one hand, and our inevitable yearning for stability and order on the other.

David's reflection places individuals, not organisations, at the core of change. He is happy to embrace an alternative view of change informed by new insights from the studies of complexity – enabling him to explore how change in organisations is driven by individual choices. Observing that the totality of experiences and aspirations for the future of actors and participants shapes our thinking, in both conscious and unconscious ways, David is able to put together the foundations for a new approach to change, which is informed by individuals and their choices rather than being driven by processes and coercion.

The reflection of those who have experienced change can thus be developed into an informed exploration of how choice can form the basis for successful change journeys. Bentley is then able to draw on the insights in order to propose a new theory based on choosing to change in the face of the unknown and unpredictable. While David is unable to offer an explicit map, he is well positioned to draw upon a far more potent instrument, the power and influence of narrative learning and storytelling. Narratives offer enhanced and directed communication that places people back in the centre of change. Narratives and communication are far more powerful than perspectives focused on machines and prescriptions; they enable change to be adopted as the new normal way of working. Choosing to change can thus overcome resistance and reform change-weary organisations into coalitions of choice in search of improvement, development and growth.

The insights from complexity thinking allow change to emerge from the interaction between people in a continuous fashion, allowing expectations to grow through self-reinforcement. Choosing to change is clearly placed at the core of David's approach and can thereby become a new habit that emerges from and welcomes interaction, communication and informed choice.

The future mapping of complexity

Mapping still has the potential to offer highly prized patterns for improvement; however, rather than propose prescription and pre-identified idealised routes, there is a need to accommodate the complex relationship between reality and human descriptions and understanding of the world. Mapping cannot be undertaken to be a purely physical endeavour as human values, understanding and social and political analysis must play a key part in making sense and deriving the new realities informed by our current explorations.

Turnbull and Watson (1993) suggest that the map is a metaphor not only for the territory it represents but also for the culture that created it. Maps take on the meaning of the territory and its importance in that culture. Cosgrove (1999) notes that the representational processes of mapping have constructed the spaces of modernity since the early Renaissance. Mapping is further evolving as a critical dialogue between research and evolving practice (Dodge et al., 2011). Rankin (2016) identifies a new emphasis on simplicity, reliability and convenience in place of the old fixation with truth and objectivity. Fields (2004) also observes a reinvigorated interest in techniques and theories related to mapping in the fields of complex systems, theoretical biology and cosmology. Mapping can therefore change its focus to create rather than merely represent, as it seeks to endow new meaning in a postmodern setting (King, 1996).

Cartography can also be viewed not as a science of map-making but as a highly socialised and politicised artistic endeavour, which savours the individual and their discourses and practices. This allows maps to evolve from representations of space to a space of representation (Siegert, 2011). Thrower observes that 'cartography, like architecture, has attributes of both a scientific and an artistic pursuit, a dichotomy not satisfactorily reconciled in all presentations' (2018: p. 1). Maps can then develop a social and political dimension, which will allow them to both relate and realign the world.

Maps increasingly have the potential to become more dynamic, allowing for experimentation and impact assessment of engagement. Indeed, land surveying technology and electronic navigation systems combined with more sophisticated tools can allow for new forms of engagement, exploration and charting from an individual perspective. Meanwhile, current thinking in geography emphasises post-representational perspectives that largely eschew material artefacts, preferring instead to accentuate *mapping* and the practices that bring it into being, thereby encouraging a processual turn fuelled by ethnographic inquiries and approaches (Dodge & Perkins, 2015). Advancing from a representational to a processual perspective allows *mapping* to be viewed as a process of constant re-territorialisation, so that maps are never fully formed, and can be considered to be transitory, fleeting, contingent and context-dependent (Kitchin & Dodge, 2007).

Projecting into the future, modern perspectives may indeed play a part in blurring the distinction between the map and the terrain allowing for new approaches to discovery and the co-creation of alternatives, preferences and decisions. Extending the analysis and the metaphor, if our maps can be addressed as a dynamic form of communication alongside narrative, mapping may yet be able to transform into a potent pictorial alternative that allows for enduring interaction, engagement and exploration in the face of complexity and can bring together participants and explorers seeking change and improvement. Emerging new approaches such as open source mapping, map hacking and map mash-up can allow activities and stakeholders to engage, interact and co-create as they learn, play, change and improve. Such rapid experimentation and sharing can develop the basis for continually developing a clearer and better-informed understanding of the complex territories, relationships and impacts of our actions, and ultimately lead to improved engagement and co-shaping of our change undertakings and dynamic change maps by willing, informed and engaged participants.

References

Adams, J. (1995). *Risk*. London: University College London Press.

Akerman, J. R., & Karrow, R. W. (2007). *Maps: Finding our place in the world*. Chicago, IL: University of Chicago Press.

Barber, P., & Harper, T. (2010). *Magnificent maps: Power, propaganda and art*. London: British Library.

Bentley, D. (2018). *Choosing to change: An alternative understanding of change management*. Abingdon: Routledge.

Black, J. (2000). *Maps and politics*. Chicago, IL: University of Chicago Press.

Bonini, C. P. (1963). *Simulation of Information and decision system in the firm*. Englewood Cliffs, NJ: Prentice-Hall.

Brooke-Hitching, E. (2016). *The phantom atlas: The greatest myths, lies and blunders in maps*. London: Simon & Schuster.

Carroll, L., & Furniss, H. (1893/1988). *Sylvie and Bruno concluded*. London: Macmillan.

Cleland, D. I., & King, W. R. (1975). *Systems analysis and project management*. New York: McGraw-Hill.

Cosgrove, D. (1999). *Mappings*. London: Reaktion Books.

Dalcher, D. (2018). Strategy as learning to discover the way forward. *PM World Journal*, 7(1), 1–12.

Dodge, M., Kitchin, R., & Perkins, C. (Eds.). (2011). *Rethinking maps: New frontiers in cartographic theory*. New York: Routledge.

Dodge, M., & Perkins, C. (2015). Reflecting on JB Harley's influence and what he missed in 'Deconstructing the Map'. *Cartographica: The International Journal for Geographic Information and Geovisualization, 50*(1), 37–40.

Dutton, J. M., & Starbuck, W. H. (1971). Computer simulation models of human behavior: A history of an intellectual technology. *IEEE Transactions on Systems, Man, and Cybernetics, 1*(2), 128–171.

Fields, K. (2004). The map is the territory, in *7th International Consciousness Reframed Conference, 2004*, p. 7.

Hammond, K. R. (2007). *Beyond rationality: The search for wisdom in a troubled time*. New York: Oxford University Press.

Harley, J. B. (1989). Deconstructing the map. *Cartographica: The International Journal for Geographic Information and Geovisualization, 26*(2), 1–20.

Harré, R. (1984). *The philosophies of science*. Oxford: Oxford University Press.

Harrison, E. F. (1987). *The managerial decision-making process*. Boston, MA: Houghton Mifflin.

Hessler, J. (2015). *Map: Exploring the world*. London: Phaidon Press.

King, G. (1996). *Mapping reality*. New York: St. Martin's Press.

Kitchin, R., & Dodge, M. (2007). Rethinking maps. *Progress in Human Geography, 31*(3), 331–344.

Klinghoffer, A. J. (2006). *The power of projections: How maps reflect global politics and history*. Westport, CT: Greenwood Publishing Group.

Korzybski, A. (1931). A non-Aristotelian system and its necessity for rigour in mathematics and physics. Paper presented at the American Mathematical Society meeting at New Orleans, *Louisiana meeting of the American Association for the Advancement of Science*, December 28, 1931. Reprinted in *Science and Sanity*, 1933, pp. 747–761.

Korzybski, A. (1933/1958). *Science and sanity: An introduction to non-Aristotelian systems and general semantics*. New York: Institute of General Semantics.

Levins, R. (1966). The strategy of model building in population biology. *American Scientist*, *54*(4), 421–431.

Monmonier, M. (2010). *No dig, no fly, no go: How maps restrict and control*. Chicago, IL: University of Chicago Press.

Monmonier, M. (2014). *How to lie with maps*. Chicago, IL: University of Chicago Press.

Rankin, W. (2016). *After the map: Cartography, navigation, and the transformation of territory in the twentieth century*. Chicago: University of Chicago Press.

Robinson, A. H. (1952). *The look of maps: An examination*. Madison, WI: University of Wisconsin Press.

Siegert, B. (2011). The map is the territory. *Radical Philosophy*, *169*, 13–16.

Snyder, J. P. (1997). *Flattening the Earth: Two thousand years of map projections*. Chicago, IL: University of Chicago Press.

Starbuck, W. H. (1983). Computer simulation of human behavior. *Systems Research and Behavioral Science*, *28*(2), 154–165.

Thrower, N. J. (2018). *Maps and civilization: Cartography in culture and society*. Chicago, IL: University of Chicago Press.

Turnbull, D., & Watson, H. (1993). *Maps are territories: Science is an atlas: A portfolio of exhibits*. Chicago, IL: University of Chicago Press.

Valéry, P. (1937). Notre destin et les lettres. *Journal de l'université des Annales*, *19*, 341–354.

Weizenbaum, J. (1976). *Computer power and human reason: From judgment to calculation*. New York: W. H. Freeman.

Wood, D., & Fels, J. (1992). *The power of maps*. New York: Guilford Press.

Wood, D. (2010). *Rethinking the power of maps*. New York: Guilford Press.

Choosing to change

David Bentley

The profession of project management is in its widest sense that of facilitating change. Whatever the context, it is essentially a process of creating something new from an existing situation. How we should best manage the process of change and create the best possible outcome has exercised management thinking for many decades.

It is one of the eternal paradoxes of life, that through the ages we constantly seek the security of continuity, sticking to the status quo, whilst life, and the world that we live in, inevitably changes. Politicians and financiers call for stability in the economy, markets and international relations knowing full well that it can't and does not happen. Harold MacMillan, UK Prime Minister from 1957–63, is reputed to have answered the question put to him by a journalist 'What is most likely to blow governments off course?' saying 'Events, dear boy, events'. The exact words spoken and indeed the attribution is questioned, but the observation is clear. The best-formulated policies and detailed planning will always be victim to the unpredictable. The events that continually emerge creating unexpected change.

Over the course of the past half century I have witnessed a rapid and accelerating pace of change. In technology, the advent of the computer and the revolution in access to information through the internet. In transport, from the post-war spread of the motor car replacing horse-drawn transport to the prospect of driverless cars and in health, evidenced by the extension of life expectancy. In all areas of modern life, we are constantly experiencing change but still we tend to be taken by surprise when it happens and resist it happening.

My professional career has been spent managing many facets of change. As a construction project manager I was involved in the planning and creating of change. Whilst it was, on the face of it, the physical change of building roads, utility plants and buildings, it was in fact that most of my time in that role was spent dealing with the unexpected. However detailed the planning and scheduling of the work, a three-dimensional structure is being created from a two-dimensional plan or nowadays perhaps a virtual image. The interpretation of the detail required will always mean that the building created is emergent from those plans and change will be an integral part of the process. The time spent on crafting contracts and resolving disputes arising from the changes that happen are testament to that. Working now in organisational change the same applies. We can plan the change in great detail and strive to make the communication of the change as clear and widespread as possible. We can follow the latest model for change management but the unexpected will always happen. People will react in unpredictable ways. Sometimes resisting change that would appear, on the face of it, to be of clear benefit to them. Other times changing in ways that they did not expect themselves and being highly successful.

Whilst pursuing my career in change management I have been challenged to radically change my views on the nature of organisations, to re-evaluate what I was doing when planning a construction project and how I understood the reactions of the people that I was working with and the cultural changes. By chance I happened to choose to do an MBA course at the University of Hertfordshire that included taking a view of management theory that was developing out of complexity theory. A view that accepts unpredictability, takes human interaction as the basis of organisation and pays attention to what is actually happening rather than creating a model of what we think should be happening. It is in taking this complexity-based view that provides us with an understanding of what motivates people to accept or reject change. Providing an approach to managing change that works with individuals to make the choice to change and determines the way that change happens.

The mainstream approach to contemporary management and organisational theory that has been developed over the course of the 20th century is founded on the application of scientific research principles. That is, by conducting experiments, taking measurements and analysing data we can come to a theory of how something works and then use that knowledge to predict and influence what may happen in the future. The ultimate assumption of this way of thinking being that, given sufficient time and research effort we will eventually discover the 'theory of everything' that will enable us to control our destiny.

If we apply that to organisations, then the theory suggests that by studying how they perform under given conditions, measuring changes in performance and observing behaviour we can understand how they function. We can then develop models of how they should be managed and plan actions for change accordingly.

By tracing the origins of the current theories of change management we can see how organisations have come to be seen as systems that can be manipulated and redesigned by an external process of management. Rooted in Kurt Lewin's classic three-stage approach to managing change, the treatment of organisations 'as-if' they are systems that can be re-engineered and reset to a new course has dominated the thinking on change management throughout the 20th century. The mindset of systems theory that dominates management thinking is of mechanics. We talk about leverage and turning the wheels of industry and we seek to measure the performance of the system. The assumption is of linear cause and effect, rationality and shared company culture. In change management we talk of having tools with which to bring about change and the movement from one state of equilibrium to another. With thinking on leadership reflecting this same view, change is considered to be a top-down driven process that can be project managed through clear visions, communication and careful planning.

At the same time as the dominant theory of management was becoming embedded in organisational thinking, others were approaching the subject from the perspective of social behaviour. Herbert Mead, the early 20th-century philosopher, sociologist and psychologist pioneered thinking in social research and the development of action research in the understanding of organisations. Mead's philosophy was aligned to the thinking of the school of American pragmatism, a view that reality is not something that exists independently of the individual but is created by the way in which those individuals act in relation to it. Put simply, an object, such as a chair, only has meaning through the way we interact with it, in this case by sitting on it.

Contemporary research in neuroscience has shown that we form an understanding of the world in which we live from birth by exploration and observation of what is happening around us. That reality is held in that part of our brains that works unconsciously to enable us to function without the need to expend energy on conscious thought. For example, we don't have to think about how we walk across a room; we just do it. In this way we construct the reality of our world only by the way that we interact with it and in order to understand the nature of any shared reality, we need to observe what people actually do and how they respond to the world around them. We gain a shared understanding as we grow up, of what a chair is by observing the way we all use it. The pragmatic approach to understanding is, then, through close contact and immersion in the everyday activities of people and observing how they construct their everyday reality through their interaction with the world around them.

To understand the nature of change in organisations we can take an approach based on the principles of pragmatism. Using narrative accounts of how people interact with change and how they respond to the challenges presented by change we are able to pay attention to what is actually going on in a change situation and how it is that people make the choice to change and when they resist. By taking this approach we start with the organisation 'as-is', that is, as a group of interacting individuals sharing a common goal of delivering a product or service rather than some form of pseudo machine. We need to understand organisations by observation of what is actually happening. Paying attention to how people in the organisation are interacting and how they are creating meaning.

Mead's thinking was influenced by his interest in developments in the early 20th century in brain research. At that time, the subject was in its very early stages of understanding and Mead's thinking was primarily observational of social interaction. He was particularly focused on the role that the brain and the central nervous system might play in anticipating future actions. At this stage of understanding, the role of conscious thought was predominant and assumed to be the driver of behaviour. Mead's life and career came to an end in the early 1970s as the explosion in computing power was getting underway. In contemporary research we can now use neuroimaging to identify areas of activity in the brain under particular conditions. Whilst we cannot, at this stage, map the immense number of neurons in the brain and the seemingly endless number of potential connections between them, we can see which parts of the brain are responding to certain stimuli. This has shown the role of the unconscious areas of the brain in managing the day-to-day functions of life and storing our individual map of reality that determines our understanding.

In his book, published by his students in 1932, Mead reasoned that the future is perpetually constructed in, what he termed, the specious present (now more commonly termed the living present), where our actions in the immediate present are continually formed and reformed by our developing perception of the past and our current expectation of the future. So, for each individual, the meaning ascribed to any situation and the action we take, in the present, is constantly being formed and reformed by our interaction with those around us, our environment and our internal selves. So, we are all influenced in the way we act in the present by a combination of our perception of our past experience and our expectation of what the future will hold. It is important here to note that our memory of the past is not fixed, as in the nature of a collection of photographs or video, but is constantly revised by our ongoing reflection on our experience. We re-evaluate the past in the light of the present.

It is the unconscious reality that we construct from birth that drives our behaviour in the present. It is the key to how we interact with each other in our organisations and in life generally. In reality, life in organisations is not the acting out of a set pattern of pre-determined and rational processes; it is an ongoing process of gestures and responses that happen in the immediate present. How we form those gestures and responses in the instant is an unconscious reaction driven by our individual reality that determines how we react to the prospect of change. The ongoing pattern of change is the emergent and unpredictable process arising from that interaction. In taking this view, we can pay attention to what is actually happening and start to work with that in the change process.

The revolution in computing and the memory capacity that has facilitated neurological research and advanced our understanding of memory has also made possible simulations of complex networks, i.e. interacting, non-linear networks of connected individuals that react according to internal adaptive rule-sets. It has shown how these networks create over time novel patterns of behaviour as the connectivity increases, that is, the degree to which each individual is able to influence the behaviour of those that it interacts with. This is seen in nature, in phenomena such as the flocking of birds and, in the longer term, the evolution of species.

If you have been lucky enough to witness a large flock of birds giving an awesome display of aerial acrobatics when coming down to roost at dusk, you will recall the ever-changing patterns that are formed. Each individual bird is responding to the birds that are closest to it and changing its course accordingly. The response of each bird to changes in its neighbour's flight path, in a dynamic situation like that, will not be linear. It may accelerate or decelerate, curve one way or the other, all non-linear responses. Their relative positions, how close they are, will affect how strongly or quickly they respond to their neighbours' changes and how many of them they are responding to. The patterns that emerge are not predetermined but the spontaneous outcome of all the ongoing actions and reactions of the individual birds. The display is unpredictable and ever changing but at the same time recognisable for what it is.

The changes in the behaviour of complex networks are influenced by what are termed attractors; factors that draw individual behaviour towards a particular state. A simple example of this is the changing gait of a horse as it increases its speed of movement from walking to trotting and on to galloping. The patterns of motion are tending towards a state of lowest energy consumption and as the pace is increased the pattern changes from one cycle of leg movements to another. Each gait is drawn by an attractor of movement for lowest energy at that pace.

We can also recognise these phenomena in human behaviour and use this knowledge to inform our understanding of organisations and change. It is the forming and constant reforming of our personal realities that is fundamental to the way we interact with each other and how change emerges from that. Change and the reaction to change is a complex process rather than a managed and externally directed activity. The key to understanding how this process works and what drives the emergence of change and our response to it lies in the ongoing way in which we make choices and react to our environment.

Stepping away from the systems view of organisations towards a complexity perspective, we see organisations as patterns of communicative interaction between independent individuals, or in other words, ongoing conversations, where its future state is constantly emergent. The organisation cannot be isolated from its context, redesigned and then re-connected. Change is a perpetual process that emerges from those conversations and the interactions of the individuals, employees, stakeholders, customers and all those linked to the organisation. Change is a consequence of the collective choices made by individuals.

The unpredictable and emergent nature of behaviour arises from the meaning found in gesture and response, i.e. the way that we act in relation to each other. Organisations are self-organising patterns of conversations in which meaning emerges. Individual realities, in the context of the organisation, are constantly formed and reformed. Thus, we are now working with what is actually happening in the organisation.

We have considered the view of organisations that is prompted by the scientific management theory that they act 'as-if' they are discreet systems that can be manipulated when we want to bring about a change in their state. A process that creates a need to change, implements a new state, perhaps a new way of working or behaving, and then cements that into everyday practice. A view that tends to treat organisations as a form of sentient organism capable of holding values and a social conscience and so able to change in itself. I suggest, though, that if we take away the individuals we are not left with anything that is capable of acting in that way. In the absence of artificial intelligence, without the individuals we only have a collection of buildings, machinery, stock and products. Further, what makes it an organisation is not even just the individuals themselves but the way they interact and particularly the activity that emerges from that interaction.

The insights gained from modern neuroscience help us to see how Mead's description of acting in the living present through an ongoing sequence of gesture and response creates, in an organisation as with all social groupings, the behavioural patterns described by complexity theory. The personal reality that we build and constantly rebuild in our unconscious brain, together with our expectations of the future, are expressed in our gestures and responses in the present. By paying attention to what is actually happening in those organisations we see that the only variable is the ongoing conversation of those gestures and responses.

A complexity understanding of what is actually happening with individuals interacting in organisations and the unpredictable and emergent nature of change puts individual choice at the centre of change management. It is the unconscious reality that drives choice and by making that explicit we can influence the narrative shared in the organisation to promote the emergence of positive change. Having challenging conversations and employing narrative learning in organisations enables groups to move to a position of creativity; the point where they can embrace the emergent and unpredictable nature of change and make the choice to change with confidence.

So, an organisation is a complex network of individuals where each individual is connected in local interactions, in the present, from which patterns of behaviour and activity emerge on an ongoing basis. This view of organisations is supported by the observation of patterns of difference and self-similarity. Life is similar day to day but is always different. Life is unpredictable and non-linear as things escalate out of seemingly nowhere whilst other things that appear, at first, to be very important fade into insignificance. We are drawn, unconsciously, to certain strange attractors such as maintaining the status-quo in the face of change as that is the line of least effort. We tend to respond to anxiety, particularly when faced with change, by adopting the attractors of basic assumption behaviour, such as fight or flight, to lower that anxiety. So, if that is what organisations actually are then we need to approach change or the creation of change in an organisation from that perspective rather than that of the systems and scientific management view.

7

Shadow working

Working in the shadows

Exposing our inner demons

Darren Dalcher

The previous chapter focused on the complexity of the terrain and the difficulty in mapping and making sense of the full scale of reality. An earlier chapter advocated the creation of a culture of cooperation between different disciplines. This chapter shifts attention to the complexity of individuals, and the cultures and organisations within which they operate. In particular, it highlights the role of light and shadows in determining what we can see and do.

Shadows may conjure up childhood images of playful finger and hand shapes of animals and magical creatures projected onto a wall in front of a torch, flashlight or fire, or perhaps invoke memories of elongated shapes manipulated at dusk, which lengthen as the twilight descends, until they are subsumed by the surrounding darkness when the sun is no longer visible.

The Oxford Dictionary offers two pertinent definitions: 'a dark area or shape produced by a body coming between rays of light and a surface', or a term 'used in reference to proximity, ominous oppressiveness, or sadness and gloom'. Upon reflection, it thus becomes possible to focus on two main types of shadows:

- **The darkness that forms**: the former description offered by the Oxford Dictionary refers to the shadow created when an opaque, or translucent, object casts a shadow, as it does not allow the light projected from a source to pass straight through it.
- **The darkness that lurks**: The latter definition acknowledges a more profound phenomena that could refer to a shadow of war impacting a country; a shadow of performance-enhancing drugs that blights a particular sport; a shadow cast by pests, vermin or disease, or some other threat; or even a more ominous shadow in the mind that encases the soul in darkness. Certain cultures, religions and mythologies also associate shadows with ghosts, demons or the underworld.

The common feature across both types of shadow is the absence of light, which manifests itself as a certain kind of emerging darkness.

Searching under the lamppost

Light seems to play an important part in driving local inquiry and emboldening the search for knowledge, while shadows and darkness stifle the local search.

There is an old parable and joke about a police officer who observes a drunken man furiously searching under a streetlight. After a few minutes the police officer approaches to discover that the man had lost his house keys. The officer joins the search, as they both thoroughly and systematically comb the area underneath the streetlight. After repeating the search three or four times, the police officer asks the man if he is absolutely certain he lost the keys there, to which the man replies, 'no, I lost them over there in the park'.

The officer proceeds to ask why he is searching in that particular spot, and the man replies that 'this is where the light is'.

Searching under the lamppost is also known as 'the streetlight effect' or the drunkard's search. It was popularised by Abraham Kaplan (1964), and has become an increasingly acknowledged and recognised observational bias where people search by looking in the easiest places. Farris (1969) observes that no matter where behavioural scientists have dropped their keys, they prefer to continue to search for them where it appears lighter, while Freedman maintains that 'researchers tend to look for answers where the looking is good, rather than where the answers are likely to be hiding' (2010).

The temptation to look under the light, where it is easier to organise a search, continues to appeal to many disciplines (see for example, Shanto & William, 1993; McKenna, Singh & Richardson, 2008). Indeed, Noam Chomsky dryly reasons in a 1993 letter that

> Science is a bit like the joke about the drunk who is looking under a lamppost for a key that he has lost on the other side of the street, because that's where the light is. It has no other choice.
>
> (reported in Barsky, 1998: p. 95)

It would thus appear that the simplicity and convenience of the proverbial lamppost appeal to both stray dogs and researchers and scientists looking to fix their gaze.

Entering the shadow world

Carl Jung (2014) refers to the *shadow* as an unconscious aspect of the personality, which the conscious ego does not identify in itself, or alternatively, as the entirety of the unconscious. The shadow is also acknowledged as the *dark side* of personality, often associated with negative aspects such as anxieties, fears, low self-esteem and false beliefs and perceptions.

While shadow typically refers to the unknown dark side of the personality, in Jungian tradition, it typically includes everything that is outside the light of consciousness, and may therefore encompass positive as well as negative aspects that remain hidden from the light.

Stevens reasons that acceptable traits are built into the personality, while the unacceptable ones are hidden or repressed into the subconscious, where they coalesce to form another complex personality as the shadow.

> Jung felt 'shadow' to be an appropriate term for this disowned subpersonality for there is inevitably something 'shady' about it, hidden away as it is in the darker lumber-room of the Freudian unconsciousness. Unwanted though it is, it persists as a powerful dynamic that we take with us wherever we go as a dark companion which dogs our steps – just like a shadow in fact. Much of the time we manage to ignore it, but it has an uncomfortable way of reminding us of its presence.
>
> (Stevens, 2001: p. 64)

Extending the previous metaphor, the personality is identified under the lamppost, whilst the *shadow*, containing other aspects, lurks outside the main focus of our lamppost.

Working the shadow side

The shadow side is not limited to individuals. Analysis of failure cases within organisations often reveals surprising patterns in behaviour that defy the espoused norms and expectations of the organisation. Special favours, unexplained deals, broken rules, politics, undocumented procedures, workarounds, escalation of commitment, unjustified promotions and unexplained hirings and firings often feature through special strategic initiatives, projects, as well as business as usual. Such covert, undiscussable and unmentionable actions appear to defy organisational logic and prescriptive manuals; yet, they are inevitably found whenever one starts delving into the organisational dynamics as they are applied in practice.

Egan posits that the shadow side consists of 'all the important activities and arrangements that do not get identified, discussed and managed' (1994: p. 4). Since shadow side factors are not normally discussed, they fall outside the reach of ordinary managerial interventions, yet, are likely to impact both the productivity and the quality of work life within the organisation (ibid.: p. 5–6).

Shadow side arrangements are not limited to negative impacts, and may include informal collaborations, mentoring and support that can add value to the individuals concerned and to the wider organisation. Often they embody informal internal rules and agreements that have tacit recognition. The key feature is that they remain beneath the surface and are undiscussed.

Egan maintains that when an individual enters an organisation, they initially only see what takes place on the surface. After a while, they begin to grasp the multi-dimensional aspects of the organisation, which will typically encompass the following categories (ibid.: p. 8):

- Organisational culture;
- Personal styles and behaviours of individuals;
- Organisational social systems;
- Organisational politics; and
- The hidden organisation, including ad hoc systems and processes.

Understanding what really goes on within organisations, and inside teams, requires working below the surface. It implies giving insights to the fragmentation of organisational life, as well as the culture, relationships, politics and other dynamics that shape organisational life and reality. Systems concepts, such as rich pictures, and complexity theory notions can play a part in mapping some of the interactions, relationships, conflicts and the politics invoked in particular settings. However, there is also a critical need to borrow some of the psychological and psychoanalytical concepts and ideas required to understand how groups, teams, organisations and social systems operate, and how they can be understood, improved and developed.

Shadow working in project management

So what are the implications for project management and how do we begin to address the shadow side of projects?

The shadow side entails a creative potential to develop and grow. An informed dialogue that covers the rational and the shadow side can improve and enhance existing ideas and perspectives and strengthen motivation and work habits. However, in order to consider such aspects, project management requires an infusion of alternative thinking approaches and ideas from other disciplines, including the arts, sociology, psychology and Jungian theory. There is a particular need to develop mindfulness and conscious consideration regarding the shadow side of project undertakings. This chapter by Joana Bértholo is developed from her book *Shadow Working in Project Management: Understanding and Addressing the Irrational and Unconscious in Groups*, published by Routledge, and addresses that particular gap.

Joana acknowledges that management is not simply a result or an ideal state of affairs, but instead views it as an unfolding process and a collective opportunity for a responsible and integrated agency. The perspective she adopts eschews instrumental rationality opting instead for an inter-dependent and co-creative view of reality. In doing so, she issues an implicit challenge: If rational actors operate within shadow organisations, it behoves all of us to consider the implications and endeavour to rise beyond the assumed instrumentality and instead make sense of the fuller and wider context of project work.

Joana's work is the first book to emerge from a major initiative undertaken by the ICCPM, The International Centre for Complex Project Management. The aim of the initiative was to explore alternative perspectives on project management with a particular emphasis on cross-cultural complex project management, which enabled the research to home in on the far-reaching implications and potential of social complexity.

The position adopted by her work offers a powerful proposition for examining the relationship between the individual and the collective, exploring the cross-cultural complexity of managing projects, understanding project management as a culture and ultimately developing a richer understanding of project work. A good starting point is the recognition that people play a far more significant part in the unfolding of project experiences. One interesting implication is the consideration that projects don't fail; it is the people working in them and on them that do! This chimes with an ever-greater focus on leadership and inter-personal skills in the project space.

Joana embraces the shadow side in the context of complex projects ready to engage with the unreasonable, lazy and irrational aspects of project work. The learning journey is a five-year experiential learning expedition into the shadow side of project work which requires the author to make sense of, recognise, label and own the traits identified in the shadow side. The journey entails a rich engagement with culture, dynamics, pressures, the dark side of leadership and other features of the shadow.

Balancing light and shadow

Many individuals remain unaware of the shadow side and the potential it uncovers. Coming to terms with the shadow side often starts with reflection on the self and the impact and culture surrounding us. Organisational systems regularly emphasise governance and efficiency, while the shadow side embodies creativity, responsiveness and extraordinary leadership that can make things happen in alternative ways, despite the normal systems.

Shadow, however perceived, owes its origin to the light from which it emerges. The contradiction between light and shadow offers the potential to perceive the world differently and develop new and creative ways of engaging with and benefiting from the external environment. Indeed, Stacey (2007: p. 325) asserts that the shadow system pulls the organisation towards chaos and as it enables diversity of thought and approach it thereby harbours much of the creativity and potentiality that resides within the organisation.

Engaging with the shadow opens up new creative opportunities that overcome dysfunctional culture, rigid procedures, small powerbases and bureaucratic hierarchies. The secret lies in maintaining a dynamic balance between the rigidity of the conventional system and the flexibility enabled by the alternative arrangements. Being able to maintain such a dual operating system can harvest the edge or zone between efficiency and disruption and innovation required to generate new forms of work and methods of achievement. Ultimately, balancing light and shadow would remain a critical and ethical part of the job of every responsible leader and manager as they endeavour to work in the shadow and learn to operate beyond the comforting gaze of the lamppost.

References

Barsky, R. F. (1998). *Noam Chomsky: A life of dissent*. Cambridge, MA: MIT Press.

Bértholo, J. (2017). *Shadow working in project management: Understanding and addressing the irrational and unconscious in groups*. New York: Routledge.

Egan, G. (1994). *Working the shadow side: A guide to positive behind-the-scenes management*. San Francisco, CA: Jossey-Bass.

Farris, G. F. (1969). The drunkard's search in behavioral science. *Compensation Review, 1*(2), 29–33.

Freedman, D. H. (2010). Why scientific studies are so often wrong: The streetlight effect. *Discover Magazine, 26*, August 1st, 2010.

Jung, C. G. (2014). *The archetypes and the collective unconscious*. London: Routledge.

Kaplan, A. (1964). *The conduct of inquiry: Methodology for behavioral sciences*. San Francisco, CA: Chandler.

McKenna, S., Singh, P., & Richardson, J. (2008). The drunkard's search: Looking for 'HRM' in all the wrong places. *Management International Review, 48*(1), 115–136.

Shanto, I., & William, M. (1993). *The drunkard's search. Explorations in political psychology*. Duke Studies in Political Psychology. Durham, NC: Duke University Press.

Stacey, R. D. (2007). *Strategic management and organisational dynamics: The challenge of complexity to ways of thinking about organisations*. London: Pearson Education.

Stevens, A. (2001). *Jung: A very short introduction*. Oxford: Oxford University Press.

Shadow Working in Project Management

Towards new levels of consciousness in groups

Joana Bértholo

> I have yet to meet the famous Rational Economic Man theorists describe. Real people have always done inexplicable things from time to time, and they show no sign of stopping.
>
> —Charles Sanford Jr., US business executive, quoted in Ket De Vries, M. (2003: p. 1)

The book *Shadow Working in Project Management* (Bértholo, 2017) is the result of a research project undertaken from 2009 to 2014. It tells the story of an experiential autoethnography, the learning journey, which sought methods to address unconscious and subconscious traits as they manifest in groups/projects. After this Journey, the author was equipped to return to the literature in project management and explore the implications of the shadow, to try to answer the main research question – What are the most prevailing shadows in project management culture? For that, some auxiliary questions had to be addressed, namely:

- What is the shadow and how does it play out in the life of projects?
- To what extent and in what way is project management influenced by unconscious factors in its practice and culture?
- To what extent is the manager's role the fulfilment of a psychological projection or an archetype?
- In what ways is the shadow related to personal development and organisational change?

The varied answers draw a map of the dominant shadow-issues in project management practice and culture. In the foreword to the book *Resonant Leadership*, Goleman (2005: p. x) writes that: 'The first task in management has nothing to do with leading others; step one poses the challenge of knowing and managing oneself'. Management is not limited to outer circumstances and resources. Fundamental processes are happening within. Through internal management, the experience of the manager is less an outcome and more a process. Any situation becomes:

> an encounter with the grander, more complex system described by the new sciences and the organizational systems literature. It also demystifies the relationship to this vast unknown, depotentiates the need for willful control over the environment and over other people in other roles.
>
> (Jones, 2004)

These quotes illustrate some guidelines to the research. In addition, important premises were:

- The existence of an unconscious realm;
- The project manager as someone who participates in a shared psychological structure wherein unconscious factors play a significant role;
- Individuals deny traits that belong to them, but which stand as a threat to their sense of self or ego identity;
- These denied traits appear projected in the external environment and create conflict and tension; and
- The collective in itself as a source of tension between individual and collective needs.

The consequences are manifold. The way a project manager handles a situation cannot be solely attributed to personality, nor is it merely a result of acquired competencies and learned conduct. These rational aspects, although they are ever present, are in fact in relation to a larger totality. The shadow is a permanent part of that larger totality, and it comes up generally through conflict or emotionally charged situations; in lack of drive or motivation; addictive and compulsive behaviour occurs, sensations of strong instability; somatic bodily symptoms, diseases, nervous ticks, allergies, and all sorts of bodily manifestations, among other forms the shadow has to show itself.

What is outside of awareness plays out in our everyday lives (see Freud, Jung, Wilber, Zweig). *Projection* and *transference mechanisms* are the central mechanisms by which the shadow manifests. These terms have been retrieved from the somewhat obscure jargon of the analyst or the psychologist and are being integrated in popular discourse, as well as in PM theory. Bowles defined the *Organisation Shadow* as the 'facts which organizations wish to deny about themselves, due to the threat posed to self-image and self-understanding and, more generally, the need to be viewed in a favourable light by others' (Bowles, 1991: p. 387). It is a useful extrapolation of the definition of the individual shadow. When we speak about the shadow of a project we are speaking about the shadow of that project's active culture at play, in the sense of its values, norms, etc. Different projects carry different shadows, and the quest for a shadow-free project is fruitless, as is the quest for a shadow-free human being.

We all carry shadows, they change through time, but they are not something we can get rid of, they are something we can be aware of and that can lead us to a more mindful life. According to Jung (1966: pp. 284–5),

> [The Shadow is] the thing a person has no wish to be. It is everything that the subject refuses to acknowledge about himself and yet is always thrusting itself upon him – for instance inferior traits of character and other incompatible tendencies.

> The Shadow is that about ourselves we find unpleasant or unbearable. It contains aspects that appear contrary to the ego ideal or to the ego identity. Therefore, it becomes a reservoir of untapped potential, rich in raw emotions and primal drives, the disavowed, poorly developed and undervalued contents of the individual psyche – but also our highest morality, creativity and power (the *Light Shadow*). When the disliked qualities are removed from view (positive or negative traits) they are also removed from supervision. They do not stop existing. Instead, they play out in unpredictable ways, usually erupting unexpectedly, potentially in hurtful forms to self or others. Afterwards, a deep sense of humiliation, shame, or guilt can be experienced. These are clear shadow-pointers. 'Confrontation with the shadow produces at first a dead balance, a standstill that hampers moral decisions and makes convictions ineffective or even impossible. Everything becomes doubtful.

> (Jung, 1963; para 708)

The most prevalent shadow of the discipline is arguably the one that puts the discipline at stake: What if ultimately nothing can be managed? Management can be called to hold the tension of that which cannot be managed, paradoxical as it may sound. In paradox lies the ultimate task of all shadow processes. Unmanageability is intolerable because it puts leaders and managers in a place of vulnerability. It means accepting fallibility, dealing with deep feelings of helplessness.

Argyris (1990: p. 30) explores this further in his work:

> Because defensive routines are accepted as inevitable and natural, and because they are unmanageable and not to be influenced, it is not too surprising that the most common reaction to them is a sense of helplessness about changing them. Employees in industrialised societies appear as fatalistic about them as peasants do about poverty.

That refers to one of the crucial issues: exploring our resistance to change. The many defence mechanisms, including self-boycott, that individuals and groups engage with just to be able to keep face. What the techniques experienced must offer are creative strategies to allow safety in bringing down those barriers, so a communication between these undesirable traits and the centre of the

Self can be established, and new boundaries drawn. In this sense, after shadow-work, a project expands in scope and possibilities.

Another important finding was that the unconscious communicates through imagery, symbols and metaphors. This is relevant if we consider how much the dominance of text, speech and discourse in project management practice relates largely to the conscious mind. The subconscious mind, however, communicates through feelings, emotions, body symptoms, active imagination, sensations and dreams, as confirmed in the learning journey.

The learning journey took inspiration from Roth and Kleiner's *Learning History*, as a first-person narrative encompassing many voices. It focused on forms of shadow-work (techniques to handle the shadow) and the cultures surrounding them. These practices were taught in a more or less dogmatic format: rules, fixed forms and expectations for how participants should behave. Nonetheless, flexibility and openness towards learning in the field of transformative practices were found to be high, in the sense that many people attend many different experiences and share their stories from setting to setting. Often facilitators and coaches experiment with each other's methods, integrating what seems to be appropriate for their own work. Being a very wide field of practice, there are many schools, many traditions and many faiths. Most of the practitioners interviewed showed a strong conviction that the technique they mastered was the one that had the strongest impact. Nevertheless, most showed interest in learning about other techniques. That helps explain why certain features, such as role-playing, can be found across very different methods. As said, what all these tools aim at is to build a new channel of communication between different parts of the self. The main Shadow practices consider a complex and multifaceted individual who needs change to be simultaneously profound in terms of depth (vertical) as well as across-realms in terms of scope (horizontal). There is a prevailing mindset that tends to move towards a combination of factors and away from one-way approaches. Some techniques are fast and intense, others demand months of continuous practice, while others call for a space of retreat. Deep and sustainable change seems to be something that cannot be achieved in an isolated workshop experience. Interviews as well as direct observation indicated that change takes commitment, continuity – and time. This is something to consider in project management, where most managers express the need for fast changes and immediate results in their teams.

It became evident along the learning journey that we seem to know less about the unconscious on a discursive level than on a practical one. That means that even when we lack the language to explain the mystery of change, we nevertheless have the tools. It also became clear that it is relatively easy to spot the shadow; what is truly difficult is to *own it*. Integration of the shadow means that what was once perceived as an outside object ('his rage', 'her arrogance', 'their incompetence', etc.) becomes accepted as a less than ideal part of the Self, but a part of oneself ('my rage', 'my arrogance', 'my incompetence'.

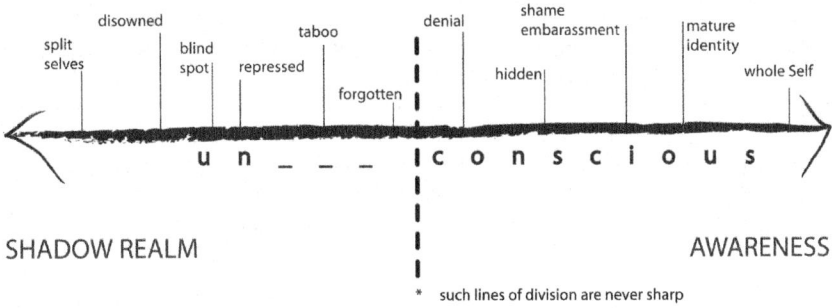

Figure 7.1 The polysemy of the shadow.

Depending on the contents, the work of integration with groups can bring about havoc and feelings of *malaise*. But the goal is wholeness and higher levels of collective consciousness.

Different levels of consciousness lead to very different styles of management. In later stages of development we encounter depictions of the organisational system as 'having a consciousness of its own', references to its 'generative powers' and descriptions of the system as 'engaging in adaptive and evolutionary activities'.

Figure 7.1 shows the polysemy of the shadow: The shadow, a plural phenomena, is dynamic and exists in a scale. The terms used are not synonymous as they stand in different places of the shadow scale, but they are all addressed as being part of the overarching group of shadow manifestations.

The ability to manage polarities and deal with paradox is essential for the integration of the shadow. 'I alone must become myself but I cannot become myself alone' is not merely a logic paradox, it is pertinent to understand individuality within a group/project. Interdependence makes the space of projects even more valid socially and culturally, for the fact that we get together, organise and make ideas come true. But it clashes with inbred needs of validation and individuality. Ultimately, what one wants and what the group desires rarely ever match.

References

Argyris, C. (1990). *Overcoming organizational defenses: Facilitating organizational learning.* Boston, MA: Allyn & Bacon.

Bértholo, J. (2017). *Shadow working in project management: Understanding and addressing the irrational and unconscious in groups.* New York: Routledge.

Bowles, M. L. (1991). The organization shadow. *Organization Studies, 12*(3), 387–404.

Goleman, D. (2005). Forward. In R. Boyatzis, & A. McKee (Eds.), *Resonant leadership: Renewing yourself and connecting with others through mindfulness, hope and compassion.* Harvard, MA: Harvard Business Press.

Jones, A. (2004). *An absence of being: A Jungian-based model for understanding situational management In public organizations* (PhD dissertation), Virginia Polytechnic Institute, 290 pages.

Jung, C. (1966). Psychology and literature, in *Collected work of C. G. Jung* (CW16), paragraph 470, Princeton, NJ: Princeton University Press.

Jung, C. (1963). Mysterium Coniunctionis, subtitled An inquiry into the separation and synthesis of psychic opposites in alchemy, in *Collected work of C. G. Jung* (CW14), paragraph 708, Princeton, NJ: Princeton University Press.

Vaill, P. B. (1991). The inherent spirituality of organizations. Paper prepared for the Academy of Management meeting, Miami Beach, FL, August 3–7.

8

Implementation

Strategy execution

Overcoming the alignment trap

Darren Dalcher

In the realm of strategy, the success of a vision is only as enduring as its execution. There is perhaps nothing more frustrating than to observe a beautiful strategy conceived in response to a promising big opportunity or cutting-edge innovation, which succumbs to the vagaries and twists of life during an attempt at executing it.

> A brilliant strategy, blockbuster product or breakthrough technology can put you on the competitive map, but only solid execution can keep you there. You have to be able to deliver on your intent. Unfortunately, the majority of companies aren't very good at it, by their own admission.
> (Neilson, Martin & Powers, 2008; p. 60)

Sir John Reginald Hartnell Bond, who retired as Chairman of HSBC Holdings plc, after 45 years with the bank, famously remarked that 'there are few original strategies in banking; there's only execution'.

Indeed, strategy execution appears to be difficult to carry out successfully. Sull, Homkes and Sull (2015: p. 60) refer to a survey of more than 400 global CEOs that found that executional excellence is the leading challenge facing corporate leaders in Asia, Europe and the United States, topping a list of over 80 issues, including geopolitical instability, top-line growth and innovation. The authors further concede that multiple studies indicate that between two-thirds and three-quarters of large organisations struggle to implement their strategies. Similar figures are regularly quoted in most strategy textbooks.

> If execution is so important, why is it so neglected? To be sure, people in business aren't totally oblivious to it. But what they are mostly aware of is its absence. They know deep down that something is missing when decisions don't get made or followed through or when commitments don't get met. They search and struggle for answers, benchmarking companies that are known to deliver on their commitments, looking for the answers in the organizational structure or processes or culture. But they rarely

apprehend the underlying lesson, because execution hasn't yet been rec-
ognized or taught as a discipline. They literally don't know what they are
looking for.

(Bossidy & Charan, 2002: p. 31)

The problem with execution

Beer and Eisenstat (2000) note that while successful companies comprehend
that they need a good strategy before proceeding to appropriately realign structure, systems, leadership behaviour, human resource policies, culture, values
and management processes, many obstacles lie between the ideal alignment and
the reality of implementation.

> For one thing, senior managers get lulled into believing that a well-
> conceived strategy communicated to the organization equals implementa-
> tion. For another, they approach change in a narrow, non-systemic and
> programmatic manner that does not address root causes.
>
> (ibid.: p. 29)

Beer and Eisenstat point out that doctors refer to high cholesterol as a 'silent
killer' because it blocks arteries with no obvious outward symptoms. They
contend that organisations similarly have their own *silent killers* operating below
the surface (i.e. within the shadow side of the organisation). These mutually
reinforcing barriers block strategy implementation and organisational learning
required for successful innovation, development and growth.

Beer and Eisenstat's research identifies the most often mentioned major
barriers to strategy implementation observed within the organisations they
studied. The six 'silent killers' (ibid.: p. 32) are:

- Top-down or laissez-faire senior management style;
- Unclear strategy and conflicting priorities;
- An ineffective senior management team;
- Poor vertical communication;
- Poor coordination across functions, businesses or borders; and
- Inadequate down-the-line leadership skills and development.

> Employees saw the overall problem rooted in fundamental management
> issues of leadership, teamwork and strategic direction, not in the commit-
> ment of people or their functional competence. Successful implementa-
> tion needs more than a leader; it requires teamwork from a leadership
> group that, through dialogue and collaboration, stays connected to the
> knowledge embedded in lower levels.
>
> (ibid.: p. 31)

The barriers are neither acknowledged nor explicitly addressed in most organisations. Moreover, factors such as 'poor vertical communication' not only hinder strategy implementation, but also prohibit and dampen any attempts to discuss and explore the barriers themselves; leaving the factors buried deeply into the shadow side of the organisation.

Beer and Eisenstat (ibid.: p. 32) note that the barriers are troubling in isolation, but can combine to make powerful vicious circles that could be difficult to overcome. The barriers represent key organisational stress points needed to successfully transition to higher levels of performance, speed and responsiveness (ibid.: p. 34). The conclusion they reach is that organisations 'can become fast and agile only if the six silent killers are met head-on and transformed into six core capabilities' (ibid.: p. 35).

Effective strategy implementation thus relies on the six core capabilities matching the six silent killers stress points:

- Engaged leadership;
- Clear and compelling business direction;
- Effective senior management team;
- Open fact-based dialogue;
- Realigning roles, responsibilities and accountabilities with strategy; and
- Strong leadership with a general management perspective.

Drawing insights from their own extensive research, Sull, Homkes and Sull (2015) identify several erroneous yet widely held beliefs about how to implement strategy. The five myths they endeavour to debunk are tabulated below together with paraphrased comments about the results observed in practice and what action might be needed to improve strategy execution capability (see Table 8.1).

Converging on the alignment trap

Many managers try to address execution problems by reducing them to a single dimension that can be partially resolved. Often such efforts focus on tightening alignment up and down the organisation (Sull et al., 2015: p. 66), but ultimately this is likely to prove to be an insufficient substitute for the coordination, agility and flexibility needed to support effective and responsive execution.

> If managers focus too narrowly on improving alignment, they risk developing ever more refined answers to the wrong question.
>
> (ibid.)

The alignment trap is a scenario where execution fails and managers respond by enforcing further alignment measures, such as adding more performance tracking measures and demanding more-frequent meetings to monitor progress

Table 8.1 Myths related to strategy execution

Myth	Observations and solutions
1. Execution equals alignment	In practice: Failure to coordinate across functions and units Needed: More structure in the processes to coordinate activities horizontally across units
2. Execution means sticking to the plan	In practice: Strategic roadmaps rarely survive contact with reality Needed: Strategy execution entails seizing opportunities and adapting to facts on the ground Execution at its best requires creative solutions to unforeseen problems or exploitation of unexpected opportunities Yet, agility should not be used as an excuse to chase every opportunity
3. Communication equals understanding	In practice: Strategic objectives are poorly understood; they seem unrelated to one another and disconnected from the overall strategy; many executives have no clear sense of how initiatives fit together Needed: Focus on understanding gained, not volume of communication outputs Focused, directed and undiluted message featuring only key strategic objectives
4. A performance culture drives execution	In practice: Despite robust performance cultures companies struggle to execute strategy; corporate cultures often fail to support the candid discussion needed to enable agility and responsiveness; more critically, companies fail to foster the co-ordination essential for execution Needed: Greater focus on ability to collaborate; and not past performance
5. Execution should be driven from the top	Top-down execution can unravel; decisions can be delayed; interventions encourage managers to defer rather than resolve depleting local capability Needed: Distributed leaders not executives; Decisions need to be made by local experts who can respond more quickly; Guided from the top, driven from the middle

and instruct the team. Such measures stifle the creativity and experimentation required to drive agility and innovation. When execution falls further adrift, additional scrutiny measures may be imposed, until companies find themselves trapped in a downward spiral in which more alignment leads to worse results (ibid.: p. 66).

> Execution is a notorious and perennial challenge. Even at the companies that are best at it – what we call 'resilient organizations' – just two-thirds of employees agree that important strategic and operational decisions are quickly translated into action. As long as companies continue to attack their execution problems primarily or solely with structural or motivational initiatives, they will continue to fail. As we've seen, they may enjoy short-term results, but they will inevitably slip

back into old habits because they won't have addressed the root causes of failure.

(Neilson et al., 2008)

Ironically, these dynamics would also appear to give rise to a hitherto unacknowledged, yet pervasive *alignment paradox*: When strategy and the structures, systems, values and processes needed for efficient execution are in optimal alignment with each other, there remains very little scope for out of the ordinary innovation or variation. However, when the strategy and the structures are out of line, the responses by senior management are likely to lead to an alignment trap and subsequently into the downward spiral, where forced efforts are made to align the two, resulting in squeezing out any opportunities for creative exploration. Alignment, it would appear, can banish creativity and innovation, regardless of whether it is working or not.

> Alignment is fine – if the world isn't changing. But perfect alignment destroys any chance of innovation, because it brooks no dissent and allows no alternatives. Alignment is the enemy of business concept innovation.
>
> (Hamel, 2002: p. 154)

In search of strategy implementation guidance

Strategy in the abstract is devoid of any potential for progress. Strategy implementation or execution thus relies on translating words, promises and appealing narrative into an explicit reality. However, this art of translation appears to be the elusive constituent that is neither shared nor understood.

> Since Michael Porter's seminal work in the 1980s we have had a clear and widely accepted definition of what strategy is – but we know a lot less about translating a strategy into results. Books and articles on strategy outnumber those on execution by an order of magnitude. And what little has been written on execution tends to focus on tactics or generalize from a single case. So what do we know about strategy execution?
>
> (Sull et al., 2015: p. 60)

Strategy execution poses an immense leadership challenge, and yet very little advice and guidance appear in the literature. Kurt Verweire, this month's guest author, steps into this void, offering fresh insights and new perspectives into strategy implementation. The chapter is derived from his book *Strategy Implementation*, published by Routledge. Kurt acknowledges the enormity of the challenge faced by strategy execution and duly sets out to provide new thinking frames and ideas that will enable leaders to turn strategy into purposeful and focused action.

Drawing on his research, Dr Verweire develops sophisticated tools, models and frameworks for engaging with strategy execution. For example, in addition to strategy and alignment, he links organisational and contextual factors in order to develop a set of levers for achieving competitive advantage and a winning performance. Verweire stresses the critical role of commitment alongside strategy and alignment, thereby elevating human and organisational performance and motivational aspects to the enterprise level consideration as a determinant of successful execution. Commitment and involvement are influenced by how a firm is managed; achievement of strategic objectives relies on an organisation's ability to engender such commitment. Verweire's work considers the underpinning decisions that address fundamental strategic questions required for strategy formulation, and the role of strategic alignment in achieving strategic implementation. Through his writing and research, he has also enhanced established strategy concepts and developed a rich diversity of thinking models and support tools that enable leaders to cultivate performance-driven implementation.

Implementation and its purpose can be understood in different ways. Verweire's multiple perspectives encompass consideration of operational excellence, product leadership and customer intimacy, making it possible to consider different operating models and perspectives on performance and thereby enhance the meaning of effective implementation. Each of the perspectives requires different organisational and strategic arrangements; offering a diversity of thought and richness of detail not found elsewhere. Verweire's work is steeped in insights, delivering much-needed guidance for driving and leading the implementation journey. The range of choices and conceptual models available enables informed tailoring of solutions to the practical problems of implementation.

What next: The future of implementation

Success remains an important goal in the business arena. Success in innovation, projects and change initiatives does not come from breakthrough products, technologies or strategies. Success emerges through, and some time despite, the execution process. Given that success is not a promised destination but a guided journey, execution extends beyond intentions and constraints enabling participants to take advantage of emerging and unfolding conditions and insights.

> If common beliefs about execution are incomplete at best and dangerous at worst, what should take their place?
>
> (Sull et al., 2015: p. 66)

In closing their paper, Sull et al. (ibid.) agitate for new and fresh thinking around strategy execution, a concept that chimes with Verweire's reframing of the ideas of implementation.

> The starting point is a fundamental redefinition of execution as the ability to seize opportunities aligned with strategy while coordinating with other parts of the organization on an ongoing basis. Reframing execution in those terms can help managers pinpoint why it is stalling. Armed with a more comprehensive understanding, they can avoid pitfalls such as the

alignment trap and focus on the factors that matter most for translating strategy into results.

(Sull et al., 2015: p. 66)

Progressing the dialogue around strategy and its execution, and addressing the meaning of success in such contexts may benefit from new strands of thinking. For instance, Rumelt (2012) contends that a leader's most important responsibility is in identifying the biggest challenges to progress and devising a coherent approach to overcoming them. The direct implication is that strategies 'belong to' challenges, and not the organisation per se (MacLean & MacIntosh, 2015: p. 73). The most important aspect of crafting a strategy may well be the articulation and framing of the challenge likely to be faced in order to avoid 'solving the wrong problems with intricate but inaccurate solutions' (Mitroff & Silvers, 2010). Thinking more widely, an alternative framing may well focus on the great opportunity, the range of uncovered options, or the emerging potential embedded within a new perspective, insight or discovery.

The direct implication may lie in liberating the strategy exploration process from a tightly coupled and rationally planned alignment towards a more emergent and flexible arrangement that is capable of changing course, responding to challenges, recognising the great opportunities and delivering an increasingly pertinent, meaningful, and dare we say, value-based execution. In doing so, we may begin the journey towards envisaging, establishing and delivering a more enduring vision of innovative and strategic success enabled through our execution discipline.

References

Beer, M., & Eisenstat, R. A. (2000). The silent killers of strategy implementation and learning. *Sloan Management Review, 41*(4), 29–40.

Bossidy, L., & Charan, R. (2002). *Execution: The discipline of getting things done*. London: Random House.

Hamel, G. (2002). *Leading the revolution: How to thrive in turbulent times by making innovation a way of life* (updated edition). Boston, MA: Harvard Business School Press.

MacLean, D., & MacIntosh, R. (2015). Planning reconsidered: Paradox, poetry and people at the edge of strategy. *European Management Journal, 33*(2), 72–78.

Mitroff, I. I., & Silvers, A. (2010). *Dirty rotten strategies: How we trick ourselves and others into solving the wrong problems precisely*. Palo Alto, CA: Stanford University Press.

Neilson, G. L., Martin, K. L., & Powers, E. (2008). The secrets to successful strategy execution. *Harvard Business Review, 86*(6), 60–71.

Rumelt, R. P. (2012). *Good strategy/bad strategy: The difference and why it matters*. London: Profile Books.

Sull, D., Homkes, R., & Sull, C. (2015). Why strategy execution unravels–and what to do about it. *Harvard Business Review, 93*(3), 57–66.

Verweire, K. (2014). *Strategy implementation*. New York: Routledge.

The challenges of implementing strategy

Kurt Verweire

Strategy implementation is a hot topic today. Managers spend billions of dollars on consulting and training in the hope of creating brilliant strategies. But all too often brilliant strategies do not translate into brilliant performance. Strategy implementation ranks high on top managers' agendas but is a topic that has not received sufficient attention in the academic world. It seems like academics assume that if a firm has a strategy, it gets implemented automatically. But talk with managers and most will admit that their organisation is experiencing significant problems with translating their strategy into concrete activities and results.

Why do so many companies struggle with strategy implementation? And what can be done about it? In this chapter, I first present five root causes why strategy implementation is so hard. Some of these root causes deal with the quality of the strategy itself, the others deal with the topic of implementation. Then I present a new model that tackles many of these issues. This model consists of three building blocks and is called the Strategy-Alignment-Commitment model. The chapter zooms in on each of the three building blocks and provides useful suggestions on how to increase the success rate of your strategy implementation programs.

Why do strategy implementation initiatives fail?

In my discussions with managers who struggle with strategy implementation, I have discovered that there are five root causes for an unsuccessful strategy implementation:

Too much focus on financials in strategy discussions. Strategy implementation only succeeds if a company has a well-formulated strategy in the first place. In reality, however, few companies have a genuine strategy. According to Michael Porter (2006) – one of the most influential writers in the field – managers often rely on a flawed definition of strategy. For example, managers confuse strategy with aspiration. How many times have we heard or read: 'Our strategy is to be #1 or #2 in that particular industry', or 'Our strategy is to grow shareholder value by 30% in the next three years'. But those statements are not strategies – they're goals or aspirations. These statements say what the company wants to be or achieve, not *how* it will get there. Goals are important, but they do not substitute for strategy. Great strategies provide guidance and coherence to the organisation; financial goals, unfortunately, do not!

Functional strategies are no substitute for a business strategy. One of the major reasons why it's difficult to reach consensus on a clear business strategy is that the focus in many organisations is on the development of functional strategies. Companies have a strategy for operations, for sales, for marketing, for HR and so on. But the more you break strategy up into various functional strategies, the less likely you will have a winning business strategy. There is a great risk for sub-optimisation and conflicts among departments over resources and conflicting goals.

Strategy implementation is too fragmented. While companies face significant problems formulating a compelling strategy, the issue of strategy implementation itself also poses some challenges. What actually is strategy implementation? Some management authors see strategy implementation as a performance measurement and management exercise, where you translate strategies into key performance indicators that you cascade further down in the organisation. Others see strategy implementation as creating an organisational culture that empowers people to act in line with the strategy. And still others see implementation as strategic project portfolio management. As I will show later, strategy implementation is all of that, and even more. Too often managers address only one item of the whole strategy implementation challenge, and they tackle execution in a way that is too fragmented.

Managers communicate about strategy but forget to translate strategy into action. While strategy implementation is about aligning different activities, it is also about creating commitment throughout the entire organisation. Commitment is created when employees see where and how they can make a difference and are stimulated to take action within the boundaries set by the strategy. But it takes time to create an organisational context that stimulates widespread action-taking. All too often, managers do not take the time to create that context.

Strategy implementation requires leadership capabilities. The four points outlined above indicate that the implementation job requires leaders, not just managers (De Flander, 2010). Strategy implementation is not about delegating the bits and pieces of a strategy to the functional managers, so that the marketing manager tackles the marketing issues and the operations manager manages the operational issues. The Chief Implementation Officer should be the business manager, or at least somebody from the business management team. Strategy implementation is difficult because it forces people to change their behaviour. So, it's a job that should not be delegated to lower-level managers.

The Strategy-Alignment-Commitment Model

Over the last few years, I've conducted extensive research on how firms turn strategy into results. From my research findings, I've constructed a model,

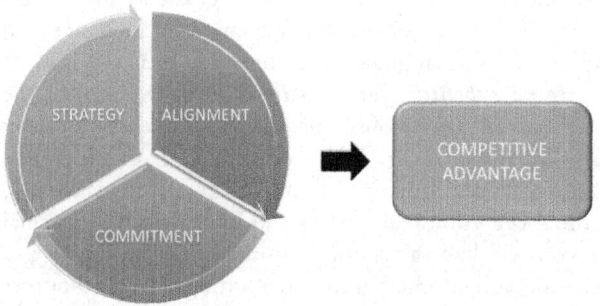

Figure 8.1 Strategy implementation model.

shown in Figure 8.1, to capture the essential elements of what constitutes effective strategy implementation. Although there is no step-by-step formula to turn strategies into great results, I have seen common patterns in how companies implement winning strategies and translate them into great performance.

In order to achieve a competitive advantage, firms need a clear, winning *strategy*. A winning strategy makes the choices explicit that the company has made to win in the marketplace. The second component is called *alignment* and defines which activities your company should set up to make the strategy concrete. Successful firms spend time to build up a powerful management infrastructure that facilitates the implementation of the strategy. The last lever to achieve competitive advantage – *commitment* – is often overlooked in the strategic management literature. What is the behaviour that winning companies instil in their organisation? We should not forget that strategy implementation takes place within an organisational environment that is shaped by the leaders of the organisation. It is that organisational environment that produces the behaviour that you can observe in companies (Markides, 2000; 2004).

Developing a winning business strategy

Effective strategy implementation only occurs if the quality of the strategy is high. In the numerous strategy workshops I've done with executive teams, I've learned that 80 percent struggle not only with the implementation but also with the formulation challenge. In the previous section, I already argued that a strategy is different from a goal. A business strategy outlines how to achieve the goals. Only after a firm has developed a business strategy should it develop functional strategies.

A business strategy is a coherent, integrated set of choices that addresses four fundamental questions, as presented in Figure 8.2: (1) Who do we serve? (2) What do we provide? (3) What is our value proposition? And (4) What is our operating model?

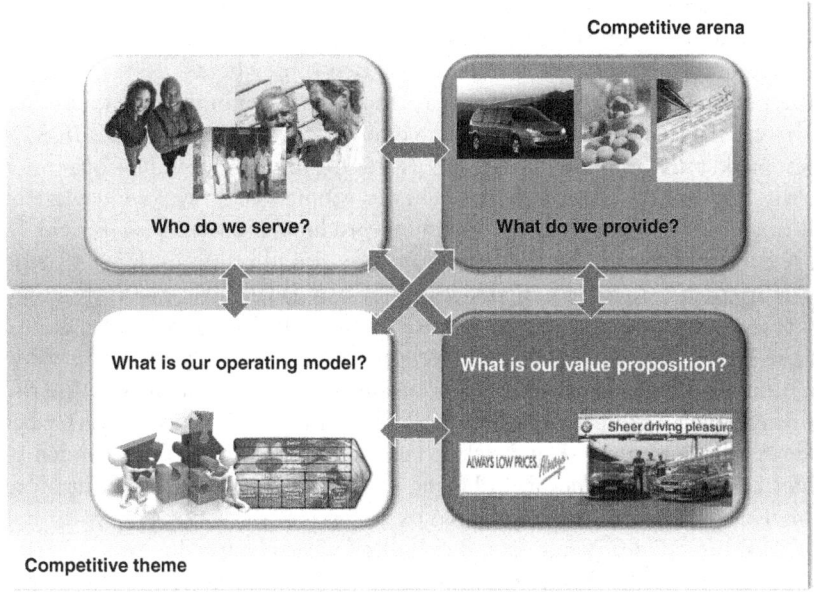

Figure 8.2 Vlerick Strategy Formulation Framework.

The answers to the first two questions specify where a company wants to play – they set the firm's *competitive arena*. For example, easyJet and Ryanair have carved out a very specific competitive arena in the European airline industry. Both companies have chosen to provide point-to-point flights on short-haul routes in Europe and the Mediterranean region. EasyJet and Ryanair do not fly to the United States or to Asia, nor do they offer cargo or any other services. The motorcycle market provides another example. Ducati has focused on the sport bike market, in which its customers are 'racing aficionados' who seek extreme performance and top functionality. Harley-Davidson, on the other hand, is strong in the cruiser and touring bike market, and its customers are the 'easy riders' who associate the motorcycle with a particular lifestyle.

The questions 'What is our value proposition' and 'What is our operating model' force a company to specify how it can win in its chosen competitive arena. Answers to these questions describe the *competitive theme* to both customers and employees. Customers are interested in a good value proposition, while employees need to understand what the company's operating model is. The *Strategy Implementation* book (Verweire, 2014) provides some interesting frameworks and exercises to help you to make the necessary choices here.

Answering these questions implies that managers can articulate who not to serve, and what not to provide. Furthermore, it's important to define what is not your value proposition – where are you happy to follow the competition – and what is not your operating model. The essence of strategy is choosing what not to do. A proper strategy sets boundaries for what activities the organisation does and does not perform. I have the feeling that most managers opt for being mediocre everywhere rather than being the best somewhere.

It is not only important to make clear choices for each of the four questions, but it's crucial that the answers form a coherent whole. For example, IKEA's target market ('whom do we serve') is young, primarily white-collar, not wealthy, and likely to have children. These customers can buy a wide range of well-designed, functional home furnishing products ('what do we provide'). IKEA attracts customers by providing low-priced but stylish products. Its customers are treated to a fun experience as they wander through a visually exciting store. They can take the item home or have it delivered the same day, because IKEA carries an extensive inventory at each store ('what is our value proposition'). IKEA is able to meet its customers' needs profitably because the company benefits from economies of scale and efficiencies of replication ('what is our operating model') (Hambrick & Fredrickson, 2001). Although much of its low-cost position comes from having the customers assemble the furniture themselves, IKEA offers a number of extra services that competitors do not offer. In-store childcare and extended hours ('what is our value proposition') are perfectly aligned with the needs of its target segment. In summary, coherence is essential to achieve a competitive advantage.

Implementing strategy through alignment

Once a clear strategy is defined, a company needs to take actions in support of that strategy. An organisation can be seen as interconnected sets of processes – and processes are a collection of tasks and activities that together transform inputs into outputs. Within organisations, inputs and outputs can be materials, information and people (Garvin, 1998). I have identified five major sets of processes, shown in Figure 8.3, that managers must master to make strategy work. These are the five substantive levers you must pull to make strategy happen, and they constitute our Strategy Implementation Framework.

Direction and goal setting processes include those processes that translate the strategy into clear departmental goals, targets and action plans.

Operational processes are the processes that create, produce and deliver the products and services that the company provides; they generate the revenues for the organisation. Michael Porter calls them the primary activities.

Support processes help improve the effectiveness and efficiency of the operational processes. They do not produce output for external customers, but are necessary for running the business. Support activities include workforce planning and resource allocation, information technology support, and the definition of rules and methods in order to facilitate internal communication.

Evaluation and control processes ensure that the organisation is performing as planned. They detect perturbations, initiate corrective action and restore the

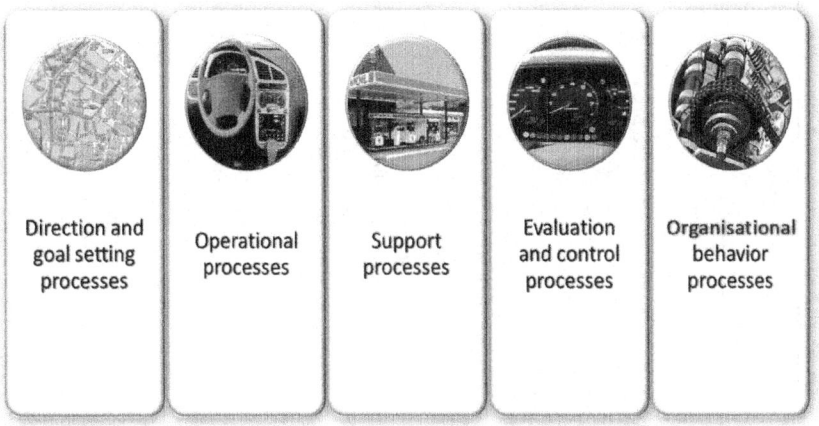

Figure 8.3 Vlerick Strategy Formulation Framework (De Cnudde et al., 2004).

organisation to its previous equilibrium. Audit, risk management and management control are examples of evaluation and control processes.

Organisational behaviour processes affect the form, substance and character of operational processes by shaping how they are carried out. These processes direct motives, influence and attitudes.

Alignment means that an organisation takes actions in line with its competitive theme, as defined by its strategy. Table 8.2 illustrates that when organisations choose different competitive themes, they should also emphasise different sets of actions. In other words, the management infrastructure for building an operational excellence organisation is very different from building a product leadership or customer intimacy organisation.

In my book *Strategy Implementation* (Verweire, 2014), I've built toolkits that calculate the level of alignment for each of the three models and I have found significant correlations between the level of alignment and financial performance. Companies that have set up a powerful management infrastructure have higher sales growth and higher margins. I found significant correlations in my three databases – the operational excellence, the product leadership and the customer intimacy database. So alignment matters!

Implementing strategy through commitment

While the concept of strategic alignment is well known in the strategic management literature, the concept of commitment is a rather neglected aspect of strategy implementation. Nevertheless, if managers want to implement a strategy successfully, they must also create an appropriate organisational environment that facilitates the implementation of that strategy.

Table 8.2 The power of alignment

	Operational excellence	Product leadership	Customer intimacy
Competitive theme	Best price Best access ('are we fast, easy and painless?')	Best product	Best service Best connectivity (relationship orientation)
Direction and goal setting	Efficiency through process thinking Zero-defect service	Best product through continuous product innovation Clear innovation strategy: where to place our bets?	Understanding the broader problem Having expertise about the customers' business Customers carefully selected
Operational processes	The operations department drives the company Attention paid to process speed and quality	R&D is key: idea management is important Marketing is also key: educate people with a missionary zeal Get engineers, designers and marketers systematically together	Demonstrate expertise and experience Strengthen the relationship with your key customers Build loyalty: focus on customer retention
Support processes	Highly automated processes Information systems increase control and coordination and streamline tasks World-class supply chain management	Clear innovation governance process Systematic process for allocating resources to innovation programs Knowledge sharing and networks	Systematic collection of customer and market information (through Customer Relationship Management)
Evaluation and control processes	Rigid, centralised control Detailed measures on various aspects of the process Setting higher thresholds	Innovation performance measures Control, learning and experimentation	Detailed measures about account penetration and loyalty Lifetime value of the customer
Organisational behaviour processes	Centralised structure Organisation structured around core processes Culture of continuous improvement	Fluid organisation structure Stimulate diversity, tolerate mavericks Low levels of formalisation Entrepreneurial culture	Decentralised organisation Employee retention Go the extra mile for customers who deserve it

One of the key lessons of my research is that firms can be classified not only according to their competitive theme and their operating model – operational excellence, customer intimacy, product leadership or none-of-these-three – but also by their *management maturity* level. The management maturity is the extent to which operational and management processes are set up and managed so that managers and employees are committed to making strategy work. The concept of 'maturity' was borrowed from the various Capability and Maturity Models (CMM) that are applied to management processes such as software development, HR, process management, strategic management and innovation.

I have identified four levels of maturity for strategy implementation: (1) the entrepreneurial organisation, (2) the structured organisation, (3) the connected organisation and (4) the committed organisation. The four maturity levels present four different stages of organisational development. Organisations always start as entrepreneurial organisations, but they can advance over time to the next level and become structured organisations. Some organisations move on to Level 3 and become connected. A minority even make it to the last level – the level of the committed organisation. The higher the maturity level, the more organisations build a powerful context for strategy implementation.

In the entrepreneurial phase, the emphasis is on creating both a product and a market. There is no clear strategy and there are no clear goals. Attention is paid to operational issues, but this leads to short-termism and often a lack of strategic insights. Do not bother managers of entrepreneurial organisations with advanced planning and control systems. In such an organisation, formal planning is minimal or even non-existent. Entrepreneurial organisations are very flexible and agile, and can be successful if an enthusiastic crew is in place to help grow the company. My research has shown that about 40 percent of firms can be classified as 'entrepreneurial'.

When firms reach a particular stage – let's say the company has grown to 50 or 100 employees – this entrepreneurial mindset can become a liability rather than an asset. In that case, managers start to pay more attention to managing the company more professionally. In this stage, the company has grown large enough to require functional managers. The organisation is no longer a collection of individuals but a *collection of departments*. The company introduces strategic planning, separates and structures the core activities and gradually builds supporting activities. The operational budget is the main *control and evaluation* tool. Financial performance data are collected on a regular basis. Adding structure to an organisation is not necessarily a bad thing, but some organisations grow into rigid bureaucracies that lack flexibility and suffer from a silo mentality. In those over-structured organisations, the enemy is no longer the competition; instead, it is the people from the sales department, or the employees of the back office. Forty percent of companies qualify as structured – and sometimes over-structured – organisations.

Firms can tackle this challenge by moving to the next maturity level. In a connected organisation, a company starts to think and act strategically.

Business managers are increasingly aware that success is achieved not only when departments perform well but when they perform well *together*. The organisation is no longer a collection of departments: the managers connect the departments around a competitive theme. Such firms build integration mechanisms to link the operational and management activities of the various departments. Managers make clear strategic choices and discuss how this strategy impacts the rest of the organisation, e.g., in performance management and in training and selection. This creates a positive organisational climate, in which managers from different levels take action and are committed to delivering results. The output is what counts. (In bureaucratic organisations, it is the input that counts.)

Some firms take the next step to reach the final maturity level. But my research has shown this is only a minority of companies – only around 2 percent of companies – would become 'committed'. The organisation is no longer a connection of departments, but a *connection of individuals*. This is a truly exceptional organisation. Bound together by a strong set of values, there is a drive to continuously perform better throughout the entire organisation. In a committed organisation, responsibilities and authorities are assigned to the lowest hierarchical levels. All employees are closely involved in monitoring the results and are encouraged to provide suggestions for improving performance. The employees work closely together in teams and 'delegating' is an important leadership attribute. Leaders and employees are engaged in a continuous dialogue founded on a team-based culture.

In 2006 I conducted a research project to empirically test whether management maturity and performance are correlated. In that research project, I examined the financial results of a large sample of Belgian insurance companies and investigated what drove the performance of Belgian insurance companies. The study showed that management maturity was positively correlated to the profitability of the insurance companies (Verweire et al., 2006).

Alignment and commitment as drivers of success

My research has shown that alignment and commitment are correlated. Companies with high levels of alignment also have a more mature management infrastructure. Maturity helps a company to achieve higher levels of alignment.

Figure 8.4 shows that the true product leaders, customer intimacy firms and operational excellence organisations are at least connected or committed. Entrepreneurial firms or structured firms often have not made clear choices with regard to their value proposition and operating model. Entrepreneurial firms do not see the need to make these choices; they are too occupied with solving operational issues or they have not yet specified their competitive arena. Structured organisations find it difficult to make these choices because they are too inward-focused. They're working on professionalising and structuring their organisation, but they often forget to take the customer's perspective into consideration.

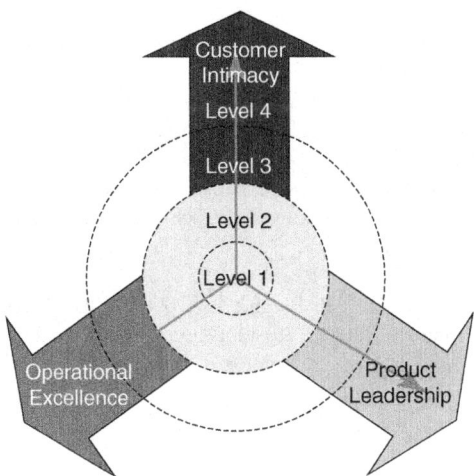

Figure 8.4 Linking alignment with commitment.

Conclusion

Strategy implementation is an important but challenging topic for managers today. In this chapter, I have explained why this is the case. I have listed five major root causes why firms struggle. Some of the root causes deal with the quality of the strategy, others deal with the quality of the implementation efforts. A final one deals with the quality of the leaders, a topic that we have not tackled in great detail here.

Despite decades of management publications and consulting help, firms still struggle with defining a clear and winning strategy. This is caused partly by the lack of clarity as to what constitutes a genuine strategy, and partly because the essence of strategy is choice; and many managers hate to make choices.

In this chapter, I have elaborated on the implementation challenge. I have argued that strategy implementation is about creating alignment and commitment. Both concepts are powerful notions that can help companies to get better results, even in today's turbulent times.

References

De Cnudde, P., Hindryckx, B., Bauwens, M., Carrette, B., & Verweire, K. (2004). Introducing maturity alignment: Basic concepts. In K. Verweire, & L. A. A. Van den Berghe (Eds.), *Integrated performance management: A guide to strategy implementation*. London: Sage Publications Ltd.

De Flander, J. (2010). *Strategy execution heroes: Business strategy implementation and strategic management demystified*. Brussels: The performance factory.

Garvin, D. A. (1998). The processes of organization and management. *Sloan Management Review*, Summer, 33–50.

Hambrick, D. C., & Fredrickson, J. W. (2001). Are you sure you have a strategy? *The Academy of Management Executive*, *15*(4), 48–59.

Markides, C. C. (2000). *All the right moves*. Boston, MA: Harvard Business School Press.

Markides, C. C. (2004). What is strategy and how do you know if you have one? *Business Strategy Review*, *15*(2), 5–12.

Porter, M. (2006). Michael Porter asks, and answers: Why good managers set bad strategies. Knowledge@Wharton, 1 November 2006, http://knowledge.wharton.upenn.edu/article.cfm?articleid=1594, accessed 14 December 2018.

Verweire, K. (2014). *Strategy implementation*. New York: Routledge.

Verweire, K., Roelandt, P., De Grande, J., & Van den Berghe, L. (2006). What drives performance in the Belgian insurance industry? *Research Report*. Gent: Vlerick Business.

9

Connecting

Conclusion

Connecting for business and social innovation

Darren Dalcher

According to the Oxford Dictionary, to connect is 'to bring together or into contact so that a real or notional link is established', or 'to associate or relate something in some respect'. The derivation appears to be from Late Middle English in the sense of being united physically. The dictionary further adds that the etymological root is from the Latin *connectere*, in the form of con – which implies 'together', and nectere, to 'bind'. The Cambridge English Dictionary simply explains to connect as 'to join or be joined with something else', while the Merriam Webster Dictionary offers the brief definition 'to join (two or more things) together'.

Connecting can thus be defined as joining, linking or being joined. Over time the use of the term appears to have expanded from a physical sense of binding together to a more logical set of connections that are being made between objects, things and people. The Oxford English Dictionary thus defines a connection as a 'relationship in which a person or thing is linked or associated with something else', while the Cambridge Dictionary relates to 'the state of being related to someone or something else'. The Oxford Dictionary also provides a somewhat more contemporary definition of connections, as 'people with whom one has social or professional contact or to whom one is related, especially those with influence and able to offer one help'.

The transformation of *connecting* from a physical-material point of view towards a more social sphere appears to be in train. In the age of social media, connecting can enable new forms of arranging, organising and engaging for novel types of action and improvement. Ultimately, connecting can enable radical and beneficial transformation that empowers change subjects to engage, influence and shape whilst ensuring that communities buy into, co-create and make use of the budding change.

Projects for the community: The Eden Project

The Eden Project, located near St. Austell on a site of a former china clay mine, is an extremely popular visitor attraction in Cornwall, England. The £141m project to reclaim and regenerate a neglected brownfield site, in Cornwall, which has the UK's highest proportion of derelict mines, was the brainchild of Sir Tim Smit. Sir Tim previously restored the Lost Gardens of Heligan in Cornwall, neglected since the Second World War, which gave him the inspiration to create the regenerative concept of the Eden Project (Petherick, Eclare & Smit, 2004; Smit, 1999; 2016).

The Eden Project is a dramatic global garden housed in tropical biomes that nestle in a crater the size of 30 football pitches. The two enormous biomes consist of hundreds of hexagonal and pentagonal inflated plastic cells, supported by a steel framework. The site, which was opened in March 2001, has welcomed its 20 millionth visitor in 2018. The Eden Project, often marketed as the eighth wonder of the world, affords a gateway to the relationship between people and plants, offering a fascinating insight into the story of mankind's connection to and dependence on plant life (Eden, 2016).

The Eden Project is a new kind of visitor garden. The rainforest biome, the world's largest greenhouse and indoor rainforest at 3.9 acres, enables visitors to experience the sights, smells and scale of the rainforests and to discover the tropical plants that are used to produce everyday products from fruiting banana, coffee and rubber plants to giant bamboo. The Mediterranean biome offers the chance to explore more temperate and arid climates, including lemon trees, olive groves and gnarled vines, while the 30-acre outdoor botanical garden offers the opportunity to see tea, lavender, hops, hemp, sunflower and other plants that will change our future, flourishing under the Cornish sun.

The Eden Project recognises, and shares, the importance of sustainability to local communities and takes into account the economic, environmental and social benefits to be considered when making decisions. It has improved the image of the local area and rapidly transformed a derelict former mine into one of the UK's top tourist destinations, averaging well over a million visitors per year and contributing in excess of £2 billion to the Cornish economy. It employs over 700 local people, the majority of whom were previously unemployed, and uses over 2,500 local farmers and suppliers. Indeed, all food and drink is locally sourced from Cornwall and the South West. The project has transformed the local economy, decreased unemployment by 6 percent and introduced a growing demand for holidays and accommodation, whilst also boosting attendance at the other local and regional attractions and resorts.

The Eden Project is fast emerging as a unique resource for education, knowledge and innovation towards a sustainable future. The latest addition to the site is the Core, a sustainable education centre built to educate future generations, as well as businesses and entrepreneurs, about the benefits of sustainable development.

The core has been built as an education facility incorporating classrooms and exhibition spaces designed to convey the central message about the relationship between people and plants. The building has taken its inspiration from plants, capped by the soaring timber roof, which gives the building its distinctive shape. Schools and other groups can utilise the facility for extended periods and are also welcome to make use of the local youth hostel which was specially made out of repurposed shipping containers.

The Core is also a home to art exhibitions and special projects and installations, which support the educational mission of the facility. The Eden Project offers environmental education focusing on the interdependence of plants and people. It is also concerned with generating a better understanding of how humans can 'manage' behaviours and ecosystems to live more sustainably, thereby complementing the physical facility with long-term education and improved understanding and skills related to responsible and sustainable practices.

The Eden Project: Global impact and vision

Revolutions come in different shapes and sizes… The success of the Eden Project has encouraged wider aspirations and further initiatives. In order to continue to raise environmental consciousness across the globe, the newly established Eden Project International Foundation will sprout spinoff centres in an English motorway service station, a Tasmanian warehouse, a Chinese docklands and amongst the giant sequoia trees of the Sierra Nevada mountains of the US (Kennedy, 2017). The grand vision is for a collection of oases of change that will engender a fever of excitement and wonder about our interconnection to the natural world.

The intention is not to create a string of theme parks, but instead to offer the space for observation, reflection and thinking. The projects can thus tackle different domains and challenges. For example, a future project on the River Foyle in Derry, the second largest city in Northern Ireland, is intended to link three old walled gardens – one catholic, one protestant and one state-owned. The centres aim to continue to challenge thinking on sustainability, and the one planned for the motorway services at Junction 27 of the M5 motorway will be linked to the railway station of Tiverton Parkway, Devon with visitors arriving by fast train and hiring electric cars to explore the surrounding countryside. According to Sir Tim, the intention is to create 'the best motorway service station in the world' (ibid.).

But the most immediate plans are for establishing a new centre in China. Construction will begin in 2018 on Eden Qingdao, the port city on the east coast of China. The new facility will cost £150m and focus on the theme of water and its importance for life. It is due to open to the public in 2020 and to feature the world's highest indoor waterfall, matching the height of the Niagara Falls (Morris, 2018). The site secured for the project is a large area of reclaimed and damaged land originally used for salt production at the confluence of two rivers and will feature a large biome and a series of streams and lakes. It is hoped that the site will encourage environmental and sustainability consideration and a reflection on the role of water and its relationship with human society.

Future plans for additional centres in China include: a new facility in the city of Yan'an – the place where Mao Zedong's Long March came to an end – to transform a blighted valley just outside the city into a showcase for agriculture, craft and education; the conversion of a former limestone mine near Tianjin into an environmental centre and a further development for the Sheng Lu vineyard in Beijing, to fight the persistent opaque local fog pollution (Kennedy, 2017) and provide an oasis for citizens wishing to reconnect with nature (Morris, 2018).

Creative community engagement: The Eden Project

Engagement extends beyond space and physical facilities. The transformation of the scarred landscape in Cornwall and the creation of the Eden Project biomes were only the early part of the activities emerging from the mission to engage with the public around the area of sustainability. Success beyond the actual delivery of the assets requires continued attention to usage and the value that is being delivered. Attracting over 20 million visitors in the first 17 years of operation implies success not just in the delivery but also in establishing and embedding the new facilities and in attracting significant usage patterns. However, the Eden Project mission to engage goes deeper than visitor numbers. Environmental education provides additional business and engagement activities, however, the educational facilities and new relationships forged from the use of the facility generate novel opportunities for engagement and development.

The Eden Project is developing new ways for engaging with visitors, as well as with the wider community, by taking some of what has worked in their facility into new neighbourhoods and areas. The use of art, music, story telling, humour and hands-on activities has proved effective in engaging both individual visitors and complete communities and plays a key part in involving people in influencing the future of where they live. Many of the ideas and approaches developed by the Eden Project have been applied in planning events for local improvement in Cornwall and beyond, and in other developmental initiatives.

The range of activities is re-shaping the ideas for engagement with communities, encompassing, for example:

- Drop-in community planning days, designed like local fêtes;
- Film-making workshops with local stakeholders;
- Learning journeys to other communities; and
- Practical training on everything from gardening to business skills.

The philosophy that underpins the events extends beyond the normal focus on the products and artefacts of consultation and engagement, placing a greater focus on the processes that lead to engagement. Indeed, a process view has the potential to enable a longer-term engagement with participants, stakeholder groups and communities and support the building of long-term relationships and meaningful alliances.

The benefits of the ambition to value the process of engagement over specific artefacts and products include the ability to:

- **Establish a real sense of participation**: by giving people tangible ways to provide input to the day, such as setting up 'washing lines' or 'rant pinboards' where they can add their comments.
- **Encourage new people to get involved**: by reaching out to as many age groups as possible by providing a convivial setting (often with tea, cake and bunting!) in a venue that's easily accessible.
- **Inspire new thinking**: by creating an inspirational space and offering practical activities – such as contributing to ideas scrapbooks – and trying to raise people's aspirations of what may be possible.
- **Catalyse partnerships**: by convening different people, from residents to service providers to community groups, in a neutral space where they can find common ground.

The discussions and engagement resulting from the creative approaches to engage and involve potential partners and participants enable communities to kick start meaningful conversations about where people live and work and get involved in neighbourhood planning and environmental improvement initiatives. More crucially, they play a part in enabling people to reflect upon, communicate about and even begin to co-shape their future.

There are many examples of initiatives where the use of Eden expertise had enabled participants to transform traditional planning models. One example is the case of seven local Cornish towns, which have worked with an established theatre company to develop new ways to engage with a wider community about future improvements. The idea of *Imaginary Journeys* enabled the seven locations to: provide access to the arts across Cornwall, and build and communicate with new audiences and support town-centre regeneration. Under the scheme, 24 local artists used town-centre premises ranging from empty shops to community centres to apply and develop the metaphor of a travel agency to encourage interaction with non-traditional arts audiences. As the project was drawn from the community, each of the localities developed its own sense of ownership and perspective, which were reflected in their particular installation. The value of the activities was in exploring the pride of place in the local community, valuing memory and the past, facilitating the imaginative expression of dreams, hopes and aspirations and imagining potential futures.

Other initiatives utilised creative techniques to: design nature-based play space for local families in Ayr, build a recreation ground in Kingsbridge, devise better outdoor play access on the Lizard Peninsula and the Isle of Scilly, strengthen community links in the West Midlands, use outdoor activities to connect older people in care homes with their local community or make use of empty space in the East End of London. The success of the engagement activities was in being able to offer new perspectives, ideas and inspiration for new endeavours and in instilling future-focused and community-aware methods for thinking about, planning for, co-creating and engaging with a better future.

Connect to lead

Other businesses continue to grapple with their role in public engagement. Lord John Browne of Madingely, former Chief Executive of BP and President of the Royal Academy of Engineering, observes a significantly altered business landscape. Reflecting on the big rift between big business and the rest of society, he identifies a critical and urgent need for business to connect with society in order to avoid the mistakes of the past (Browne, Nuttall & Stadlen, 2016: p. x). Lord Browne recognises an enormous potential prize for the companies, which choose to meet the new demands for unremitting transparency with respect, authenticity and openness so that they can reflect society's needs as part of their changing business model. The new imperative is for companies to directly connect with society.

The business environment is increasingly becoming more demanding. Mirvis and Googins (2017) assert that businesses face three interlocking challenges:

- Shareholder demands for growth;
- Employee desire for meaning from work; and
- Rising public expectations to address social, economic, and environmental concerns.

> A renewed connection with the external world is only possible if business people are willing to adopt an entirely new attitude. They need … to engage radically. This means being brave enough to embrace genuine openness, far sighted enough to make friends before they need them and to communicate in a language that exudes authenticity rather than propaganda.
>
> (Browne et al., 2016: p. xv)

Browne puts forward a simple agenda in the form of four fundamental tenets needed to underpin the new relationship and connect with the external world. The framework is based on the collective wisdom and reflection of a group of senior leaders engaged during a two-year research effort. Framed as *connected leadership*, it calls for the integration of societal and environmental considerations into core-business decision making at every level of the company. Connected leadership is predicated on engaging effectively and sustainably with the external world through four basic tenets (Browne et al., 2016: p. 14):

- Map your world;
- Define your contribution;

- Apply world-class management; and
- Engage radically.

Browne agitates for the development of a constructive alliance between business and society. While the specific issues may change and the cultural values of participants may evolve, the fundamental importance of a constructive alliance will remain critically essential to address the needs of both parties. He notes that succeeding at applying the four tenets requires a profoundly different point of view and the courage to question the status quo.

> I am acutely aware that when I succeeded in business it was so often because I engaged effectively and sustainably with the external world. When I failed it was usually because I got this wrong. My ambition is to change the way people think about business. Business is the most powerful tool we possess in our quest for progress and prosperity. In my view we need to take more care of it, whether we are executives inside companies, citizens observing from outside or government leaders tasked with oversight.
>
> (ibid.: p. 15)

New forms of creative engagement are possible as has been proven by the Eden Project and other progressive organisations trying to bridge the gap and engage stakeholders and the wider community in radical new ways.

The new business imperative: People rising

Connected leadership offers the potential to connect and shape in meaningful new ways. However, Lord Browne identifies three major forthcoming shifts that will accelerate the imperative to connect business with society. The shifts, which are likely to fundamentally alter the relationship between business and society and will therefore need to be addressed proactively, are (ibid.: p. 215):

1 **The rise of disruptive technologies in general and of artificial intelligence (AI) in particular**: While AI promises radical solutions, it places extraordinary power in corporate hands and could trigger a new level of distrust in organisations.
2 **The shift in the economic centre of gravity towards emerging economies**: The main theatre of action for interaction between big business and society will be in the emerging new world replete with attitudes and cultures which are altogether different from those of the West.
3 **The emergence of a new global generation that will demand more than ever from business**: The demand is likely to be fuelled by increasing wealth, education and access to information, as well as shrinking government budgets. The growth of emerging markets will further add to the pool of potential commentators, critics, stakeholders and interested participants.

These three trends will change the nature of the business–society relationship, creating a moving target that even the most enlightened companies will have to chase with a commitment to renewal and learning. Above all, the trends will amplify the relevance of this relationship to the successful future of both sides.

(ibid.: p. 215)

There appears to be one additional factor that merits consideration: The growing impact, availability, accessibility and power of **technology** appears to add a further complicating factor that can underpin, support and give a voice to wider communities. Technology can also play a part in exposing, and then sharing widely practices that are not compatible with the wishes of the community, the values that it holds or the expectations that it may harbour. Moreover, technology can provide a platform through social media for campaigning, commenting, influencing and participating that can drive the agenda and empower society, or even small players and specific interest groups within it, to object to or battle companies in new and far more public ways.

Nonetheless, technology can ultimately provide the best response and the means for effective and engaged campaigns to address concerns and mismatches. In this way technology can deliver the infrastructure, provide the means to engage and also determine the future for the interactions, relationship and connections between business and the community. In other words, technology certainly appears to have the potential to shape the relationship of business to its various stakeholders.

Technology: Placing people at the core

What are the implications of the newfound emphasis on technology?

Given that we find ourselves in a post information age, with technology enabling organisations to report, chart, analyse and potentially and controversially even influence and determine, does technology have a mediating role in our relationship with society? Given its aggregating capacity and overseeing perspective, does it rule out or diminish the influence of people?

Ultimately, with the rising importance of technology, is the age of the individual over?

The chapter by Dale Roberts endeavours to respond to the challenge and address the impact and role of technology. The chapter is based on Dale Roberts' and Rooven Pakkiri's book *Decision Sourcing: Decision Making for the Agile Social Enterprise*, published by Routledge. Roberts recognises the liberating impact of the digital economy, yet, rather than focus on the products, structures and processes, he places the focus on the way business organises, communicates and behaves.

Technology enables unprecedented levels of interaction and connection but has been used to cement and institutionalise structures and procedures arresting the potential for significant development. The widely popular process–centric perspective on management begets individual transactions; Roberts laments the transactional nature of business relationships with customers, pointing instead to technology as an enabler and facilitator. Indeed, ignoring the connection potential of social technologies imperils organisations that are not attuned to their consumers. Social tools offer businesses the possibility to become more human and Roberts makes a case for wider interaction within systems as a preferred mode of explaining and planning for connections.

Agile aficionados may recognise the manifesto call for people over process, but the narrative adopts a historical orientation to consider the shifting balance between the process and people within the business. Through his discussion, Roberts raises some thought-provoking issues related to connections, relationships and how we position things, such as how consumers and customers may feel about being included in some company's selling cycle, instead of driving their own initiated buying endeavour that they may wish to shape and direct.

The key contribution of Roberts' thesis is in drawing attention to how decisions are made within organisations. Transactions support hierarchical structures and formal decisions by the highest established authority. Yet, the emergence of social technology enables a richer diversity of views, opinions and participants; it also encourages the concerned parties to become involved. In other words, social technologies provide the glue needed to connect the business with its internal participants, external stakeholders and other relevant parties. While his work offers insights regarding social listening, engaged decisions and the relationship between different technologies and the level of interaction, it brings home the need to consider how decisions can be sourced and improved.

Participation comes at different levels and Roberts is therefore able to identify the diverse roles of contributors. Broader participation as advocated through his writing enables better-informed and more creative forms of inclusive decision making as befits a changing social and business context. Social technology supports broad and more representative participation in decision making. Social technology can thus be utilised to facilitate wider inclusion and improve decisions that can be sourced through collaboration with wider communities of interested individuals and groups. It also offers the potential to engage the workforce, customers and other interest groups and begin to envisage new ways of making better-informed and more comprehensive decisions whilst trying to create a better future. Crucially, therefore, technology puts people back in the driving seat, ready and able to participate, shape, influence, drive and deliver. Rather than signal the end of individual participation, social media and technology are thus able to position people at the very core of beneficial and relevant change efforts.

Connecting with people and communities

Social tools challenge organisations and hierarchies. As Roberts has demonstrated, they return the focus back to people. While they enable potential opportunities for growth and agility through new forms of informed, aligned and inclusive decision making, they play a key part in emphasising the community and the need to connect and engage more widely. They also encourage consideration and inclusion of the workforce, different participants and diverse communities who may have an interest in the decisions. Wider inclusion of interested communities can also offer more creative and more sustainable solutions that address real needs and issues.

Social entrepreneurs have long tried to address the needs of communities through appealing to individuals. Their approaches emphasise and empower individuals as the key players in understanding their own condition and acting to improve upon it through small-scale engagements, short experiments and positive experiences that can be built upon and scaled up to involve increasingly larger constituencies and interest groups.

> Social connection is such a basic feature of human experience that when we are deprived of it, we suffer.
>
> Leonard Mlodinow

Connecting is an essential part of human existence and a crucial part of our ability to organise into groups and networks. Connecting seems to encompass two main components encapsulating the material and the emotional. The material level may entail physical or increasingly likely digital connections and links, which may have social, tribal or organisational implications; while the emotional builds on relationships, needs and expectations. US physician Dean Ornish observed that 'the need for connection and community is primal, as fundamental as the need for air, water, and food'. Others, including US author David Shields, note that being a part of a group is essential as 'we hunger for connection to a larger community'.

The topic of community is closely related to the need to connect and appears to be tightly woven into the ways we organise and socialise. Nonetheless, to impact communities, we need to develop ways of connecting and engaging.

> Where there is no human connection, there is no compassion. Without compassion, then community, commitment, loving-kindness, human understanding, and peace all shrivel. Individuals become isolated, the isolated turn cruel, and the tragic hovers in the forms of domestic and civil violence. Art and literature are antidotes to that.
>
> Susan Vreeland

Non-governmental organisations (NGOs) and organisations such as the Eden Project have shown how the power of art and literature can be utilised in connecting, engaging and encouraging wider participation and overcoming some of the fundamental challenges highlighted by Lord Browne. The power to influence and connect through the emphasis of human emotions and needs has long been noted. Angela Ahrendts, American businesswoman and Senior Vice-President for Retail at Apple, observes that 'at their core, an influencer creates an empowering human connection'.

Connecting appears to have a fundamental role in achieving and influencing. Canadian writer and motivational speaker Robin S. Sharma maintains that 'the business of business is relationships; the business of life is human connection'. Dr Marshall Goldsmith, a leading researcher and executive coach, suggests that the project managers and shapers of the future will be more facilitators than experts. Project Eden has proved that effective advocacy can engage, facilitate, influence and help to change hearts and minds.

What then are the parameters for responsible, engaged and connected facilitation?

Drawing partially on the Gettysburg Address by President Abraham Lincoln, we may define connecting as the responsible leadership, facilitation and stewardship informed by the need to act for the people, with the people and by the people.

Acting for the people may prove to be the only way to continue to maintain the trust and respect between business and society as indicated by Lord Browne and his approach to connected leadership as we map, define, apply and radically engage with respect and authenticity.

Acting with the people requires the engagement and creativity achieved by Project Eden in getting people to explore, question, participate, encourage, inspire and catalyse partnerships.

Acting by the people remains a massive challenge that entails getting individuals and communities to co-create and drive their own change initiatives, often invoking the principles of social innovation and social entrepreneurship that have been used to transform lives and communities one step at a time.

Getting people involved can be facilitated through social media and technology. In reality it often requires individuals and communities to engage through a series of activities that embed commitment, deliver marginal improvement and thereby continue to point to future possibilities and further improvement. The momentum, and funding, for such initiatives may need to come from business and other national or regional initiatives concerned with improvement, development and social innovation.

Connecting for social innovation

Connecting is instrumental to developing new ways forward. German writer and statesman Johann Wolfgang von Goethe reflects that 'in nature we never see anything isolated, but everything in connection with something else which is before it, beside it, under it and over it'.

Lord Browne observes an ongoing failure of many business leaders to learn from the past as well as a failure of the systems established by organisations to ensure they remain connected and relevant.

Corporate Social Responsibility, 'CSR', has failed in its role as the system for handling external relationships because it is so disconnected from commercial activity and from the needs of real people. I believe CSR is dead. The connection between business and the world can only thrive if companies integrate social and environmental issues deeply into their core business strategy and operations. Critically, as traditional sources of competitive advantage are eroded, connection with society represents a final frontier of competitiveness: An opportunity to build lasting distinctiveness.

(Browne et al., 2016: pp. xiii–xiv)

Reflecting upon the failure of CSR, Lord Browne draws four main criticisms of CSR (ibid.: pp. 136–7):

1 CSR ambitions are rarely realised because they lack the active participation from big spending organisational functions such as production and marketing;
2 Centralised CSR ignores local managers and takes too narrow a view of the relevant external stakeholders;
3 CSR is overly focused on limiting the downside; and
4 CSR programmes tend to be limited and short-lived.

Lord Browne's solution is to apply the tenets of connected leadership (ibid.: pp. 143–4) as an alternative approach that requires organisations to:

• Understand the trends that are shaping their context;
• Quantify the value at stake (and to discover what stakeholders want and need);
• Professionally manage the connection between business and society; and
• Engage radically so as to earn trust and credibility and build lasting relationships.

Lord Browne concludes that connected leadership can do significantly more than generate mutual advantage for society and the private sector. In his view, connection with society offers the new frontier of competitive advantage, providing a means of success for those who learn to address it (ibid.: p. 145).

Mirvis and Googins (2017: p. 1) posit that addressing the challenges faced by business requires turning to Corporate Social Innovation. They observe effective organisations that are able to invest in new innovation sources and methods, including partnerships with social entrepreneurs and internal employee 'intrapreneurs'. Such organisations are able to generate new products, unlock markets and engage in creative philanthropy, thereby addressing key social challenges while supporting business reputation and growth.

Much in common with the Eden Project, Corporate Social Innovation recognises that social issues provide enormous opportunity to refocus, collaborate with multiple parties, gain from the diversity of views, connect with different parties and engage new communities. Addressing societal problems in meaningful ways requires multi-party collaboration, bringing in a diversity of skills, attitudes, capabilities and perspectives. Most importantly, meeting social challenges requires new and innovative ways of doing things. The Eden Project has developed a range of innovative approaches for engaging, communicating and proposing new ideas. Connecting underpins the ability to develop sustained relationships. Refreshing the modes of engagement and developing new and more engaging ways for connecting, innovating, co-creating and existing side by side could become part of a new balance between business and society. Connecting and continuing to connect may ultimately hold the key to developing a prosperous, lasting and sustained co-existence.

References

Browne, J., Nuttall, R., & Stadlen, T. (2016). *Connect: How companies succeed by engaging radically with society*. London: Random House.

Eden (2016). *Eden Project: The guide*. St Austell, Cornwall: Eden Project Books.

Kennedy, M. (2017). Eden Project branches out with plans for Chinese and US sites. *Guardian*, 28 July 2017, https://www.theguardian.com/uk-news/2017/jul/28/eden-project-branches-out-with-plans-for-chinese-and-us-sites, accessed 14 December 2018.

Mirvis, P., & Googins, B. (2017). The new business of business: Innovating for a better world. In *Giving Thoughts, Conference Board*. March 2017, pp. 1–19.

Morris, S. (2018). Chinese Eden Project to feature world's highest indoor waterfall. *Guardian*, 2 February 2018, https://www.theguardian.com/uk-news/2018/feb/02/chinese-eden-project-to-feature-worlds-highest-indoor-waterfall, accessed 14 December 2018.

Petherick, T., Eclare, M., & Smit, T. (2004). *Heligan: A portrait of the lost gardens*. London: Weidenfeld & Nicolson.

Roberts, D., & Pakkiri, R. (2016). *Decision sourcing: Decision making for the agile social enterprise*. Abingdon: Routledge.

Smit, T. (1999). *The lost gardens of Heligan*. London: Orion Books.

Smit, T. (2016). *Eden: Updated 15th anniversary edition*. London: Eden Project Books.

The digital social workplace, people over process

Dale Roberts

Workplace computing has, for the last three decades, been about automating process. The result is that we work together in ways that are stilted. In information science terms, they are nothing more than transactional. Digital social tools are changing the way we work, share and collaborate but surprisingly in a way that is more, not less natural. Paradoxically, technology is making organisations, teams and projects human again.

The end of advantage through scalable process

'I understand why you would think that', my executive contact acknowledged at a recent customer meeting, 'that our competitors are businesses like ours, other [so-called] fast moving consumer goods businesses'. The threat to their €50B turnover, it would seem was clearly going to be less obvious than my earlier posseting of the name of their biggest competitor. He went on: 'Rather, it is the vast crowd of small, innovative brands that are no longer held back by barriers to scale, even globally'. No one competitor was going to bring this behemoth down, it would seem. Rather, it was vulnerable to a thousand cuts from the long tail of artisanal sourdough and locally made soaps.

In a digital economy, businesses are no longer secure by virtue of their size. Our high streets are slowly emptying of lumbering giants. A decade ago the financial services landscape was populated by a handful of titans, whilst today they are under threat from small, pioneering insurgents commonly referred to as 'challenger banks'. One unsurprising reaction has been for incumbent businesses to buy-up and absorb the new players but they may be making a fundamental miscalculation. They are typically acquiring technology, customers or brand but overlooking the critical ingredient: Their agile ethos.

Today, competitive edge is more about how businesses organise, communicate and behave rather than their products, services or the technology they use. It is less about web sites and mobile apps and more about people.

Organisational interaction has changed

Human interaction has reached an electronic tipping point. It is digital, omnipresent, instant, permanent, analysable and searchable. It's a shame that existential issues of privacy aside, the most successful change agent and so-called social tool is Facebook because their usefulness is far broader. *The Conversation Prism*, an infographic co-authored by Brian Solis and now at version 5 (2013), lists hundreds of such tools supporting everyday human interactions from organising events to crowd funding. Whatever a group of people need to do, it can be done on-line or with the help of an app.

Business tools such as Slack have revolutionised the way we interact in the workplace as much as Facebook changed the way we maintain personal connections. Indeed, the term social is spectacularly misleading. It isn't the adjective that describes the act of enjoying activities outside of work. It is attributive. It relates to society or organisations. A social group. Businesses and projects are social constructs. They are a group of people organising around a common purpose albeit an economic one.

Enterprise social tools are permitting new workplace norms. Communication doesn't require being in the same room or even the same building. I consult often but today there is a reasonable chance that at least one person in my meeting will be in their pyjamas, providing it is a teleconference. Physical meetings are still important to forge closer working partnerships but they are only part of the mix. Indeed, on one recent occasion, I and a colleague travelled 140 miles for a meeting with a team of seven to find that only one of them was physically present, the others joining virtually through a conference phone occupying a single spot in the centre of the table.

A decade ago, when managing projects, I would strongly recommend and sometimes insist on co-location and a project office. Today, the natural beat of project communication barely slows down when the team don't even share a time zone.

Systems of process, systems of engagement

Until the advent of social tools, computing played little part in the way we related to one another. Outside of electronic mail and SMS, computing power was entirely directed at the chain of tasks and activities that ultimately culminated in a service or product.

Running a business was achieved through an automated, predictable and repeatable process. Efficiencies here, through the use of business process management software, lead to reduced costs, competitive advantage, growth, even market dominance. This was the process world.

By the beginning of the 21st century, the process world had evolved into one of exemplary efficiency. Wasteful, repetitive or error-prone processes had been or were soon to be outsourced, off-shored or re-engineered. This created an unprecedented demand for Enterprise Resource Planning (ERP) software and prodigious software businesses such as Oracle, SAP and the corporate divisions of IBM and Microsoft.

The time it took to conduct an activity, process cycle time, was continuously reduced and exceptions eliminated. Six Sigma, an approach developed by Motorola in the 1980s, aimed to drive out exceptions to a point where 99.99966 percent of products are free of defects. That's a mere 3.4 defects per million items.

Management driven by process, not people

Businesses, though, followed processes to the point that they lost sight of people. Customers and co-workers took second place. Organisations scaled but became incomprehensible.

Yves Morieux, a senior partner of Boston Consulting Group (BSG), explains in an article published in the *Harvard Business Review* entitled *Smart Rules: Six Ways to Get People to Solve Problems Without You*, that BSG created an 'index of complicatedness'. It shows that across US and European companies that processes are undermining not improving corporate productivity. In fact, in the 20 percent of organisations that are the most complicated, managers spend 40 percent of their time writing reports and as much as 60 percent of it coordinating meetings. That leaves little, if any, time for them to work with their teams or their customers. The reason is that over the past 15 years there has been as much as a three and a half times increase in the procedures, vertical layers, interface structures, coordination bodies and decision approvals needed in each of those businesses (Morieux, 2011).

The same index is referred to in Lisa Bodell's book *Kill the Company: End the Status Quo*. Bodell, CEO of futurethink, describes how she has encountered companies so wedded to their procedures that they have allowed their processes to become their culture. Efficient, accountable, but rigid and inflexible. Corporate culture actually discouraged creative thinking. The very processes and procedures companies put in place to become efficient and productive discouraged the act of thinking itself and the result was stasis. Businesses froze whilst the customers they served continued to change (Bodell, 2012).

Customers, vote out process

The relentless pursuit of process eventually led to computer systems that would encompass customer interaction. In the interest of efficiency, businesses evolved into systems of customer relationship management (CRM).

However, interaction cannot be modelled on customer service flow-charts. There are too many arrows, decisions and exceptions. Jeff Kober describes the problem with trying to build a process that delivers their legendary customer service levels.

> The typical tendency for leaders is to try and map out all the possible behaviours their employees should demonstrate when working with

customers. This approach is flawed for two important reasons. First, such behaviours tend to come across as rote, rather than genuine. Second, it is impossible to map out all the potential behaviours individuals should demonstrate for future unforeseen circumstance.

(Kober, 2007)

Kober was rejecting the process world because it didn't deliver what customers, or guests, had come to expect from one of the world's most loved brands: Open, genuine, reciprocal and human exchange: Interaction.

As more and more businesses rolled out CRM systems, it became increasingly apparent that there was a growing dissatisfaction with the process world. The upward trend in CRM correlated with a downward trend in customer satisfaction. Businesses took the process outside the organisation and forced it on the customer and they did not like it much. Being the subject of a process is objectifying rather than humanising and whilst employees were paid to live in the process world customers were not. They didn't, for example, see any reason for them to accept being marched through someone else's selling process. It seemed supremely one sided to refer to a 'sales' cycle. Surely, from the customer's perspective, it's a 'buying' cycle. In fact, the customer wasn't even sure they liked being dealt with in a 'cycle'. Once the customer had been 'closed' they were subjected to more processes. Customer services or customer support routes commonly incentivised agents on first call resolution (FCR). Measurable metrics, such as FCR, could easily result in unintended consequences or blatant abuse. In this case, returning customers might find themselves starting from scratch to make the metrics look good assuming they had made their way past the long wait-time and the automated messages assuring them that their call was important.

Customers soon began to tire of increasingly transactional encounters, such as businesses going through the motions to get the task checked off, the process completed and the metric right. And when customers started voting with their feet businesses took a long hard look at their systems and conceded that they had been built from their own perspective. Louis Gerstner, CEO of IBM from 1993 until 2002, articulated the problem at a major conference and expo in the winter of 2001. In his book, *Smart Mobs*, Howard Rheingold describes how Gerstner told business leaders that they needed to focus on *interaction* rather than *transaction*. Gerstner was quoted as saying that the 'technology was easy' presumably if you hired IBM to help you, but more importantly that 'the hard part is re-conceptualising management models' (Rheingold, 2002: p. 17).

Action, transaction, interaction

Gerstner's view that we should eschew the transaction can be illuminated by looking through the lens of information science. Information science is a discipline that concerns itself with the retrieval and dissemination of organisational information along with the way people collaborate around it. A 1973 paper

Figure 9.1 Action, transaction, interaction.

by William F Eadie of Purdue University, Indiana, based on work by the philosopher and psychologist John Dewey and political scientist Arthur Bentley, distinguishes three forms of communication: Action, transaction and interaction (see Figure 9.1).

Action

Communication as action is described as an act involving independent actors. Action is something one party simply does to another. In communication terms this is the equivalent of an exasperated parent declaring 'because I said so'. This doesn't sound like a communication strategy that sustains a relationship or allows groups to collaborate willingly for any length of time.

Transaction

Communication as transaction is described by Eadie (1973) as functional. It takes the form of active inquiry at some stages but held in reserve in others. It is an occasional exchange sufficiently equitable in the long run to keep most individuals in the relationship. If 'sufficiently equitable' sounds like the bare minimum, that's because it is. It describes a somewhat narrow, restricted relationship between businesses and their customers and their workforce.

Interaction

Information science views interaction as reciprocal role taking involving empathic behaviours. The goal of interaction is the merger of self and others to anticipate, predict and behave based on joint rather than individual needs.

Systems of interaction

Customers had grown tired of their functional role in the transaction and they suddenly had the tools to force interaction. They tweeted, they reviewed and they posted. Million dollar advertising campaigns for thousand dollar TVs could be undermined by a single reviewer pointing out that there were not enough HDMI slots.

The power dynamic had shifted forever. Customers had as much information and as much of a voice as the corporation. In a world of comparison sites and online reviews, businesses had to find a way to compete beyond price, product and marketing budgets. Businesses could only sustain through deeper, empathic relationships with their customers.

Management is interaction

The pressure for businesses to interact rather than transact didn't stop at the revolving front door. Business processes need managing, changing, improving, evolving and fixing when they break.

This is the world of decision making. Organisationally, it sits distinct and separate to the process world in order for the processes to be observed and controlled. At its simplest level, decision making might itself be described as a process to identify a problem, gather a list of possible solutions and then select and implement the most optimal. However, it is on closer inspection a set of interactions. Decisions require the gathering of relevant information, analysis, debate, discourse and deliberation before finally reaching a conclusion and implementing whatever determination was made. And how is it implemented? Again, by interaction.

Management by hierarchical interaction

The prevailing method of organising, managing and making decisions has chiefly been through hierarchy. This can be functional (marketing, sales or finance) grouped around a product or service, or, as is common in the Financial Services sector, around a specific customer category. Barclays, whose divisions include Retail Banking and Corporate, is a good example of this. Geography may also play a part so that regional structures can manage across locations and international boundaries. Decisions are made by layers of management at each level of the hierarchy, which we might refer to as decision nodes. A Senior Management team, answerable to the board of directors and shareholders, sits at the top.

This form of management relies on a simple, single flow of information upwards until the right point of the org chart is reached, at which point a decision is made, and then flows down.

Knowledge is not hierarchical

When the hierarchical structure served us well, the Head of Engineering was probably a former Engineer. A shift manager in a factory was probably a former machinist and a Tailor was probably a Tailor's hand five years previously. If an important decision was needed, the further up the hierarchy you went, the more knowledge and experience was going into the decision. Today, this is not true. The environment is changing too quickly. Fifteen years ago, Facebook didn't exist. By 2018, it had more than two billion users and was on the radar of every marketing team. Before 2010, there was no such thing as an iPad. Now there are 350 million and counting. A little over a decade ago there was no such job as Community Manager, Search Engine Optimisation Specialist, Sustainability Manager and there were no User Experience Managers, App Developers, Uber Drivers or Driverless Car Engineers. None.

Today, managers may be managing individuals in roles that they have never fulfilled using tools and platforms that did not exist when they were moving into management. Community managers are all managed by individuals, few of whom have been community managers. Many software engineers have a manager who has never been a software engineer, at least not in terms of the current technologies. It is no longer safe to assume that knowledge and experience can automatically be found by searching up the hierarchy. Instead it exists in alternative networks, undocumented by the single dimension organisational chart.

Organising without hierarchy

If the hierarchy isn't necessary for knowledge, surely it is essential for coordinating the activities of the business. Surely, organisations don't organise themselves. Except, there are many examples of where they do exactly that.

One business that is built on self-organisation is Semco, a Brazilian manufacturing conglomerate. The business, which manufactures over 2,000 products including dishwashers, marine pumps and mixing equipment, is built around self-managed teams. Ricardo Semler, CEO, wanted to share decision making with the people doing the work and connect them to the customer. Semco employees, Associates, make both tactical and strategic decisions including those that might relate to product or new plant locations. There are no receptionists and no personal assistants. Semco staff arrange their own appointments and draft their own correspondence. There are very few rules too. Staff set their own time hours and pay. The Semco policy manual is a 20-page booklet with cartoons and brief declarations. According to Semler, in his book *Maverick: The Success Story Behind the World's Most Unusual Workplace,* rules and regulations only serve to divert attention from the company's objectives, provide a false sense of security for executives and create work for bean counters.

Businesses may need fewer rules and co-operate more naturally than we think. Semco's revenues are around $200 million a year, it employs around 3,000 people and has been visited by at least 150 of the Fortune 500 in an effort to understand just how it is done. Says Semler (1999), 'I am often asked how do you control a system like this'? I answer, 'I don't. I let the system work for itself'.

Network decision roles

Organisational decisions are rarely made in isolation. I run the risk of stating what is obvious here in order to reinforce the point that organisational decisions are different to decisions we make as individuals for that very reason. They are decisions made by groups for groups.

Hierarchical decision making is out of step with fast-moving, highly participative businesses. Information is lost, checks and balances missed and many that should be consulted are not. Some, perhaps even those impacted by the decisions, are often not informed until after the fact.

Understanding the roles individuals play in contemporary organisational decision making is complex. The single line in an organisation chart is inadequate in the same way that some social platforms did not initially distinguish relationship types.

Paul Adams, a Facebook Product Manager and former social researcher at Google, led a study of social groups and concluded that the one-size-fits-all, 'Friends' category was simply unhelpful (Adams, 2011). We have family relationships, relationships with our colleagues and closer 'best' friends. We also have relationships that are built during life stages (university) or around hobbies (football teams, diving) and those that are built because of locality (neighbours). As part of his research, Adams built up a picture of over 300 groups, 85 percent of which did not even contain the word friend.

This is true of the workplace too. Decision making in modern and agile businesses counter-intuitively involve more rather than fewer participants. Narrow, top-down management is replaced by inclusive, dynamic and informed collaboration. And, at the centre of it are digital social tools that are making interaction frictionless. Decision constituency today is often extended beyond the unnatural limits of enterprise walls to include customers and prospective customers through Twitter, Facebook and the thousand tools that orbit around them. Social tools; part cause, part effect, are making networked decisions commonplace.

Participation is the power of networked decisions

To understand the power of networked decisions, compare how little an organisational chart reflects the reality of interaction and participation in a typical decision. One team member may initiate the need for a decision by raising an issue, an exception, a problem or an opportunity and is therefore the **originator**. That same individual may co-ordinate the activity involved in progressing the decision to a conclusion as a **facilitator**. The decision will require information provided by others in the business, perhaps business partners such as finance analysts or data scientists or simply those with specific knowledge to either frame the decision or **inform** alternatives. Others still will be **contributors**, either because they possess related knowledge or can

Table 9.1 Decision roles

Role	Description
Originator	Identified the problem or opportunity and started the framing process.
Facilitator	Co-ordinate the interactions of the other actors through the process of making the decision. Often but not always the originator.
Adjudicator	Has the responsibility to make the call and will be accountable for it usually as a result of capital responsibility. Shared in a consensus but not necessarily in collaborative decisions. If the group is made by a committee then the adjudicator will be the chair.
Analyst	Provides explicit information to help frame the decision or inform the alternatives.
Contributor	Trusted contributors provide tacit knowledge, opinion, creative input or contrary views with the sole purpose of improving decision quality.
Consultee	Consulted because they are affected by the decision. Implementers would typically be consultees.
Approver	Where formal approval is required. Executives with legal or regulatory compliance responsibility.
Implementer	Implements the decision. Inclusive decision making assumes that implementers are also consultees so that decisions are arrived at with implementation considered.

provide ideas or simply because their opinion is trusted and valued. Some will be **consulted**, perhaps because they will be affected by the decision or because they will eventually be **implementers**, carrying out the decision once it is concluded. There may be others involved in formal **approver** processes, particularly in regulated industries, and finally, the **adjudicator**, the 'reports-to' in our hierarchical decision, will make the final call. The different decision roles are summarised in Table 9.1 (Roberts & Pakkiri, 2016: p. 70).

Networked decisions, thanks to the digital tools that support them, are not slowed down by the increased level of involvement. In fact, the ease with which stakeholders can become active results in their more frequent association. Networked decisions offer better quality than hierarchical decisions, not just because they are less at risk to individual bias but also because they are better informed by the wider participation and are ultimately executed by a more included and therefore more engaged team.

Strategic decisions and bias

New forms of digital interaction can have a hugely positive impact on decision quality. To illustrate this, let's examine a major challenge with the bigger, strategic decision making process. According to research conducted by Sidney Finkelstein, in the publication of his book *Think Again: Why Good Leaders Make Bad Decisions and How to Keep It From Happening to You*, human decisions, particularly high-stake organisational ones that rely on experience, are subject to many forms of bias and pre-judgment (Finkelstein et al., 2008). More than that, today the factors behind them are increasingly complex and nuanced and relying on all the relevant information flowing upwards so that good decisions can flow downwards is becoming increasingly unlikely to yield the best possible outcomes.

Thankfully, organisations provide an abundant resource to neutralise both bias and the absence of detail; other people. Others can challenge, debate, inform, analyse, govern and share. And let's not forget the small matter of getting things done when the decision is made. However, until the introduction of digital and social tools, this would have slowed things down. Today though, these interactions are easy and fast so that decisions are not just safeguarded, they are optimised. Higher participation decision making creates more decision alternatives, tests more hypotheses, considers more variables, weighs more pros and cons and carries more contributors through the process.

Social tools an opportunity to be more human

We are seeing hierarchies erode and not just in high technology businesses. Dennis Bakke, former CEO of AES, a global energy company based in Arlington, Virginia, described their philosophical foundations in the *Harvard Business Review* article 'Organising for Empowerment'. Their system, according to Bakke, 'starts with a lack of hierarchy. We abhor layers. We avoid them like the plague'. And the rationale, according to Bakke, is that 'the more authority figures you have above you, the more likely it is that you won't make decisions yourself' (Sant & Bakke, 1999: p. 114).

The revolution in information sharing and digital interaction is accelerating flatter, fairer organisational alternatives such as *Holocracy*, which distributes decisions, information and authority. Making the most of opportunity or dealing with problems requires creativity and innovation, none of which is the job of one person. Diversity in background and skills unleash potential only present, by definition, in teams.

Social tools represent an exciting opportunity for business to be more agile and innovative whilst also being engaging places to work. People are at the centre rather than the process. Distributed collaboration means that we can reject business practices that reduce us to consumers and workers in the interests of scale. The rise of digital social tools is an opportunity to connect, to interact rather than transact. Social is an opportunity for businesses, workplaces and the projects we run to be more human.

References

Adams, P. (2011). *Grouped. How small groups of friends are key to influence on the social web.* Berkeley, CA: New Riders.

Bodell, L. (2012). *Kill the company: End the status quo, start an innovation revolution*. Brookline, MA: Bibliomotion.

Eadie, W. F. (Nov 1973). *Action, interaction and transaction: Three means of viewing the communications world*, West Lafayette, IN: Department of Communication, Purdue University.

Finkelstein, S., Whitehead, J., and Campbell, A. (2008). *Think again: Why good leaders make bad decisions and how to keep it from happening to you*. Boston, MA: Harvard Business.

Kober, J. (2007). Disney Service Basics. *Mouse Planet*, 29 November 2007. http://www.mouseplanet.com/6978/Disney_Service_Basics, accessed 4 June 2012.

Morieux, Y. (2011). Smart rules: Six ways to get people to solve problems without you. *Harvard Business Review*, 89(9), 78–86.

Rheingold, H. (2002). *Smart mobs*. New York: Basic Books.

Roberts, D., & Pakkiri, R. (2016). *Decision sourcing: Decision making for the agile social enterprise*. Abingdon: Routledge.

Semler, R. (1999). *Maverick: The success story behind the world's most unusual workplace*. New York: Random House.

Silverberg, M. (2010). Semco: Democracy in the Workplace. Case Study, 14 Sept. 2010. https://www.asone.org/asone/stories/casestudy.html?uuid=c28fbc91-245e-417a-9b35-9bf483b9130c, accessed 5 June 2012.

Solis, B. (2013). https://conversationprism.com, accessed 15 October 2018.

Westlaufer, S., with Sant, R., & Bakke, D. (1999). Organizing for empowerment: An interview with AES's Roger Sant and Dennis Bakke. Interview by Suzy Wetlaufer. *Harvard Business Review*, 77(1), 110–123.

Conclusion

Reframing the new agenda

Darren Dalcher

In a revolution, as in a novel, the most difficult part to invent is the end.
—Alexis de Tocqueville

The writing in this volume offers new ways of thinking about and approaching a diverse set of areas ranging from leadership, teams and culture, to strategy, complexity and implementation. While conventional project management practice seems to retain a distinct preference for predictable and planned approaches to optimisation and managing, the authors look further afield into a more eclectic and wider ranging selection of new ideas, insights and perspectives before relating them to the realities of life in modern business settings, organisations and projects. The challenges of contemporary environments defy the simplified logic of normative instrumental solutions, and the authors emphasise the richness, diversity and flexibility that can be harnessed from the new ways of thinking and working.

The volume advances and broadens project scholarship by extending the focus, augmenting the vocabulary and energising the potential skillset available to practitioners. More importantly, however, it encourages the development of a new mindset that recognises the challenges and opportunities in the project space and is open to considerations of contingency, change, culture and complexity. One clear message that resonates throughout the writing is the centrality of people and the need to place them back into the project context. People seem to defy logic, resent change, apply defensive routines and work on the shadow side of the organisation: They can make the most perfect plans obsolete and irrelevant in a single heart beat. Managing (and leading) projects as if people mattered could pose a strong antidote to the pervasive preoccupation with recipes for success, established 'best practices', and standardised KPIs and CSFs. Instead it requires less formal arrangements that are contingent, responsive and opportunistic, infused with commitment, courage, passion and a good dose of resilience.

The title of the book invokes the metaphor of a revolution and the rest of this brief concluding essay will highlight some of the implications of adopting that metaphor as a lens and perspective for considering the health and potential development of the discipline. French post-imperialist artist Paul Gauguin prominently reflected that art is either plagiarism or revolution. The plagiarism side is easily covered: Project management has excelled at sharing and replicating certain practices and approaches codified in the bodies of knowledge, professional qualification frameworks and mandated methodologies. Thus far it has failed to embrace the revolution and rethink the methods, approaches, success criteria or even begin to question the ultimate purpose and impact of project work. This book encourages thinking beyond imitation and thus endeavours to focus on the management of projects, people and change required to deliver beneficial, impactful and sustained results.

The problem is that plagiarism and imitation sell, revolution not so much. Revolution has to be embraced, subscribed to. It starts with the few and has to be explained, conveyed and 'sold' to the many. Moreover, whilst imitation appears to be safe, revolution is more exposed, more risky. Saul Alinsky (1971), considered by many to be the father of modern community organising, explains that there are no rules for revolutions; no simple manuals and guidebooks exist. Given the need to transform and engage with political and social systems and human actors, the outcome is largely uncertain, and the means unclear and open to interpretation.

In recognition of the complexities of social environments, Alinsky advocates realistic radicalism in preference to rhetorical radicalisation. Realistic radicals and activists who want to change their world must understand the central and universal concepts of action in human politics. This enables a pragmatic attack on the system, rather than the mere espousal of dogma or resentment. Activists need to be steeped in the art of communication so that they can communicate within the experience of their audience. This enables those who want to change to do the social thing 'for and with the people' (ibid.: p. xix). The emergence of social media and technology offers new opportunities to engage, agitate, direct, lead the quest for a better future, and benefit from the power, wisdom and energy of the crowds.

Effective activism, or advocacy, requires pragmatism and the ability to respond to challenges. Indeed, Jamie Bartlett (2017) reasons that systems, such as democracies, require fresh ideas to survive the emerging and increasingly scary challenges they face. Bill Lucas expounds the need to develop adaptive expertise in order to continue to thrive in crazy and increasingly demanding times. Pragmatism, resilience and adaptive capability provide the flexibility needed to understand different potential positions and to adjust and trade-off whilst pursuing beneficial goals, targets or a better future. Lucas (2009: p. 3) puts forward 'the capacity to imagine futures, to reframe situations, and to conduct, with others, a series of on-going experiments into the way we live our lives' as the requisite new skills for thriving in increasingly turbulent times.

It is often said that a revolution is not an event; it is an unfolding process, and it takes time for it to run its course. In many ways a revolution is akin to a much desired but long-awaited paradigm shift. Paradigms embody a current state of affairs in understanding and reasoning. They encompass explicit laws, models, theoretical assumptions, as well as the general direction and expectations and some tacit knowledge. Most critically perhaps, they have a lot of invested emotional and intellectual capital, often accompanied by persistent structures, systems and mechanisms that defy any attempts to challenge, question or dethrone the residing point of view. Like other forms of change and transformation, shifting a paradigm is difficult precisely because it is entrenched, which means it has had time to develop the underpinning culture, in addition to the overwhelming structures which rebuff any attempts to overhaul it. Those operating within the system may be working in the shadows and utilising workarounds and other compromise measures devised to cope whilst avoiding any major challenges to the accepted logic.

Paradigm shifts are hard to engender, partly because they require consensus that the overriding logic is flawed and ought to be replaced: Any change to the logic is difficult to justify, if it can only be contended using that same prevailing logic. Over time, inconsistencies, surprises and discrepancies continue to accumulate until their cumulative influence and impact are sufficient to trigger a 'crisis' state. The 'crisis' is resolved when a radical change, transformation or revolution leads to the birth of a new normal paradigm, which is adopted by the wider community.

Pioneers, radicals, activists and early adopters are similarly familiar with the need to find creative ways of establishing and proving new knowledge, ideas or discoveries and engaging with the wider community. Pragmatic pioneers, realistic radicals and adaptation-conscious activists recognise that the key lies in effective communication and dialogue. The authors of the individual chapters endeavour to highlight some of the potential ways and new approaches required to reframe the human dynamics of successful projects. They openly acknowledge and embrace the role of people in social endeavours, whilst exploring new thinking frameworks and perspectives related to leadership, culture, change, strategy and behaviour.

Radicals and revolutionaries are often boldly challenged to improve their communication skills and define their proposed change. Del Gandio observes that while radicals have important messages to deliver, they often become so caught up in the passion of their causes that they lose sight of effective communication leading to a significant gap (2008: p. 2). Consequently, activists suffer from a rhetorical crisis; a credibility gap because of the lack of a coherent message and a strategy for its delivery (ibid.: p. 1). If interaction creates the social world, the ability to communicate clear messages may hold the key to changing and improving that world. In the spirit of Del Gandio's call to rhetorical action, we conclude this book with the re-articulation of the key observations from the volume, rearranged as a manifesto for change in project thinking.

The radical manifesto for change in projects

People are essential to the success of projects, change initiatives and social development. Traditional sources within project management often neglect this critical aspect. However, this is the time for significant and meaningful rethinking of our practice.

The writing throughout the book pursues a progressive agenda that encourages new ways of thinking about people in projects operating in change ridden, turbulent and dynamic environments with significant social and political and societal implications. The corresponding shift in values advocated through the work could be summarised as a series of moves:

- From a static toolset, towards flexible skillsets and pragmatic mindsets;
- From the pursuit of process, towards an appreciation of people;
- From technical and instrumental rationality, towards a wider social, cultural, political and institutional awareness; and
- From passive conformance, towards professional reflection, agility, flexibility and adaptability.

Delivering sustainable and enduring results through projects, programmes and portfolios of change depends on our ability to deliver projects as if people matter. This book and the ideas put forward by the individual authors is hopefully the beginning of an important and enduring dialogue about people in and around projects.

References

Alinsky, S. D. (1971). *Rules for radicals: A primer for realistic radicals*. New York: Vintage Books.

Bartlett, J. (2017). *Radicals: Outsiders changing the world*. London: William Heinemann.

Del Gandio, J. (2008). *Rhetoric for radicals: A handbook for 21st century activists*. Gabriola Island, BC, Canada: New Society Publishers.

Lucas, B. (2009). *rEvolution: How to thrive in crazy times*. Carmerthen, Wales: Crown House Publishing.

Index